PSYCHOLOGICAL ISSUES

Vol. IV, No. 1   Monograph 13

THE INFLUENCE OF FREUD ON AMERICAN PSYCHOLOGY

by

DAVID SHAKOW and DAVID RAPAPORT

INTERNATIONAL UNIVERSITIES PRESS, INC.
227 West 13 Street   ·   New York, N.Y. 10011

Copyright 1964, by International Universities Press, Inc.
Library of Congress Catalog Card Number: 64-21456

PSYCHOLOGICAL ISSUES

GEORGE S. KLEIN, *Editor*

Editorial Board

MARGARET BRENMAN   ROBERT R. HOLT

ERIK H. ERIKSON   MARIE JAHODA

SIBYLLE ESCALONA   GEORGE S. KLEIN

CHARLES FISHER   GARDNER LINDZEY

MERTON M. GILL   ROY SCHAFER

ROBERT S. WALLERSTEIN

SUZETTE H. ANNIN, *Editorial Assistant*

Annual Subscription per Volume, $10.00
Single copies of this Number, $3.50

CONTENTS

Preface		1
INTRODUCTION		5
1	THE PROBLEM OF THE ASSESSMENT OF INFLUENCE	7
2	DARWIN AND FREUD: A COMPARISON OF RECEPTIONS	14
	The Three Historical Blows	14
	Reception of the Theories	16
	Reception of *On the Origin of the Species*	18
	Reception of Freud's Ideas	20
	Factors Contributing to Reception	22
	Intrinsic Factors	23
	Extrinsic Factors	28
	Summary	32
3	NINETEENTH AND EARLY TWENTIETH CENTURY BACKGROUND	33
	The Helmholtz Program	33
	Interpretation of the Program	35
	Psychology's Commitment	36
	Freud's Commitment	41
	Implications of Commitments	47
	Freud and Dynamic Psychology	51
	Overview	52
4	GENERAL ASPECTS OF TWENTIETH CENTURY DEVELOPMENTS: INFLUENCE AND OBSTACLES TO INFLUENCE AND UNDERSTANDING	55
	Indirect Influences	55
	Sources	55
	Response to Influence	63

Direct Influences 65
The Responses of Selected Psychologists 65
Obstacles to Influence and Understanding 78
General Causes of Conflict 78
Primary Sources of Psychoanalysis 86
Secondary Sources 87
Summary 95

5 THE UNCONSCIOUS AND MOTIVATION 98

The Unconscious 98
Freud's Own Concept 98
Precursors and Contemporaries 100
Three Symposia 108
Knight Dunlap 111
Summary 112
Motivation 112
Freud's Concept of Instinctual Drive 112
General Background: The Polarities 113
Relation to Other Theories of Motivation 119
Predecessors' Theories 119
Contemporaries' Theories 120
Descendants' Theories 121
Piaget 121
Lewin 125
Thorndike Followers: General 132
Thorndike Followers: Hull and Yale Group 135
The Instinct Controversy 142
Rivers 142
McDougall 143
J. B. Watson 148
E. C. Tolman 149
Woodworth 150
Dynamic Psychologists 154
F. L. Wells 154
H. A. Murray 157
Other Dynamic Psychologists 158
Summary 158

6	APPRAISALS, SURVEYS, AND REFERENCE WORKS BY PSYCHOLOGISTS DEALING WITH PSYCHOANALYSIS	161
	Appraisals of Psychoanalysis	161
	Surveys of Experiments Testing Psychoanalytic Theory	167
	Articles on Psychoanalytic Themes in the *Psychological Bulletin*	174
	Histories of Psychology	180
	Readings	186
	Dictionaries	189
	Summary	190
7	CONCLUSIONS	191
Bibliography		203
Index		227
About the Authors		245

PREFACE

In the spring of 1955, David Rapaport was approached by Heinz Hartmann with the request that he prepare a chapter on the influence of Freud on American psychology for the Freud centenary volume he was then planning. Rapaport did some preliminary thinking about the chapter and began working on it. He and I discussed the project at length, if somewhat at random, during his visit to Bethesda in November, 1955, and he became interested in how well my ideas complemented his own. He subsequently invited me to co-author the article, and early in 1956 I agreed to participate. Through a number of personal conferences and much correspondence between Stockbridge and Bethesda, a first draft was finished sometime in June, 1956, and sent out to a group of readers. Although there was still the possibility of keeping the study as an article for the centenary volume, it became increasingly clear that the paper called for considerable expansion. When other commitments delayed its completion for the projected publication date, it was decided to extend the article to monograph length and publish it separately.

As our respective schedules permitted, Rapaport and I worked together on the volume for a period of approximately five years. He often had to drop his active involvement because of other professional commitments. In addition to writing *The Structure of Psychoanalytic Theory* (1959) and "On the Psychoanalytic Theory of Motivation" (1960a) during this time, he was carrying a heavy teaching burden at the Western New England Institute for Psychoanalysis and was in great demand all over the country for his unique scholarly lectures on metapsychology and ego psychology. He nevertheless managed to put in a considerable amount of work on the monograph, and had just started to work on a "last" revision of a draft I had returned to him, when he died. For the approximately two years since his death, I have carried on, as my own program permitted, essentially along the lines we had outlined together. There was still, however, a great deal to be done; some of it we had not even had the opportunity to discuss together.

Those acquainted with David Rapaport's theoretical insight and scholarship will have little difficulty in recognizing his substantial contribution to the monograph. I have tried to maintain his standards in so far as I have been able, but these standards are not easily matched. I trust I have succeeded in producing a volume to which he would not have taken too much exception, one that is reasonably worthy of such a "junior" author!

In the discussions dealing with Rapaport's own work—particularly *Emotions and Memory* (1942a) and *The Structure of Psychoanalytic Theory*—I have either inserted new comments, or taken the liberty of otherwise modifying Rapaport's essentially matter-of-fact description of them. If the reader recognizes there a trace of high praise, he should be made aware that it is entirely mine.

Since this volume is dedicated to Rapaport's memory, I do not hesitate to quote a short excerpt from the citation read at the presentation to him of the Distinguished Contribution Award in Clinical Psychology by the Division of Clinical Psychology of the American Psychological Association in 1960—only three and one half months before his death.

Rapaport, the citation said, ". . . will probably be remembered most as a profound scholar and systematist. His almost frightening comprehension of Freudian thought has resulted in his being called the leading contemporary student of psychoanalysis. In monumental works whose footnotes frequently deserve to be texts, he has not only discovered, through his systematic analysis, more in Freud than Freud probably realized was there, but also he has effectively integrated the psychoanalytic developments into the general body of psychological theory. In some of this work he does not give himself enough credit for originality in the extension of ideas stimulated by Freud. A primary contribution of this sort is his emphasis on ego psychology . . . A teacher extraordinary, he has always set high standards for his students, stretching them to fullest capacity and leaving them later grateful for a unique educational experience."

PREFACE

As we have indicated in the introduction to Chapter 6, the present volume has been unavoidably limited in its coverage of the many areas of psychology that have been influenced by Freud. We should also perhaps forewarn the reader that in some sections the original intention to limit ourselves to the period up to 1950 could not quite prevail against the temptation to deal with what seemed to us obviously relevant material that appeared later. I trust that the reader will forgive the ragged edges which occur with increasing frequency as we approach the present date.

Since readers so frequently come to a work hoping to find what they would like to have written themselves, it is perhaps wise at this point to say what the volume is, as well as what it is not, about. It *is* what its title indicates: a study of *Freud's* influence on American psychology. It makes no effort to detail the forces which influenced Freud except when they seem particularly pertinent. Neither is it a discussion of the influence of various psychoanalytic schools, other than the Freudian, on psychology. Those who expect to find a discussion of Jung, Horney, Rank, Sullivan, or Fromm will therefore be disappointed.

About any particular bias that may be present in our study, we can only say that such, we suppose, is unavoidable and, perhaps, even desirable. It will become clear that we believe that Freud is the most significant figure in the history of psychology, and that he has not received his proper acceptance in this field. If these are biases, we hold them nevertheless. Even so, in the context of these attitudes, we have tried to evaluate the history of Freud's relationship with psychology as fairly as possible. Speaking for myself as an American psychologist whose particular hero is William James, I must admit that there are occasions when I cannot avoid some feeling of antagonism toward Freud. The grounds for this that come to mind immediately are his attitude toward the United States and toward academic psychology. Which, I suppose, may indicate that I should not be involved in writing a history that concerns Freud!

Several persons were kind enough to read and comment upon the penultimate draft of this monograph. I have profited especially from the criticisms of two. Dr. E. G. Boring generously gave his time in the midst of an impossibly heavy schedule to go over the manuscript in detail. His critical historical insights and candor in pointing out slippages from the exalted platform on which the historian ought to dwell were made easier to accept by his deep interest in the work. Dr. Merton Gill, in his similarly thoughtful reading of the manuscript, made a contribution which was both corroborative of, and complementary to, Boring's. His equal candor, his monumental knowledge of the Freudian literature, and his keen and detailed comments have helped to clarify many passages. I also accepted his advice about certain changes in the structure of the monograph.

Dr. Fred L. Wells was not only helpful in checking the passages referring to him, but was sufficiently kind, at some cost to himself, to read the full manuscript and to give most valuable suggestions. Dr. Henry Murray, Dr. Max Schur, and Dr. John Burnham each read the manuscript from the vantage point of his own special knowledge and offered improving suggestions. It goes without saying, however, that any errors of fact and judgment are mine, not those of the persons I have just mentioned.

I owe a different order of thanks to my two "Smithies," Harriet Basseches and Donna Greenough, who have served in the capacity of editorial assistants on this task. Together and in succession they have worked most devotedly and intelligently on every aspect of the volume. Much of whatever clarity of expression and accuracy of reference the volume may have is due to them. The volume also owes a great deal to Suzette Annin, who, first as Dr. Rapaport's research assistant, and then as Editorial Assistant for *Psychological Issues*, did so much along the same lines.

The project has also been fortunate in having the services of Miss Jessie Honn on the references and the excerpts, and the succession of conscientious typists—Irene Byrne, Sadie Fishman, Virginia Masterson, and Joan Zweben—who patiently saw the manuscript through more drafts than one can bear to contemplate.

David Shakow
Bethesda, Md.
August 1, 1963

INTRODUCTION

Psychologists who study the general history of psychology can with reason view the kind of intricate relationships involved as importantly affected by the *Zeitgeist*. The study of a specific problem, such as Freud's influence on psychology, requires both a detailed examination of these complex interrelationships and an attempt to trace the various processes which compose the totality called the *Zeitgeist*. Ideally, the tracing of these historical trends calls for students who have competence both in the substantive knowledge of the field, in psychological-genetic knowledge, and in knowledge of the history of scientific concepts, ideas, theories, and discoveries. The present authors are limited in meeting this combination of qualifications. As psychologists we are able to avoid judging a person who comes to us for help while tracing a genetic trend in him. We do not, however, have the analogous ability to maintain distance from trends in the history of ideas with which we are still involved as participants, whether as protagonists or antagonists. Owing to the nature of our material, it has not always been possible to avoid those points at which distance from the trends is too short for objectivity. Where it has not been possible we have stated our judgment directly.[1]

Our study has another shortcoming of a more contentual nature: we focus mainly on the influence of Freud on psychology in the United States, with resultant neglect of the greater part of European psychology. With respect to continental European psychology, this omission is not entirely a matter of choice, for the American material is far more readily available. Two world wars and dictator-

[1] We are indebted to E. G. Boring, who read the first draft of this study, for pointing out several such judgments which had not been stated directly. It is, of course, Boring's *History of Experimental Psychology* (1929, 1950b) which made the *Zeitgeist* part of psychology. See also Boring (1950a, 1954a, 1955).

ships, as well as the consequent mass emigrations, decimated psychology in much of Europe and disrupted its continuity.[2] Further, most of psychology on the West European continent since the end of World War II has grown up in the shadow of either American psychology or of existentialism. Although the factors we have mentioned do not apply to British psychology, we shall not attempt a special study of Freudian influence in Britain. Such a study would require the exploration of a unique and complex set of circumstances which we do not feel ourselves prepared to undertake. We shall nonetheless consider a number of outstanding British psychologists in their particular relationship to the American scene. We trust that others will try to document the influence of Freud on European psychology.

Despite such difficulties we believe that an assessment of Freud's influence on American psychology is possible and desirable.

In assessing the impact that Freud has had on psychology, we shall first discuss the problem of influence itself. We shall then plunge directly into some concrete aspects of influence by a comparison of Darwin and Freud. This will be followed by an examination of the nineteenth century milieu in which both Freud and psychology developed. Then we shall attempt to trace both the direct and indirect influences of Freud in the first half of the present century. To complement the general survey of Freud's influence, we shall make a detailed analysis of a few specific areas where the influence was particularly important. At appropriate places in the volume we shall attempt what Boring has called a "retroperspective"—an overview of Freud's influence on the aspect of psychology under consideration.

---

[2] During the same period, the migration of European psychoanalysts to the United States became one of the important vehicles of Freudian influence on American psychology.

1

THE PROBLEM OF THE ASSESSMENT OF INFLUENCE

When the word "influence" appears in a scientific context, the reader may naturally expect a discussion of the general problem of how ideas in science gain acceptance. We must from the very beginning disclaim any attempt to achieve such an ambitious goal. It is our purpose here merely to lay a foundation sufficient to guide a detailed examination of the vicissitudes of the theories of one man—Freud—within one field—psychology. This volume may be considered as a single case history in the study of influence.

In making a genetic study of a trend or a phenomenon in an individual life, we customarily search for prior trends similar to it. Some of these prove to be genetic predecessors, others parallel developments arising from the same roots, and still others entirely independent trends. Moreover, we usually find some tendencies which are full-fledged derivatives of original trends, others which are merely vestigial or abortive forms, and still others which derive from related or unrelated predecessors. Even in the most clear-cut case, however, any statement about such relationships must contain some element of conjecture, owing to the complexities and uncertainties of historical evidence.

In the case of Freud's influence on psychology, the general situation seems to be of this kind. The history of psychology (and philosophy) shows many ideas which bear a resemblance to Freud's theories. Some of them, for instance the earlier theories of the unconscious of Herbart, von Hartmann, and Carpenter, appear to have had little direct effect on the development of Freud's concept of the unconscious, although Freud was probably familiar with a few of them from his youth and was very likely influenced by them in a general way. What seems certain, however, is that they helped to shape the *Zeitgeist,* and their influence made the *Zeitgeist* ultimately receptive to Freud's influence. These relationships will be discussed in Chapter 5, when we consider Freud's concept of the unconscious.

Throughout this monograph we shall be using not only "concept," but "conception." We make a sharp distinction between them. By conception we mean the broad matrix from which theories and concepts crystallize. Concepts have definitions; conceptions make use of any term, and apply concepts in a common-sense way in disregard, or even in ignorance, of their definitions. Theories by and large use only terms which have a conceptual status. When terms (for instance, relativity, libido, survival of the fittest) are used outside of the theory they become conceptions, as they may have been before the theory gave them definitions as concepts.

The ideas of Freud's immediate forebears, including Meynert, Brücke, Charcot, Breuer, Bernheim, Brentano, Fechner, Hering, T. Lipps, seem to have had considerable influence on Freud, although they were not predecessors of his central ideas. They contributed to the intellectual development of the period, a development which came to a culmination with the impact of Freud's theories.

The ideas of Freud's early contemporaries, such as the functionalists (James, Dewey, Angell), while they do not seem to have influenced Freud directly, were precursors of some of his central ideas, and helped to pave the way for the acceptance of Freud's conceptions. James played an especially important role by his anticipation[1] of some of Freud's particular insights, and by his influence on the thinking of his students: Holt, Woodworth, Thorndike, and others.

The various concepts of the "subconscious" held by Freud's contemporaries—Janet, Prince, and Sidis, for example—affected Freud's thinking little if at all,[2] yet contributed a great deal to the receptivity in psychological circles to Freud's conception of the unconscious.

[1] See pp. 38-39.
[2] "We must avoid, too, the distinction between 'supraconscious' and 'subconscious,' . . . for such a distinction seems precisely calculated to stress the equivalence of what is psychical to what is conscious" (Freud, 1900a, p. 615).

Thus these predecessors and early contemporaries are not truly genetic antecedents of Freud. They are instead representatives of numerous parallel developments.

Those who followed Freud in time present no less complex a situation. On the one hand, many trends in psychology appeared after Freud's publications which seem to represent direct effects of his influence, but are said to derive from independent sources. For instance, Spence (1952) maintains that Hull's drive concept was derived from Thorndike.[3] Rickers-Ovsiankina, Dembo, and Heider attribute Lewin's theory of tension systems in particular, and his "affect and action psychology" in general, to the "dynamic" atmosphere of the time rather than to Freud.[4] On the other hand, many theorists who claim that their views are derived directly from Freud seem to have utilized only certain of Freud's ideas in combination with other theories. Dollard and Miller's (1950) and Mowrer's (1950) theories may be considered on the whole to fall into this category.

In the course of our presentation, we may appear to be suggesting a steady growth of Freudian influence. That such a semblance of continuity is illusory, however, should not surprise anyone who is accustomed to genetic observations and who has learned to think in terms of "epigenesis" rather than "preformation," in terms of saltatory rather than uninterrupted development, in terms of advance by developmental crises rather than along smooth growth curves.[5]

[3] See p. 135 ff.
[4] See p. 125 ff.
[5] In this connection, we undertook a rough survey of the first fifty volumes of the *Journal of Abnormal and Social Psychology*. This analysis showed that, beginning around 1909-1910, there was a quick rise in the number of Freudian contributions and discussions. Beginning in 1920-1921, articles opposing psychoanalysis tended to preponderate. By the middle of the 1920's indirect discussions—often without any references to Freud—became more numerous than direct ones. In the 1930's both direct and indirect discussions became less frequent; only in the late 1930's did the volume of indirect discussions again begin to increase slowly, a tendency which appears to have persisted to the present. In 1943, Herma, Kris, and Shor (1943, p. 331) characterized the more qualitative aspects of the development of Freud's influence as follows: "Parts of Freud's theory are being integrated into the general body of knowledge. Acceptance tends therefore to be anonymous, while rejection is personalized."

J. C. Burnham, a student of the history of Freud's influence on American civilization, suggests (personal communication, June 17, 1956) that the above trends may represent changing editorial policy more than anything else, and that

Forewarned against the simplistic assumption, we notice not only the obvious, increasing respect which finally reaches a crescendo of homage to Freud the man and his conception of man, but also some of the other attitudes which color whatever acceptance his work has gained.

1. What is accepted is Freud's new view of man and his pioneering in new areas for psychological study. There has been a slow realization that Freud awakened interest in human nature, in infancy and childhood, in the irrational in man; that he is the fountainhead of dynamic psychology in general, and of psychology's present-day conceptions of motivation and of the unconscious in particular.

2. Although there are many striking exceptions, it is for the most part his *conception* of these fields of study and his *observations* in them, not his *concepts* and *theories* about them, which have been accepted.

3. When the theory itself is referred to, it is usually transformed into some "common-sense" version or is taken at the level of its clinical referents. In either case it is likely to be criticized. It can even be said—as we shall show—that until recently, no serious efforts were made to study thoroughly or to define Freud's concepts before either "testing" them experimentally or rejecting them.

4. The methods by which Freud arrived at his theories have not been used. Only recently has there been some effort made to examine the psychoanalytic method as a tool for research.[6]

Thus, along with the nonlinear growth of influence, we find that at almost every step the increase of the influence is accompanied by opposing or confounding trends. What has occurred has been increasing acceptance without proportionate growth of conversance; acceptance of Freud's conception of man but not of the means by which he derived it; in fact, an influence that was not accompanied by true understanding.

---

an evaluation of them is complicated by the appearance on the scene of the specifically psychoanalytic journals (*Psychoanalytic Review* in 1913, *International Journal of Psycho-Analysis* in 1920, *Psychoanalytic Quarterly* in 1932). Nevertheless, editorial policy in the long run does reflect the climate of opinion. Both the upsurge of specialized psychoanalytic journals and the consequent reduction of accessibility of psychoanalytic literature to the academic psychological public are part of the vicissitudes of Freud's influence on psychology.

[6] See Benjamin (1950), Escalona (1952), Kubie (1953), Shakow (1960a).

A more explicit understanding of the problem of influence is needed. What do we mean by "influence"?

Hoffman (1957), in *Freudianism and the Literary Mind*, has expressed the view that by the time a theory reaches and influences an artist (he is talking about the creative writer) it "acquires the qualities of . . . illustration, and loses its original accuracy or 'abstract purity' " (p. 89). He points out that between the artist and the theorist stands the lecturer or popularizer and sometimes the translator. It is also likely that the artist will use and transform the theory as it suits his needs (p. 92). He believes, therefore, that "We need to determine the nature and quality of the artist's variation from exact theory" (p. 94). We are inclined to agree with Hoffman about the influence of theories on artists. In fact, we would extend his analysis to include scientists as well. Ideally, we would expect the scientist to study and gain objective knowledge about a theory, to line up all the facts, and to judge exclusively on that basis what is worth incorporating into his own thinking. It would be comforting to believe that scientists are always so rational. The fact is, however, that since scientists, like artists, are human, with rare exceptions they fall far short of this ideal.

As we shall see, in the case of psychoanalytic theory, barriers in the way of ideal rationality were numerous and weighty among psychologists. Generally speaking, the scientist, because of the limited working time available to him, tries to learn more and more about his area of specialization, and inevitably attends less and less to everything outside it. In his specialty he may try to be completely rational and objective. But outside of it—and for a long while psychoanalysis was "outside" to most psychologists—where he lacks tested knowledge, he will act, not like a scientist, but like any other person. Common experience, corroborated by Erikson (1956b) and Hartmann (1956a), indicates that when tested knowledge is not available, implicit regulations of various sorts—whether ideologies, commitments, biases, predilections, or aversions—will select and shape the understandings he gains and mold the "influences" which impinge upon him.[7] It is easy to see why many psychologists,

---

[7] In a personal communication (December 24, 1962), Boring points out that this is equally true when tested knowledge *is* available.

involved in their specialized concerns and protected by their ideologies, were immune to the influence of this new theory.

The historical influence of a theory cannot be measured by the degree of familiarity with and acceptance of it. In the case of Freud, if we were to take *precise* understanding of the theory, or any part of it, as the measure of his influence on psychology, our study would be brief and we would be forced to conclude: Freud had no influence. One is repeatedly struck by the scant theoretical grounding in psychoanalysis on which acceptance or rejection is based. The epigram written about Klopstock, the author of *Messiah*, comes to mind: *"Wer wird nicht einen Klopstock loben? Doch wird ihn jeder lesen? Nein. Wir wollen weniger erhoben und fleissiger gelesen sein."*[8]

Therefore, rather than insisting on the criterion of precise understanding, we will use a more flexible and perhaps more appropriate measure of influence, one more like Hoffman's (1957, p. 94). *Freud's influence on psychology must be gauged by the reactions of psychologists to any idea which* demonstrably *originated in Freud's observations and theories, regardless of whether the idea came from original sources, secondary sources, popularizations, or hearsay.*

Our task, then, is to trace the details of this kind of influence, and also to establish how closely the "accepted" ideas resemble the original theory. In so doing, we shall examine, among other things, the ideological commitment of Freud and the channels through which his theory was presented, and the specific ideological commitments of psychology which determined its reaction to the impingements of Freud's theory, as well as some aspects of the broader ideological situation in the United States at the time of the first impact of Freud's theory. For, while such factors are irrelevant to the appraisal of the theory itself, they nevertheless helped determine the character of Freud's influence.

And as we shall see, in a discussion of Darwin and Freud, the history of Freud's influence may not be essentially different from that of the influence of other scientific theories. Alternatively, what happened in Freud's case might be more like the history of the

---

[8] "Who would not praise a Klopstock? But would everyone read him? No. We would rather be exalted less, and more assiduously read."

influence of social or religious systems. But, just as there does not seem to be an essential difference in the way scientists and artists relate to a new theory, there is perhaps no sharp difference between the impact of new scientific theories and the impact of new religious systems.[9]

---

[9] Boring (personal communication, 1957) commented on this point: "I keep seeing similarities between Freud and Titchener and between the disciples of each, and one uses that word *disciples* as one uses the word *orthodoxy* to denote that science gets this religious connotation, or rather that the scientists do."

2

DARWIN AND FREUD:
A COMPARISON OF RECEPTIONS

THE THREE HISTORICAL BLOWS

On at least three different occasions[1] Freud implied a similarity between himself, Copernicus, and Darwin. His comparison was not actually a personal one; rather, he compared psychoanalysis with the Copernican and Darwinian theories.[2] When Abraham commented on the apparent personalness of one of these passages (Freud, 1917), Freud replied: "You are right in saying that the enumeration in my last paper may give the impression of claiming a place beside Copernicus and Darwin. But I didn't want to give up the interesting train of thought on that account, and so at least put Schopenhauer in the foreground" (Jones, 1955, p. 226).

Not only Freud, but also his biographer, Ernest Jones, seems to have been somewhat sensitive about this comparison. In 1956,

---

[1] *Introductory Lectures on Psycho-Analysis* (1916-1917, pp. 284-285), "A Difficulty in the Path of Psycho-Analysis" (1917, pp. 139-144 [originally written for the outstanding general Hungarian periodical, *Nyugat*]), "The Resistances to Psycho-Analysis" (1925a, p. 221).

[2] It is true that upon occasion Freud did make a direct comparison of himself with historical figures. One such comparison was with Columbus, whom he considered an important explorer-discoverer, but not a great man (Jones, 1955, p. 415). Barzun's (1958, pp. 85-86) view of Darwin is of interest in this connection. He holds that Darwin ". . . does not belong with the great thinkers of mankind. He belongs rather with those others—men of action and feeling and unconscious power—whom Hegel termed world-historical characters because the world after them is not as it was before." Himmelfarb (1959, p. 164) expresses a similar view. Darwin, she thinks, might very appropriately have said of himself what Freud said of himself in a letter to Fliess: ". . . I am not really a man of science, not an observer, not an experimenter, and not a thinker. I am nothing but by temperament a *conquistador* . . ." (Himmelfarb quotes this letter from Jones' biography [Jones, 1953, p. 348]. It has not been included in the volume containing the Fliess letters.) Simon (1957) offers justification for Freud's identification of himself with Oedipus, Hannibal, La Salle, and particularly with Moses.

14

Nigel Walker published an article entitled "Freud and Copernicus" in *The Listener*.[3] Although some exceptions may be taken to Walker's article on certain grounds,[4] the resulting exchange between Jones and Walker is a significant illustration of Jones' attitude. In this article Walker referred to Freud's comparison of himself with Copernicus and Darwin, but concluded that Freud more closely resembled Captain Cook (changed to "Magellan" in the reprinted version). For this, Jones took Walker to task: ". . . nothing would ["could" in original version] have been more unlike Freud" (Nelson, 1957, p. 287). This sensitivity of Freud and Jones is rather difficult to understand, considering Freud's repeated juxtaposition, if not complete identification, of psychoanalysis with the other two historical developments. Modesty of both author and biographer perhaps forbade their pointing to the amount of objective justification for the comparison.[5] As Heidbreder (1940) said in her obituary of Freud, and as so many others have repeated since, the comparison with Copernicus and Darwin has "become inevitable."[6]

In both *Introductory Lectures on Psycho-Analysis* and "A Difficulty in the Path of Psycho-Analysis" Freud made the comparison of psychoanalysis with Copernican and Darwinian theory in terms of the three historical blows which human narcissism has had to undergo: the *cosmological* blow administered by Copernicus, the *biological* blow administered by Darwin and his group, and the *psychological* blow administered by psychoanalysis. These blows jolted respectively man's geocentrism, anthropocentrism, and ego-

---

[3] Reprinted, with minor changes, as "A New Copernicus?" (Walker, 1957).

[4] For instance, Walker's emphasis on the special importance of Herbartian psychology in Freud's background. See Kris' comment about Freud and Herbart (in Freud, 1887-1902, p. 47).

[5] Although Freud perhaps never thought about himself as a genius, emphasizing instead the importance of his discoveries, Jones' reaction to Walker is rather belied by what he says about Freud in various other places. For instance, in the third volume of the biography (1957, p. 304), he says he "bestowed on Freud the title of the Darwin of the Mind." See also Jones (1955, especially Part III) and particularly his *Centenary Addresses* (1956).

[6] For example, E. D. Adrian (1954), in his Presidential Address to the British Association for the Advancement of Science on "Science and Human Nature," has briefly made this comparison. Alex Comfort (1960) has compared Darwin and Freud, calling for more interrelationships between Darwinians and Freudians —a suggestion which deserves strong support. Erikson (1956a) has sensitively compared Darwin's and Freud's problems in their respective fields of biological and individual prehistory and very briefly touched on the differing implications of each.

centrism.[7] Freud himself considered the blow to the ego's mastery of its own mind as the "most wounding blow" of the three.[8]

A detailed comparison of the effects of all three major historical contributions is beyond our scope. However, the major aspects of the impacts of the differing but related Darwinian and Freudian theories can, we believe, serve as an effective introduction to some of the problems we shall be facing in the attempt to trace Freud's influence on psychology. This comparison seems particularly appropriate during this centennial period, when there is so much discussion concerning Darwin's influence.

Reception of the Theories

A dependable evaluation of the effects of the respective blows is particularly difficult to make because of the chronological relationship of Darwin and Freud, who came within only half a century of one another. Our main concern is not, of course, the relative importance of the two theories[9] or the relative greatness of the two men. Rather, we are interested in comparing the *responses* to these two revolutionary theories in their respective historical situations.

To begin with, was there a difference in the length of time it took for each of these theories to be accepted? To say *when* a theory is "accepted" is, of course, most difficult. Perhaps the best

[7] Closely associated with Darwin's disturbance of anthropocentrism is the little-noted but important contribution Alfred Russel Wallace made to the weakening of the intimately related ethnocentrism (see Eiseley, 1959, p. 303 ff.). See also Fenichel's (1946) comments on the narcissistic blow. Actually there is need for a re-examination of the whole problem of "blows," both those considered here and the most recent "galactic" blow which has such far-reaching implications for man (Shapley, 1958).

[8] "In the course of centuries the *naïve* self-love of men has had to submit to two major blows at the hands of science. . . . This is associated in our minds with the name of Copernicus, though something similar had already been asserted by Alexandrian science. The second blow fell when biological research destroyed man's supposedly privileged place in creation and proved his descent from the animal kingdom and his ineradicable animal nature. This revaluation has been accomplished in our own days by Darwin, Wallace and their predecessors, though not without the most violent contemporary opposition. But human megalomania will have suffered its third and most wounding blow from the psychological research of the present time which seeks to prove to the ego that it is not even master in its own house, but must content itself with scanty information of what is going on unconsciously in its mind" (Freud, 1916-1917, pp. 284-285).

[9] "Freud's effect is, however, still too recent to compare with Darwin's. For that we must wait fifty years" (Boring, 1950b, p. 743).

we can do is to define as the time of acceptance the periods when the fundamental ideas seem to have passed through the usual initial period of marked opposition and to have become part of the general culture.

In both cases, approximately one generation appears to have been sufficient to make each theory a recognizable, even prominent, part of the culture.[10] Of the two theories, however, evolutionary ways of thinking have undoubtedly taken a greater hold and become a more intimate part of the culture and of man's concept of himself than have psychoanalytic ways of thinking.[11] Why is this so? The difference, we believe, cannot be accounted for merely by the four decades' seniority of the former. We must look to other factors also. From the first, Freudism seems to have met with greater opposition than did Darwinism. Let us therefore examine in some detail the nature of the differences in their reception.

---

[10] Not that opposition did not persist considerably beyond a generation, even with respect to the essential aspects of the theories. Isolated opposition to Darwinism existed even two generations later—witness the Scopes trial in the United States and Sir Ambrose Fleming in England. The Scopes trial took place in the summer of 1925. According to Keith, Sir Ambrose Fleming's attack came on January 14, 1935 in a presidential address before the Victoria Institute and Philosophical Society of Great Britain (see p. 19). "In this he maintained that the account of the creation of man given in the book of Genesis is literally true, and that the 'evolutionary theory is totally at variance with the scriptural teaching as to man's original perfection'" (Keith, 1935, p. 51). Sir Ambrose was a F.R.S., a fellow of University College, London, and a world authority on electrical engineering.

Opposition to psychoanalysis, both in the culture at large and in professional circles, still exists in even more widespread form at the present time—again several generations later. Dallenbach (1955) and Gengerelli (1957), for instance, are quite recent examples of this opposition among psychologists.

Copernicus met religious objection almost immediately (particularly from the Protestants; for example, Luther, Calvin, and Melanchthon), although it is of interest to note that he himself did not believe that his views conflicted with the Bible. But recognition of how radical his ideas actually were did not occur for at least a generation. It was only after two generations, with Giordano Bruno's emphasis on the plurality of worlds and the infinite universe implied by the theory, that the Copernican view became the center of real controversy (see Butterfield, 1949, pp. 48-50; Wightman, 1953, p. 49). Copernicus' work was banned by the Catholic Church until 1822 (Schwartz and Bishop, 1958, p. 219). For a more detailed discussion, see Kuhn (1957), *The Copernican Revolution*.

See Freud's discussion of the acceptance of new ideas in *Moses and Monotheism* (1939, pp. 103-104). Darlington (1959a) and Himmelfarb (1959, p. 292) point out that the general aspects of Darwinian ideas actually triumphed within a decade.

[11] See Sir Julian Huxley (1960) for a description of the vicissitudes of Darwinian theory, with its many very high ups and few downs.

RECEPTION OF *On the Origin of the Species*

How was the *Origin* received? As in the case of any scientific idea, certain groups were instrumental in determining its acceptance. Here four groups were involved: (1) those in the immediately concerned scientific disciplines, persons for whom evolutionary doctrines had direct professional significance—the life-scientists, such as zoologists, biologists, physiologists, and scientists involved with retrospective material, such as geologists and paleontologists; (2) those in other academic fields and sciences; (3) clergymen; (4) educated laymen.

Among those immediately concerned, the reaction to Darwin's theory was on the whole favorable.[12] Especially important support came from Darwin's four "lieutenants": Hooker, the director of Kew Gardens; Lyell, the father of modern geology (with some residual resistance); Gray, the Harvard botanist; and Huxley. And naturally there was Wallace, who shared the honors of the 1858 presentation to the Linnean Society. Other prominent persons reacted favorably: Carpenter, the physiologist; Ramsay, the geologist; Chambers, the geologist and publisher; and Galton. Some equally prominent persons were, of course, not favorably disposed. Agassiz was the most outstanding of this group which included Richard Owen, the "greatest anatomist of his time," Mivart, the Roman Catholic biologist, and Whewell (see Ellegård, 1958, Chapter 9), the leading philosopher of science.

In other parts of the academic community, the negative attitude of Herschel, the mathematician, was balanced by the positive attitude of Sir John Lubbock, the astronomer and mathematician. The attacks on the theory by physicists, however, particularly by Lord Kelvin (the greatest physicist of the nineteenth century) were especially troubling. These attacks, based on the then reasonable physical theories of the relative recency of the earth's origins, resulted in a brief period of anti-Darwinian feeling (see Eiseley, 1959, p. 233 ff.).

The most vehement opposition to the *Origin* came from the

---

[12] Some question may be raised, as it has been by several persons, about beginning an assessment of the response to Darwin's views with the publication of the *Origin*. For there was much initial opposition from a number of his associates, even his "lieutenants." This was dispelled in the period prior to 1859 by considerable correspondence and personal discussion. However, since our concern is with the response in the culture as a whole, it seems reasonable to adopt as our starting point the date when Darwin finally decided to reveal his views publicly.

clergy. To them the book became a kind of anti-Bible, probably because it epitomized the issues in the long-standing battle between religion and science dating from Copernican times. Darwinism became the symbol of the growing secularization of society and the undermining of religious institutions.[13] A few clergymen, like the Reverend Charles Kingsley of *Water Babies* fame, accepted the revolutionary doctrine quite calmly. The great majority, however, including the Reverend Adam Sedgwick, Darwin's old geology teacher, raised a storm of protest. The clergy also received reinforcements from a "religious phalanx" among scientists and physicians. In 1865 this phalanx founded the Victoria Institute, " 'to investigate fully and impartially the most important questions of Philosophy and Science, but more especially those that bear upon the great truths revealed in Holy Scripture, with the view of defending these truths against the opposition of Science, falsely so called' " (quoted by Ellegård [1958, p. 104] from the Victoria Institute *Journal*).

Against this opposition, Huxley, in England, and Haeckel, even more spiritedly, in Germany, provided a most outspoken and ultimately successful defense (see A. D. White, 1896, especially pp. 70-71, 245). Even in 1860, in the celebrated collision between Huxley and Bishop Wilberforce—perhaps the most vocal opponent of the *Origin* in the early days after publication—Huxley emerged the winner (Irvine, 1955, pp. 5-7; see also R. Moore, 1957, pp. 119-123).

Among laymen, early acceptance of Darwin's views seems to have been quite positively correlated with educational level and degree of general liberalism (Ellegård, 1958, pp. 33-35). Barzun (1958, p. 33) points out that during the middle of the Victorian era, "press and public were in the right mood for the close and protracted discussion of ideas." We know that science figured prominently in the later nineteenth century school curriculum and enjoyed prestige among educated laymen. With the increasing acceptance of Darwinism by the scientific group, and the clergy's diminishing status and reduced opposition to Darwinism, the nat-

---

[13] J. Pelikan (1960, p. 246) says: "Seldom in the history of the Christian church have theologians reacted as violently to a non-theological book as they did to Charles Darwin's *Origin of Species*." See also C. C. Gillispie (1951), John C. Greene (1959a), Ruth Moore (1957, Chapter VI), Dillenberger (1960), and Ellegård (1958, especially Chapters 5 and 8).

ural result was a gradual acceptance of Darwinian ideas by the layman.

RECEPTION OF FREUD'S IDEAS

Let us now turn to the reception of Freud's ideas. In Freud's case it is rather difficult to select a particular year to focus on. Rather, it seems most appropriate to take the decade from 1895 to 1905, in the middle of which appeared *The Interpretation of Dreams* (1900a). This period also included the appearance of an important series of Freud's papers and presentations: in May of 1896 he gave an address to the Society of Psychiatry and Neurology in Vienna on the etiology of hysteria, and in 1898 published his paper on "Sexuality in the Aetiology of the Neuroses," which included the first mention of infantile sexuality. This is also the period of *The Psychopathology of Everyday Life* (1901), *Jokes and Their Relation to the Unconscious* (1905a), and *Three Essays on the Theory of Sexuality* (1905b). With *The Interpretation of Dreams*, these works helped to establish the image of Freudian thinking.

In the reception of Freud's thought, the relevant groups, parallel to those examined for Darwin, were: (1) the professionals and scientists most directly involved—psychiatrists, neurologists, and psychologists; (2) members of the other branches of the medical profession and academic disciplines; (3) the clergy; (4) educated laymen.

The contrast with the Darwinian situation shows up most strikingly in the reactions of the primary groups involved—psychiatrists, neurologists, and psychologists. Almost all the leading figures in these professions are to be found among the opponents. A list of those who expressed vehement opposition to Freudian ideas at various times during the early period, up to about 1910, is actually a "Who's Who" of psychiatry and neurology. In the Germanic countries the array is stellar: Aschaffenburg, Bumke, Förster, Heilbronner, Isserlin, Jaspers, Kraepelin, Moll, Oppenheim, Sommer, Spielmeyer, Vogt, Weygandt, and Ziehen, to mention the most prominent.[14] On the American scene, somewhat later, were Collins,

---

[14] It is possible that a good deal of the reaction of these persons was based on their essentially antipsychotherapeutic "organic" approach to psychopathology. However, a review of the content of their opinions, so frequently vituperative,

Dercum, Sachs, Sidis, and Starr,[15] and on the French scene, Dubois. From psychology, Wilhelm Stern may be mentioned here merely as an example, since we shall be examining the situation in this field in detail later.[16]

The reactions of persons in other branches of medicine and science[17] to Freud's ideas were equally negative, as was to be expected from persons in fields that were little touched by the new theories. For in respect to psychoanalysis they were essentially laymen who, because of professional identification, tended to accept the guidance of their more involved colleagues. Jones' chapter on "Opposition" in the second volume (1955) of his biography provides one picture of the hostile reception of Freud by the professional world, particularly in the Germanic countries and in America.[18]

What about the clergy, from whom the main attack on Darwin had come? In Freud's case, the reaction of the clergy was much less evident. To some extent, the difference may have arisen from the fact that, although "morality" was deeply involved in Freudism, and its moral implications were as great as or even greater than Darwinism's,[19] it did not, as had Darwinism, make a direct attack on such concrete religious tenets as the creation. It could therefore not so easily be taken as a symbol of the increasing secularization of society. Then, too, the relative absence of material on the attitude of the clergy may in part be the result of a difference in the cultural context in which Darwin and Freud developed their ideas. A greater interrelationship seems to have existed between religion and science in Darwin's Britain, as reflected, for instance, in the parson-naturalists of that country, than in the Germanic

---

leaves the impression that much more than a reaction to psychotherapy was involved. Their arguments seem largely directed at the sex aspect of Freud's theories.

[15] Two Americans whose views were not quite so strong were S. Weir Mitchell and Southard. An example of Weir Mitchell's reaction to Freud is found in Earnest (1950, pp. 180-181). Southard's predominantly negative views of Freud are discussed by F. P. Gay (1938, pp. 194-201).

[16] See Jones (1955, pp. 107-126) for some details.

[17] See Freud's (1913, p. 182) point about biology; also see (1913, p. 166).

[18] See Bry and Rifkin (1962) who present a somewhat different picture in their analysis of the reception of Freud's discussion of male hysteria and the reviews in journals of *The Interpretation of Dreams*. Although this is a helpful corrective effort, a much more inclusive analysis of the contemporary response is still needed.

[19] See Brierley (1934-1947), Erikson (1950, 1961), Flugel (1945), and Hartmann (1960), who consider the "moral" aspects of psychoanalysis.

countries of Freud's time. Darwinism itself must certainly have made a significant contribution to the change in the tenor of the times. It may be that there was a lack of interest in the opinion of the clergy because of the lower status they held in the culture by the end of the century. And it may be that, as Jones says, "Freud lived in a period of time when the *odium theologicum* had been replaced by the *odium sexicum* and not yet by the *odium politicum*" (1955, p. 108).[20]

The strong opposition to Freudism by professional colleagues militated against its acceptance by the educated layman. Opposition among laymen was also aroused because the perversions and distortions of Freudian ideas which rapidly became current were antithetical to dominant public attitudes. It was only the next generation which found these distorted views not incompatible with other radicalisms they were accepting. Indeed, as we shall have occasion to review later, an important role was played by the educated layman in the eventual acceptance of Freud's views.

Thus we find that whereas Darwin had to contend primarily with the clergy while having strong support from other groups, particularly from his colleagues, Freud encountered opposition from almost all groups, especially from his colleagues.

Those who were drawn to psychoanalysis were almost exclusively in the group who eventually became psychoanalysts. They were mostly youngish, relatively unknown persons coming from non-academic and even nonmedical fields, frequently from the humanities. With rare exceptions they were Jews, who lived their professional lives under many handicaps, and who had relatively little power and prestige. Later a few outstanding persons, largely from the Zurich group, became associated with Freud. But the support of Jung and Bleuler, the most prominent of these, did not last.

Factors Contributing to Reception

Why did these marked differences in the reception of Darwinism and Freudism exist? Among the multiplicity of probable contributing factors, some appear intrinsic to the theories and others more accessory in nature, though it is often difficult to define the

---

[20] See Rieff (1959, p. 272), who quite flatly says that the attachment of clerics to Freud is misplaced.

forces at work as clearly belonging to one or the other of these categories.

INTRINSIC FACTORS

Perhaps the most important of the intrinsic factors was the degree to which each theory threatened to disturb man's concept of himself. As psychologists, we agree with Freud's own view that psychoanalytic theory offers a more immediate and deeper threat to fundamental narcissism,[21] for it contains potentially anxiety-arousing elements less manifest in Darwinian theory. One can perhaps "take," and live quite comfortably with, the general and rather impersonal idea of a genetic descent from animals, an idea that does not necessarily carry negative implications about man's present status. It is much more difficult, however, to deal with an idea which focuses on the omnipresent existence of the animal within oneself. Actually this idea is a natural extrapolation of Darwinian doctrine, but not one that had been emphasized in the earlier period. The dethronement of rational control which accompanied Freud's central emphasis on the unconscious made his theory especially hard to take. The shock engendered by this view was apparently so great that even among persons in the psychological professions the response aroused was highly emotional.

Still another source of anxiety stemmed from Freud's minimization of the difference between the normal and abnormal. Almost from the very first Freud argued that the distinctions between normal and abnormal were not qualitatively great. While one of his earliest and most important formulations of this view is in *The Interpretation of Dreams* (1900a, pp. 603-608), it is perhaps more simply expressed in a paper published in 1937: "But such a normal ego is, like normality in general, an ideal fiction. The abnormal ego ... is unfortunately no fiction. Now every normal person is only approximately normal: his ego resembles that of the psychotic in one point or another, in a greater or lesser degree, and its distance from one end of the scale and proximity to the other may pro-

---

[21] No matter that the immediate and obvious outburst was probably against a theory based on a dirty subject—sex—put forth by a Jew, and therefore not being worthy of serious consideration. But perhaps the projection involved in this superficial "scapegoating" hid not only the fact that one was interested in sex, but also the awareness of how deep the interest was, and to what "untouchable" persons it was directed.

visionally serve as a measure of what we have indefinitely spoken of as 'modification of the ego' " (1937, p. 337).[22]

We have presented a psychologist's view of the relative disturbance to man's concept of himself made by these two revolutionary theories.

Might not the biologist see the issues differently? Although we know of no direct attempt at comparison by a member of this discipline, the opinions of some biologists on the disturbing effect of Darwin's impact indicate that they indeed might. For instance, Simpson (1960), in his characteristically lucid and forthright address at the 1959 meeting of the American Association for the Advancement of Science, said:

> The influence of Darwin . . . has literally led us into a different world.
> . . . Perception of the truth of evolution was an enormous stride from superstition to a rational universe.
> . . . According to the higher superstition, man is something quite distinct from nature. He stands apart from all other creatures; his kinship is supernatural, not natural.
> Another subtler and even more deeply warping concept of the higher superstition was that the world was created for man. Other organisms had no separate purpose in the scheme of creation. Whether noxious or useful, they were to be seriously considered only in their relationship to the supreme creation, the image of God.
> Those elements of the higher superstition dominated European thought before publication of *The Origin of Species*. . .
> A world in which man must rely on himself, in which he is not the darling of the gods but only another, albeit extraordinary, aspect of nature, is by no means congenial to the immature or the wishful thinkers. That is plainly a major reason why even now, a hundred years after *The Origin of Species*, most people have not really entered the world into which Darwin led—alas!—only a minority of us. Life may conceivably be happier for some people in the older worlds of superstition. It is possible that some children are made happy by a belief in Santa Claus, but adults should prefer to live in a world of reality and reason.[23]

And in a personal communication of April 11, 1960 he adds: "Except for what I have said about the impact of Darwin in that article, I doubt if I can be of real help in your comparative assess-

---

[22] See Shakow (1960b) for a discussion of some present-day reverberations of this threat, as represented in the concern with "positive mental health."

[23] Some psychoanalytically oriented persons hold that for many it is through the kind of self-examination suggested by Freud that such a goal may be achieved.

ment of the influence of Darwin and Freud. . . . I feel that the Darwinian influence has been probably less superficially obvious and yet more profoundly disturbing and important."

Eiseley (1959, p. 257) states the same view of the Darwinian revolution somewhat differently: "It is my genuine belief that no greater act of the human intellect, no greater gesture of humility on the part of man has been or will be made in the long history of science."

Viewing the issue as a whole, however, a different conclusion seems not unreasonable. It would seem relatively easy to live with the blow to man's collective pride at no longer being the darling of God, and even to suffer the violation of many of one's traditional religious beliefs—for these are distant issues, impinging relatively little upon daily life. Granting the validity of Eiseley's evaluation, we might wonder whether the self-sacrifice involved is not compensated for by the warm glow of humility to which one is entitled as an acceptor of the Darwinian view. Further, and perhaps more importantly, no immediate implications for *conduct* are attached to accepting Darwin's views. They can therefore be more readily tolerated.[24]

Even if one overcomes the blow to human pride coming from Freud's reduction of the importance of reason and his minimization of the difference of normal man from both the animal and the psychotic, implications for conduct remain to be dealt with. It is easy to derive an invitation to sexual and other licenses from Freudian theory. For, instead of being recognized as the potential liberator of man from the tyranny of the unconscious, Freud was seen as a seducer of man, as one who encouraged man to give free rein to animal desires. Freud's arguments for the existence of the unconscious and his detailed description of its characteristics were widely interpreted as open advocacy of the direct satisfaction of the wishes which were uncovered. The strong moral aspect of psychoanalysis with its motto "Where id was, there shall ego be" (Freud, 1932,

---

[24] A letter from Mrs. Carlyle to Mrs. Russell, January 28, 1860, on this subject is relevant: "Even when Darwin, in a book that all the scientific world is in ecstasy over, proved the other day that we are all come from shell-fish, it didn't move me to the slightest curiosity whether we are or are not. I did not feel that the slightest light could be thrown on my practical life for me, by having it ever so logically made out that my first ancestor, millions of ages back, had been, or even had not been, an oyster" (Froude, 1883, pp. 119-120).

p. 112) was overlooked by both professional opponents and the public.[25] Barzun (1958, pp. 353-354) puts the case succinctly: "Freud's thought is a good example of the way in which work devoted to freeing man from thralldom through the use of intelligence has been blindly misinterpreted as proving the necessary slavery of man to 'unconscious urges,' and the advisability of giving loose rein to them because they were scientifically there."[26] It was in this way that Freudism gradually took on, for much of the culture, the meaning of "libertinism," and such an interpretation of Freudian theory presumably afforded the grounds for satisfaction at a concrete animal level. The acceptor thus faced a temptation to indulgence—a temptation which could arouse anxieties of a quite different character and intensity from those connected with the Darwinian view.

A different intrinsic reason for the dissimilar reception of Darwin's and Freud's ideas lies in the relative completeness and systematization of the early presentations of their respective arguments. In both these respects Darwin certainly had the advantage, despite Freud's greater skill as a writer.[27] It seems, however, that each spent

[25] Not until a somewhat later period (about 1910) did the outstanding proponents of the adaptive (in the sense of improvement) and moral aspects of psychoanalysis begin to become prominent, and even then there was some opposition from the more conventional Freudians, who were perhaps afraid that this emphasis might divert attention from the central issues. These proponents were Putnam (1915) in America, and Pfister (1913; also see 1923) and Silberer (Freud, 1900a, pp. 523-524; Freud, 1922, p. 216) on the European scene. For a description of some aspects of this development in America, see Matthews (1955, Chapter VI).

Nathan G. Hale (personal communication, April 16, 1963) believes that "there is a distinctively American interpretation of psychoanalysis—optimistic, simplified, eclectic, far more 'environmentalist' than Freud himself." This is in some ways corroborated by Putnam's views. Although this particular trend was probably most characteristic of the United States, it also existed elsewhere.

[26] Saul Rosenzweig (1935) earlier pointed out this fact in a rather obscure journal, *The Modern Thinker*.

[27] See Barzun (1958, pp. 74-75). Also see T. H. Huxley's (L. Huxley, 1900, p. 190) letter to Foster, February 14, 1888, on Darwin: "I have been reading the *Origin* slowly again for the *n*th time, with the view of picking out the essentials of the argument, for the obituary notice. Nothing entertains me more than to hear people call it easy reading.

"Exposition was not Darwin's *forte*—and his English is sometimes wonderful."

Those in a position to judge apparently have a high opinion of Freud as a writer, or at least as a stylist. In this connection, it is significant that Freud in 1930 won the Goethe Prize for Literature. Einstein wrote to Freud in 1939: "I quite specially admire your achievement [*Moses and Monotheism*], as I do with all your writings, from a literary point of view. I do not know any contemporary who has presented his subject in the German language in such a masterly fashion" (Jones, 1957, p. 243). Hyman's most interesting book, *The Tangled Bank* (1962),

a similar amount of time—a period of twenty to twenty-five years—on the development of his theories before presenting them in systematic form.

Darwin began his formulations during his fifty-seven-month voyage on the *Beagle* in the years 1831-1836. Actually his report on this voyage, published in 1839, contained many of the elements which were later included in the *Origin*. The year 1837 marks the beginning of the period of approximately two decades in which Darwin "never ceased working" on facts in preparation for *On the Origin of the Species*. This period includes the various publications relating to his voyage—the narrative, his writings on the mammalia and the fossil mammalia, coral reefs, and volcanic islands, the *Geological Observations on South America*—the two monographs on barnacles, as well as several other monographs, and of course the writing of the *Origin* itself.

As nearly as one can tell, Freud's thinking along the lines which led to the psychoanalytic formulations started at the earliest about 1882 when Freud discussed Breuer's case of Anna O. with him.[28] At that time he began to use the term "unconscious," to which he gave increased emphasis in 1893 when the case was published. During this same period (1885-1886) he went to Paris to work with Charcot. It was during this decade that the major part of his shift from neurology to psychology occurred (Freud, 1886).

Yet, as we have indicated, despite the similar time span, the initial presentations of the two theories were strikingly dissimilar both in completeness and systematic formulation. The *Origin* reflects a tremendous piling up of evidence from a great variety of sources, presented in a form generally acceptable to science.[29] In contrast, we find in Freud a relatively unsystematic succession of papers and the *Interpretation,* which volume came some eighteen years after

---

discusses Freud's rich use of metaphors—"the language of ideas." See also Jones (1955, pp. 400-402).

Both Darwin and Freud were, however, apparently guilty of what Freud exaggeratedly called *"Schlamperei"* ["sloppiness"], but which was really ambiguity. Barzun (1958, p. 74), however, makes a case for the virtue of this quality in the presentation of new ideas.

[28] See Strachey's Introduction (Breuer and Freud, 1893-1895, p. xi).

[29] As Simpson (1960) points out, and as others have pointed out before him, the "organization, understanding and conviction" with which Darwin presented his argument in the *Origin* were enough to change Huxley from an antievolutionist to an evolutionist.

Freud first began to think psychoanalytically. This volume does, of course, contain a surprisingly complete presentation of his theory and a striking mass of observational data. Unfortunately, however, neither the theory nor the observations were in a form science found easily acceptable.

The differing receptions of the two theories must also have resulted from dissimilarities in the subject matter, from their different methods of investigation, and from the contrasting nature of the evidence they provide.[30] However, a not inconsiderable part of the respective receptions may be attributed to less fundamental factors.

EXTRINSIC FACTORS

Extrinsic reasons are frequently no less important in their effect on the acceptance of ideas than those we have labeled "intrinsic" (see Barber, 1961). In the cases we are considering, the way in which the ground was laid for acceptance was of considerable importance.

Before publishing the *Origin* Darwin carried on an extensive correspondence with scientists, particularly outstanding biologists, and other significant persons. The relationships established through these contacts helped to insure a favorable reception for the *Origin* when it appeared. Darwin also made the *Origin* more palatable by avoiding a discussion of the application of the laws of evolution

---

[30] See Freud's statement to Marie Bonaparte: "Mental events seem to be immeasurable . . ." (Jones, 1955, p. 419). In the discussion of one of his early case histories Freud said:

"I have not always been a psychotherapist. Like other neuropathologists, I was trained to employ local diagnoses and electro-prognosis, and it still strikes me myself as strange that the case histories I write should read like short stories and that, as one might say, they lack the serious stamp of science. I must console myself with the reflection that the nature of the subject is evidently responsible for this, rather than any preference of my own. The fact is that local diagnosis and electrical reactions lead nowhere in the study of hysteria, whereas a detailed description of mental processes such as we are accustomed to find in the works of imaginative writers enables me, with the use of a few psychological formulas, to obtain at least some kind of insight into the course of that affection" (Breuer and Freud, 1893-1895, pp. 160-161).

The problem of the "nature of the evidence" still plagues psychology today. In the natural sciences the evidence can be marshaled in such a way that "everyone"—participant or nonparticipant—can follow the general argument. Many psychological data, on the other hand, are relatively so subtle and so dependent upon the observer as a participant that it remains difficult to convey them to the nonparticipant. This is especially true since most nonparticipants consider themselves "psychologists" as well.

to man. He did not deal with this topic at length until twelve years later, in *The Descent of Man*, by which time his propositions had been generally accepted. In the first edition of the *Origin*, Darwin merely included one sentence toward the close of the last chapter suggesting that "light will be thrown on the origin of man and his history." (In later editions of the *Origin* he added the word "much" before "light.") He inserted the statement so that "no honourable man should accuse me of concealing my views" (F. Darwin, 1887, p. 76; see also F. Darwin, 1950, p. 61). His essential conservatism thus led to a gradual presentation of his views, a presentation which in effect made acceptance of his doctrine easier. Some have held, however, that this method was solely due to his desire to have the evidence sufficiently massive and complete. Schwalbe (1909, p. 114) believes that Darwin's characteristic delaying of publication for years until he had carefully weighed all aspects of his subject—his extreme scientific conscience—restrained him from challenging the world in 1859 with a book fully setting forth the theory of the descent of man. It is possible, however, that he realized he was offering a sufficiently radical pill in his *Origin* to make it unwise at that time to develop further the theory of the descent of man. Darwin characteristically avoided controversy and, as Irvine has put it, ". . . practiced the British art of reticent and unprovocative statement" (Irvine, 1955, p. 102). This showed up particularly in his lack of response to the Butler attacks (pp. 220-224).[31]

Freud's activities in comparable circumstances were quite different. No matter how much he himself may have wished otherwise, there was no parallel correspondence with outstanding members of his profession to prepare the ground. His voluminous correspondence does not appear to have been productive along this particular line. For instance, the Fliess letters represent correspondence with a person who for many reasons was most unlikely to be influential. Beyond this, Freud's letters seem largely limited to the psychoanalytic group and to some literary persons, again not persons likely to have the kind of influence necessary to aid in the acceptance of his ideas. This seems a reasonable conclusion to draw from the relevant material in the second volume of Jones' biography. In the

---

[31] See Willey (1960, pp. 18-31). Darlington (1959b), a kind of "debunker" of Darwin, interprets Darwin's "flexible strategy" as "slippery" (p. 60), and uses such terms as "intellectual opportunism" (p. 63).

Preface to this volume Jones refers to some five thousand of Freud's letters to which he had access for the writing of the biography. Among the letters that Jones cites, one finds no evidence of the kind of correspondence we have described in the case of Darwin. The selection of letters published by Freud's son (E. L. Freud, 1960) does not alter this conclusion.

Although Freud was much more direct about the presentation of his ideas, he followed Darwin's pattern in relation to controversy and the reply to criticism (e.g., Jones, 1955, pp. 112, 120-121, 426).

A more subtle extrinsic factor affecting initial acceptance resided in Darwin's social and scientific status as compared to Freud's. In the first instance, we are dealing with a Darwin married to a Wedgwood, both belonging to a close, economically independent, intellectual elite. Add to this Darwin's own high scientific standing, as well as his family's, and imposing bases for recognition are provided. In the case of Freud, however, we are dealing with a person having no family or economic status,[32] and belonging to a rejected minority group. And for Freud there was no scientific standing. In considerable part this was because he lacked the conventional entrée in his culture to intellectual status—a "Herr-Professorship."[33]

Another, more complex, factor was predominantly extrinsic, although it also included intrinsic aspects. It is to be found in the cultural context in which each of the theories was presented. At the time of the publication of Darwin's *Origin*, some aspects of the general culture were favorable and some unfavorable to the kind of thesis he proposed (see Carter, 1957). Favorable to the theory were the widespread interest in the study of nature, the rather vague evolutionary notions already current,[34] and the harmony of the theory with the strongly competitive *laissez-faire* economics of the period. Unfavorable were sentimental reactions to various aspects of the theory: to the emphasis on competition, to the contradiction

---

[32] There is no evidence of high Jewish intellectual accomplishment in his family background (see Jones, 1953, Chapter 1; Aron, 1956). But even if there had been such accomplishment, it would not have been an aid to the kind of intellectual status which Freud was seeking.

[33] See Hughes (1958, p. 50 ff.) on the status of German professors in the 1890's. Also see Freud (1887-1902, p. 11).

[34] See J. C. Greene (1959b), who traces the rise of evolutionary views of nature in the eighteenth and nineteenth centuries, culminating in Darwin's two major works.

of the story of creation in a time of considerable religious revival—especially in Protestant England—to the hint of physical animal ancestry contained in the theory, and to the extension to biology of materialistic views, views which had heretofore been limited to the physical, nonliving world.

Of course we could say in a general way that Freud had the inestimably great advantage of being able to build upon the revolution which Darwin had already wrought and which, as we have suggested, already carried in part the seeds of the Freudian concept of the animal in man.[35] For did it not naturally follow that if man were really part of the animal series, he should also have animal psychological characteristics and be subject to instinctual domination? In this connection William Morton Wheeler's (1921) reaction to psychoanalysis, which we shall discuss at length later, is particularly relevant. An additional favorable factor was that at the time Freud put forth his ideas, there was already an interest in the unconscious and a growing respect for the importance of psychology and psychiatry as fields of inquiry and endeavor.

Unfavorable was the Victorianism of the period, characterized by smug satisfaction with middle-of-the-road positions (see Brinton, 1959, p. 350) which naturally found intolerable such extreme opinions as Freud's. Probably most unfavorable was the factor that Hughes points out (1958, pp. 3-66): Freud presented his ideas in a period in which mechanism, naturalism, and positivism were dominant in the context of a "self-satisfied cult of material progress" (p. 41). The nineteenth century versions of these attitudes were a "travestied form" of the eighteenth century tradition of enlightenment, which had combined a "flexible use of the concept of reason, and . . . [a] sympathetic understanding for 'sensibility' and 'the passions'" (p. 27). Only in the narrow sense of "intellectual" as defined during the late nineteenth century could Freud, with Durkheim, Weber,[36] Croce, and others, be considered one of

---

[35] An attempt to trace Darwin's influence on Freud, as well as a detailed comparison of the personalities of the two men, would be illuminating for the further understanding of their methods of work and the dissemination of their ideas. In the present context, however, these tasks would take us too far afield. See Brosin (1960) for some discussion of the latter topic.

[36] Frenkel-Brunswik (1954, pp. 332-335) has made an interesting comparison of Freud with Weber and Durkheim. She points out that although Weber and Durkheim have been accused of rationalism, both actually saw the foundations of society as fundamentally based on nonrational moral qualities. "Freud, on the

the prominent "anti-intellectual" forces. In spirit, Freud's ideas were actually much nearer those of the eighteenth century.[37] Trilling (1955) and Bruner (1956) have pointed out the "Romantic" streak in Freud, the details of which we shall examine later.

Summary

To summarize then, without regard for the relative importance of these two revolutionary upheavals in the history of ideas: an examination of the reception given them leads to the conclusion that the Freudian innovation had a more difficult time in being accepted. The blow was harder to tolerate, the argument was presented less effectively, the ground for acceptance was laid less adequately, the cultural climate was less receptive, and the standing of Freud and his supporters in the community was much lower than that of Darwin and his. With this appreciation of the complex factors involved in the initial reaction to Freud, let us now go on to a detailed consideration of the ways in which Freudian theory made its impact on the psychological scene.

---

other hand, has been criticized for having given too much prominence to the irrational, while in fact his one hope is the overcoming of the irrational in a society built on reason" (p. 333).

[37] Kaufman (1960, p. 309) says: ". . . [Freud] is probably the greatest among Nietzsche's heirs, a man who followed in the footsteps of Goethe, Heine, and Nietzsche by attempting to deepen and enrich the attitudes of the Enlightenment with the insights of romanticism. For Freud tried to bridge the gap between the German romantics' profound preoccupation with the irrational, on the one hand, and the Western faith in liberty, equality, and fraternity, and in science as an instrument to their realization, on the other."

Trilling (1957, p. 39) makes a similar point in his discussion of "Freud and Literature." "If Freud discovered the darkness for science he never endorsed it. On the contrary, his rationalism supports all the ideas of the Enlightenment that deny validity to myth or religion; he holds to a simple materialism, to a simple determinism, to a rather limited sort of epistemology." "Validity" must, of course, be taken in the sense in which Trilling means it in this context. According to Peter Gay (1954, p. 379), Freud "was the greatest child of the Enlightenment which our century has known . . ."

This is not to deny that Freud had something of a credulous streak which was evidenced in his interest in Lamarckism and the occult (Jones, 1957, pp. 310-311, 375-407). However, he seems to have kept such notions in a distinct compartment, well separated from his real work.

See Cassirer (1955, pp. 104-108), P. Gay (1954, especially p. 379), Freud (1927).

3

NINETEENTH AND EARLY TWENTIETH CENTURY BACKGROUND

As we have already pointed out,[1] the nineteenth century was a period in which mechanism, naturalism, and positivism were dominant, although represented in a narrower and more materialistic way than they had been during the eighteenth century Enlightenment. An appreciation of the factors which imposed limitations on Freud's influence, including the differing commitments of academic psychology and psychoanalysis, requires reaching back into the nineteenth century philosophical matrix out of which psychology grew.

A partial explanation of the separation between psychoanalysis and psychology is probably to be found in the bifurcation of philosophy into natural philosophy and moral philosophy. Out of natural philosophy grew present-day epistemology and science. Within this context arose the key topics of early psychology—perceiving and knowing. Out of moral philosophy grew present-day ethics, with its relevant psychological problems of willing, wishing, feeling—topics central to psychoanalysis.[2]

The Helmholtz Program

Of more immediate relevance for an appreciation of the influence of psychoanalysis on psychology, however, is the nature of their

[1] See p. 31.
[2] Indeed, E. B. Holt (1915), the first psychologist to write a book championing Freudian theory, centered on its significance for ethics, entitling his book *The Freudian Wish and Its Place in Ethics*.
See J. C. Burnham (1958, pp. 377-380) on the role of the good-conduct aspect of psychoanalysis in the social and political philosophy of the 1910's. See also Walter Lippmann (1913, especially p. 79) and E. R. Groves (1916a, pp. 44-49; 1916b).

respective commitments to an important scientific outgrowth of nineteenth century philosophy—to what has come to be known as "the Helmholtz program." In part it was psychology's commitment to the Helmholtz program which separated it, and even now keeps it somewhat apart, from those roots which gave rise to moral philosophy.

The Helmholtz program was a reflection of the philosophy embodied in a statement made in an 1842 letter by du Bois-Reymond: "Brücke and I pledged a solemn oath to put into power this truth, no other forces than the common physical-chemical ones are active within the organism; that, in those cases which cannot at the time be explained by these forces one has either to find the specific way or form of their action by means of the physical-mathematical method, or to assume new forces equal in dignity to the chemical-physical forces inherent in matter, reducible to the force of attraction and repulsion" (du Bois-Reymond, 1918, p. 108).[3] This statement was accepted in principle by the group which shortly came to include Helmholtz and Ludwig, known later as the Helmholtz School of Medicine.

The aim of their program was to build a science of the relationship of mind and matter which "might carry weight with the materialistic intellectualism of the times or even be satisfactory to Fechner, the one-time physicist" (Boring, 1950b, p. 280). The first expression of this aim was psychophysics, which was characterized by Fechner as " 'an exact science of the functional relations or the relations of dependency between body and mind' " (Boring, 1950b, p. 286).

Cranefield, who has gone searchingly into this topic (1957, 1959), points out that the "1847 program," as he calls the program of the Helmholtz school, had three goals: to establish an antivitalist position with the accompanying idea of intelligible causality; to provide argument for the use of observation and experiment; and to attempt to reduce physiology to physics and chemistry. After examining the evidence, he states about the achievement of these

---

[3] du Bois-Reymond (1918), *Jugendbriefe von Emil du Bois-Reymond an Eduard Hallmann*. S. Bernfeld (1944, p. 348), whose translation we have essentially used, mistakenly gives this reference as occurring on p. 19 of *another* volume (1927) of du Bois-Reymond's letters: *Zwei grosse Naturforscher des 19. Jahrhunderts. Ein Briefwechsel zwischen Emil du Bois-Reymond und Karl Ludwig*. The material in this latter communication is about quite other matters.

goals that "Never at any time did any member of the 1847 group succeed in reducing a vital phenomenon to physics and chemistry" (1957, p. 420). He concludes that "The 1847 group was vastly successful in experimental physiology, temporarily successful in putting across mechanism as against vitalism, and reasonably successful in popularizing applied physics and chemistry as techniques in physiological research. But Ludwig, Helmholtz, du Bois-Reymond and Brücke had for a short time held most of German physiology to a much bolder task, that of dissolving physiology into physics and chemistry. It was this task which Ludwig himself admitted proved 'much more difficult than we had anticipated' " (1957, p. 423).

Cranefield, in quoting from the 1842 letter mentioned earlier, does not give that part of the "oath" which accepts the assumption of "new forces equal in dignity." It would seem that the Helmholtz school had to be satisfied with physiological forces of this second kind because it was not possible to achieve the first part of the program—a truly physicalist physiology—by the molar means then available. Indeed, this reduction, within the meaning of the original goals, was not really possible until present-day molecular biophysics and chemistry (Cranefield, 1957). We find then, even on the part of the Helmholtz group, an acceptance of the "new forces equal in dignity" to the physical-chemical ones. They departed from the physicalist physiology of the first part of the oath, attacking the multiple problems of physiology by experimental methods in which physics and chemistry were used only as tools.

Interpretation of the Program

With this clearer understanding of what was actually represented by the Helmholtz program, we are ready to examine the different ways in which psychology and psychoanalysis reacted to and interpreted the philosophy of the program, and how these respective interpretations affected both the course of Freud's thinking and psychology's receptiveness to Freudian theory. If psychology or psychoanalysis were to try to carry out the Helmholtz program, they could not reasonably be expected to do more than physiology itself was then able to achieve. At most they could adopt a mechanistic-deterministic point of view, apply experimental and observational methods to their phenomena, use physical and chemical techniques, and deal with their phenomena in terms of forces which were of "equal dignity."

PSYCHOLOGY'S COMMITMENT

Psychology was at first committed by Helmholtz, a physicist, to becoming an exact science in the same sense that physics was an exact science. But, like physiology, psychology had to compromise, and settle for an experimental rather than a physicalist approach. Psychology, in the attempt to be "exact," restricted itself to the use of the experimental method and consequently to the study of phenomena about which it *could* be exact. What came to be known as sensory psychology and psychophysics appeared to be the general areas to which these methods were applicable.

As we shall see below, it was not the theoretical commitment alone, but rather this commitment in combination with the choice of the experimental method, and of the subject matter for the application of the method, which was fateful for psychology. Psychology,[4] in aiming to establish itself experimentally, came increasingly to focus upon introspective reports. This led to an intense preoccupation with the "mental elements" constituting subjective experience. Finally, in the hands of such structuralists as Titchener, the description of these "mental structures" seemed to become the very goal. When introspective data proved to be unreliable, the shortcomings of the subjects were held to be at fault. The resultant use of trained "introspectors" led to still another problem: increasing dependence of experimental results upon the research center in which the subjects were trained, with the likelihood of nonreplicable results. A crisis in experimental psychology developed.

The resolution of this crisis split psychology into two camps, one of them rather accessible, and the other much less accessible, to Freud's oncoming influence. The first to rebel against the sterility of the structuralist program were the functionalists (James, and Dewey, J. R. Angell, and their Chicago School). They believed the experimental program had miscarried because of the quest for fixed mental elements (structures).[5]

---

[4] Our discussion of this development in psychology has drawn heavily on various histories of psychology: Boring (1950b), Murphy (1949), Flugel (1951).

[5] At a later date the Gestalt group joined the functionalists in this attack on "mental elements."

We can call on William James to illustrate the more general roots of the functionalists' dissatisfaction. James (1890) characterized the exactitude of Fechner's law (and of psychophysics) as pseudo exactitude, and asserted that whatever validity it had was in physiology (Vol. 1, p. 548) rather than in psychology. He commented as follows:

> ... it would be terrible if even such a dear old man as this could saddle our Science forever with his patient whimsies, and, in a world so full of more nutritious objects of attention, compel all future students to plough through ... his ... works ... The only amusing part of it is that Fechner's critics should always feel bound, after smiting his theories hip and thigh and leaving not a stick of them standing, to wind up by saying that nevertheless to him belongs the *imperishable glory,* of first formulating them and thereby turning psychology into an *exact science* ... [Vol. 1, p. 549].

This is followed by his well-known quotation about little Peterkin from Southey's *Battle of Blenheim*.[6]

Angell stated the functionalist program in 1907, declaring that it introduced nothing wholly new. And he was right. The functionalists did not disavow the experimental program; rather, they extended it to a broader range of areas to which experimental methods had less access, and dealt with material (such as individual differences) that later contributed to applied psychology. In the spirit of Spencer's *Principles of Psychology* and Darwin's *On the Origin of the Species* (Angell, 1907, p. 62), they believed that mental operations "mediating between the environment and the needs of the organism" (p. 85) should be the subject matter of psychology's inquiry. By raising the question of the use and purpose of psychological structures and processes they became involved in issues of adaptation,[7] development, and the relationship between organism

---

[6] Boring (1950b, p. 294), however, sees the matter somewhat differently. Boring also says (personal communication, December 24, 1962): "James' mixed metaphor bears analysis. What is it that you can smite hip and thigh and leave not a stick of it standing? A scarecrow, obviously. No flesh-and-blood enemy is made of sticks. So this was only a scarecrow."

[7] James' volumes (1890, 1907, 1911), B. T. Baldwin's writings (1914, 1921; Baldwin and Stecher, 1924, 1925), and the work of G. Stanley Hall (1904) are monuments to this continuing trend which became part of psychology through the functionalist revolt.

and environment.[8] Accordingly, they contributed to the growth of naturalistic observation and developmental theorizing. The functionalists' program thus shared with Freud's program allegiances to both the Helmholtz school and to Darwinism, and initiated a trend which augured favorably for Freud's influence.

James' rebellion against the Helmholtz program and his criticism of Fechner's psychophysics reflect his personality, showing his freedom as a psychologist to look at and think about an amazingly broad range of human phenomena. Through his opposition to the limiting requirements of the "exact science" commitment he was able to face "life in the raw" and to consider all facets of life proper subject matter for psychology.

Evidence for the similarities between the functionalist and Freudian trends are especially clear in James, who in many respects appears to have anticipated Freud's ideas. Examples of James' anticipation are so abundant that their neglect[9] by both psychologists and psychoanalysts is not only puzzling but embarrassing. Here we shall limit ourselves to two examples, one substantive and one formal. James wrote:

> The fondness of the ancients and of modern Orientals for forms of unnatural vice, of which the notion affects us with horror, is probably a mere case of the way in which this instinct may be inhibited by habit. We can hardly suppose that the ancients had by gift of

[8] J. C. Burnham (1958), in discussing Freud's influence on American civilization, points to the paramount role of Darwinism in preparing the ground for this influence: "It would be difficult to exaggerate the extent to which intellectuals in the United States around the turn of the century thought in Darwinian terms" (p. 357).

[9] It would be important to establish whether this neglect is appearance or fact. Do we have another Klopstock phenomenon here? Has "the greatest psychological work ever written" not been carefully read either? (Or must one simply curb one's impatience and acknowledge again that each generation has its own ways of reading and not reading? Actually, there now seems to be a renewed interest in James' *Principles*. Note the recent Dover edition of the *Principles*.) Surely Woodworth, who, by his own statements (1932), was deeply influenced by James, and who became the first outstanding figure in academic "dynamic psychology," must have noted examples of James' anticipation, although we do not have evidence of his having done so. In the course of completing the documentation of this study, we found that Wells, at least, did note James' anticipation of Freud and apparently referred to the very passage which we have chosen as an example: "Freud considers that the ultimate sources of the submerged ideas are in trends of quite early life, many of which are most repugnant to the adult personality. For example, we should find more marked in childhood that 'germinal possibility' of abnormal sexual conduct, which William James long since attributed to most of us" (1917a, p. 108).

Nature a propensity of which we are devoid, and were all victims of what is now a pathological aberration limited to individuals. It is more probable that with them the instinct of physical aversion toward a certain class of objects was inhibited early in life by *habits*, formed under the influence of *example;* and that then a kind of sexual appetite, of which very likely most men possess the germinal possibility, developed itself in an unrestricted way [1890, Vol. 2, pp. 438-439].

Both this passage and its context—a discussion of instinct, inhibition, and habit—anticipate Freud, who apparently did not know about them either before or after he developed his theories.

As an example of the formal anticipation, James recognized the importance of the faint, the fleeting, and the devious, which are so frequently the primary data of psychoanalysis (see Shakow, 1959a). Although *The Principles of Psychology* was published in 1890, a good deal of the chapter entitled "The Stream of Thought" had already been published in *Mind* of January, 1884, entitled "On Some Omissions of Introspective Psychology." Let us quote briefly from this chapter:

Now what I contend for, and accumulate examples to show, is that 'tendencies' are not only descriptions from without, but that they are among the *objects* of the stream, which is thus aware of them from within, and must be described as in very large measure constituted of *feelings* of *tendency,* often so vague that we are unable to name them at all. It is, in short, the re-instatement of the vague to its proper place in our mental life which I am so anxious to press on the attention. . . . What must be admitted is that the definite images of traditional psychology form but the very smallest part of our minds as they actually live [1890, Vol. 1, pp. 254-255].

Somewhat later than the functionalists, the behaviorists (Watson and others)—the representatives of the second trend—rebelled against the structuralists' miscarriage of the experimental program.[10] This group turned against the introspectionist aspect of the structuralist program, restating and reinforcing the exact science program in a form even more rigorous (or should we say more rigid) than the original. They saw the fruitless, deceptive shadowboxing of the

---

[10] Boring views the behaviorist development as actually an extreme extension of functionalism (personal communication, December 24, 1962). We take the view that behaviorism was more a third force, stemming from functionalism but with distinctive enough tenets to be recognized as a separate entity.

structuralists' introspections as the cause of the sterility of their experimental program, and concluded that consciousness was an epiphenomenon. It was as if they had deliberately agreed that consciousness was not reducible to the forces of attraction and repulsion, and therefore not of the character demanded by even a modified form of the original program. Ruling out of the exact science of psychology both consciousness as a subject matter, and the use of introspection as a method, the behaviorists declared observable behavior to be the only proper subject matter. Thus they reaffirmed the constriction of the field of psychology imposed by the exact science interpretation of the original program, and exacerbated this constriction by an accompanying blindness to the possibility of "new forces equal in dignity." (It is of course clear that actually the behaviorists were relying on those forces as much as the original Helmholtzians were.) In the exclusion of consciousness and introspection from the field of psychology, the source of the data on which psychoanalysis was built was, of course, excluded from this form of scientific psychology.[11]

Thus the general result seems to have been that the functionalists, who were directing their attention to more "meaningful" areas, made only little progress toward "exactitude" and "unified theory," whereas those who remained faithful to the earlier program made equally little progress in extending their "exactitude" beyond the confines of limited laboratory problems.[12] While functionalism, through its emphasis on "use" and "adaptation," gave rise to applied psychology and the psychology of individual differences, the main stream of American psychology came to adhere to the new and extreme form[13] of what was essentially the original exact science

[11] Although strangely enough some of the theories of psychoanalysis were not (see Watson, 1913; Watson and Watson, 1928). See Boring's (1953) "A History of Introspection" for some relationships between introspection and psychoanalysis.

[12] This is a deliberately black-and-white formulation in order to make the point. Actually there was some progress toward "exactitude" on the one side and toward "relevance to life" on the other.

[13] Boring (personal communication, 1957) comments: "One has to think back to the violence with which the exact-science criterion was supported in the old days and the bitterness that experimentalists felt about Freud and Stanley Hall and William McDougall in order to realize fully how religious these exact scientists in psychology were trying to be." The Helmholtz group itself was not immune from a form of religiosity (Jones, 1953, pp. 42-43).

One of us (Shakow) was present at the 1929 International Congress of Psychology in New Haven. He still remembers the slashing attack made on McDougall by James McKeen Cattell, and recalls his feeling at the time that what was

program as interpreted by the behaviorists.[14]

In summary, then, Darwinian influence and functionalism—especially Jamesian open-mindedness[15] and genius—led to psychological thinking akin in many respects to Freud's. It seems reasonable to assume that these account for part of whatever subsequent receptiveness there was to Freud. But as we have said, functionalism was itself isolated from the main stream of American psychology, a circumstance which partially explains the reluctant acceptance of Freud in most Western psychological circles.

FREUD'S COMMITMENT

It is important to recognize that although psychology's particular interpretation of and commitment to the Helmholtz program was an obstacle to Freud's influence, it nevertheless also served as a link between psychology and psychoanalysis. As we have already indicated, Freud too was committed to the Helmholtz program. A consideration of Freud's relationship to the Helmholtz program will help explain this paradoxical situation.

As one delves more deeply into the historical literature, Freud's relationship to the Helmholtz school and the nature of his commitment become more complicated and difficult to unravel. S. Bernfeld's (1944) article, "Freud's Earliest Theories and the School of Helmholtz," is the most helpful source in showing the alignment of Freud with the Helmholtz program. Jones' (1953, pp. 40-42) discussion of the problem is based almost wholly on Bernfeld. Galdston (1956a), in a paper on "Freud and Romantic Medicine," takes almost the opposite position from Bernfeld's and Jones', holding that Freud's real identification was with Fliess and an anti-Helmholtzian

---

being attacked was a fundamental philosophy, rather than the particular "Lamarckian" experiment under consideration. One surmises that this may have been a case of the need of a functionalist to be more *"echt"* than the *"echt*est*"* of the committed to the commitment.

[14] In many respects Jacques Loeb's (1899; see Boring, 1950b, p. 625) tropistic psychology represented the most extreme identification with the Helmholtz view: it was most forthrightly physical-chemical. Of course Loeb was a pupil of Fick who was a pupil of Ludwig, so he came by his views honestly. We might note here that there are no markings in the copy of the Loeb volume which is in the portion of Freud's library in the New York Psychiatric Institute. See footnote 19, pp. 42-43.

[15] ". . . one day he [James] came to his classroom and began his lecture with the question: 'Why is it that a perfectly respectable man may dream that he has intercourse with his grandmother?' " (Hapgood, 1939, p. 77).

view in medicine.[16] Stoodley's (1959) book also argues that Freud later departed from the Helmholtz approach in the direction of a fundamental emphasis on the social frame of reference.

Although there is something in what each of these authors (particularly Bernfeld) says, in our view the issues remain confused. Neither the components of the commitment nor the actual achievement of the Helmholtz group in relation to their commitment has been sufficiently clarified. We shall attempt to define them more specifically.

As several have pointed out (Freud, 1925b, p. 8; Jones, 1953, p. 28; S. Bernfeld, 1944, p. 354) Freud, when about seventeen, was highly impressed with the moderate expression of the then prevalent *Naturphilosophie*[17] in Goethe's essay on Nature (Goethe, 1780).[18] After this experience Freud's interests, then predominantly humanistic and political, changed, and he began to focus his vocational plans on a scientific career concerned with natural objects. He subsequently took the then conventional educational path to this goal: a career in medicine. At the University of Vienna he came under the influence of Fleischl and Breuer, and especially of Brücke, the "Far Eastern" representative of the Helmholtz physical physiology school, the person who, Freud (1926b, p. 253) said, "carried more weight with me than any one else in my whole life . . ." Through his activities in physiology at the University he became strongly identified with the views of the Helmholtz school (S. Bernfeld, 1949).[19]

---

[16] See footnote 22, pp. 46-47.

[17] The *Naturphilosophie* (philosophy of nature) of the period must not be confused with the natural philosophy we have been considering. The former was based largely on Schelling's pantheistic monism and was romantic and intuitive; the latter grew out of the philosophy of the Enlightenment and was empirical and realistic.

[18] See Wittels (1931, pp. 31-34) for an English translation of this essay. Strachey (Freud, 1925b, p. 8, note) points out that "According to . . . [R. Pestalozzi] the real author of the essay (written in 1780) was G. C. Tobler, a Swiss writer. Goethe came across it half a century later, and, by a paramnesia, included it among his own works."

[19] Actually, Freud, in addition to his contact with physiology, had more contact with academic psychology than is ordinarily supposed. Ellenberger (1956) has discussed some aspects of the possible influence of Fechner on Freud. While Freud was at the University (S. Bernfeld, 1951) he had courses with Brücke, who was not only a physiologist, but who was much interested in physiological psychology. Freud also had courses with Exner, who was a physiological psychologist (see Boring, 1950b, p. 422), and a number of courses with Brentano. The relationship to Brentano is particularly interesting, but difficult to pin down. Merlan

After leaving the medical school, he reluctantly gave up his research activities in favor of clinical medicine, with the aim of going into private practice. This he did because of his engagement to Martha Bernays. For three years he divided his time among various clinical departments—internal medicine, neurology, psychiatry, dermatology, and ophthalmology—of the General Hospital. During this period (up to 1885) he still managed to continue his involvement with the anatomy, pathology, and physiology of the nervous system while he carried on the, for him, less attractive clinical work (S. Bernfeld, 1944, 1951; Brun, 1936; Jelliffe, 1931).

As we noted previously, the five years beginning with 1882 marked a turning point in Freud's career. During this time he had heard in some detail from Breuer about the latter's "peculiar" treatment of Anna O.'s hysteria. His October, 1885-February, 1886 fellowship with Charcot in Paris further stimulated his interest in hysteria and in psychopathology in general. He tried to tell Charcot about his experience with Breuer, but Charcot did not listen. On his return from Paris he re-established contact with Breuer. It was presumably at this time that his shift to the psychological was taking place, when he was probably beginning to endow the psychological

---

(1945, 1949) provides two short notes on the relationship. Barclay (1959), in a doctoral dissertation for the University of Michigan, discusses the relationship at length. His major point is that both have an "intentional metaphysics" which Freud got from Brentano. He says: "In conclusion, it is the author's opinion that no single argument, either from the viewpoint of personality analysis, literary comparison, or teaching relationship, bears a great deal of weight in itself. *But in the cumulative resolution of all evidences lies the strength of the hypothesis that the teaching of Brentano constituted an influence in the intellectual development of Sigmund Freud"* (p. 244). Schoenwald (1952), also in a doctoral dissertation (at Harvard), is, however, more doubtful about Brentano's influence. It is also possible that Freud came to know of Maudsley through Brentano, although a 1914 note added to *The Interpretation of Dreams* (1900a, p. 612) seems to indicate that he learned of Maudsley's conclusions from reading Du Prel.

Even the part of Freud's library which ended up at the New York State Psychiatric Institute (Oberndorf, 1953; Lewis and Landis, 1957)—and we are accepting here that this is indeed material from his library, the main part of which, we understand, is in London—contains many volumes on general and experimental psychology: Ebbinghaus, Stumpf, Ziehen, Wundt, Münsterberg, among others. Of these only the Ziehen *Physiologische Psychologie* is considerably marked up, with phrases such as "wie so," "dumm!", "nein," "??," etc. It is interesting that a Hall's *Adolescence* from this library is in uncut condition, as is the one which came from the William James library. Whereas James' is a complimentary copy, Freud apparently had to buy his—for three marks. We might note in passing that the most heavily annotated book in Freud's psychological collection was Romanes' 1888 volume, *Mental Evolution in Man: Origin of Human Faculty*.

forces with the "dignity" which had heretofore been reserved for the physiological.

During the next major period, 1887 to 1902, in which Freud was so closely involved with Fliess, we see an increasing emphasis on the psychological. These were the difficult years of his father's death, his psychoneurosis, the isolation and negative response from colleagues, including his estrangement from Breuer. It was essential to have a respected person on whom to try out his ideas. Fliess actually had some of the necessary qualities, and Freud, to meet his own needs, endowed him with many of the others that he lacked. For one thing, Fliess, like Freud, was a private practitioner. Further, Fliess' superficial qualities as a scientist, interested in the physiological and quantitative, had enough face validity to justify Freud's accepting him as a representative of the Helmholtz philosophy—one who could provide the "physicalist" support which Freud then needed. (It is possible that having such "physicalist" support left Freud free to devote himself to the field of his greater interest, the psychological.) Fliess had the further advantage of being a person of imagination who, since he held heterodox opinions of his own in the sexual sphere, was able to entertain those of others. Perhaps more importantly, since this was the period of his self-analysis, Freud needed a person who could be used in the role of "analyst." For Freud, Fliess became a kind of "transference figure," which may account in part for the unaccountable in the relationship.[20] He therefore fulfilled two immensely important functions during what was perhaps the most crucial phase of Freud's development.

As we have implied, this was the phase in which Freud was emancipating himself from the narrower Helmholtz view which involved at least the use of chemical and physical methods, if not a reduction to physical and chemical concepts. Emancipation was not accomplished, of course, without considerable conflict about giving up the physiological, as is revealed in the recently discovered "Project for a Scientific Psychology" (1895c). In the "Project,"

[20] For a discussion of this topic, see Kris' introduction to Freud (1887-1902, pp. 34-35, note, and p. 43) and especially the papers referred to in the note. See particularly Buxbaum (1951, 1952), Van der Heide (1952), and S. C. Bernfeld (1952). See also Erikson (1955). In this connection Freud's letter of December 4, 1896 to Fliess (Freud, 1887-1902, p. 172) is of interest. For psychoanalysts, Freud's assumption to himself of the male organ and the assignment to Fliess of the female one may offer a possible basis for their eventual disagreement.

Freud made a valiant attempt to develop a neurological theory of psychopathology and psychology, but when he "failed" in this, he turned to what amounted to a search for forces "equal in dignity"[21] in the psychological sphere. This was not, however, the sphere of academic psychology, for the problems Freud settled on— those of affectivity—were more consonant with the subject matter of moral philosophy.

In his *On Aphasia* (1891) of this period we find indications that at least implicitly Freud took seriously the "forces equal in dignity" part of the program. Stengel, in his introduction to *On Aphasia*, writes: ". . . [Freud's] proposed division of the aphasias into three groups was a bold attempt at establishing a consistent psychological system based on the theory of associations applied to speech. Considering that the current classification was then, and still is, a confusing mixture of anatomical, physiological, and psychological

---

[21] See Pribram (1962), S. Bernfeld (1949), and Erikson (1956a) on Freud's neurological theory. We do not know how much the fact that the project was "a psychology for neurologists" indicates identification with the psychological.

Two questions might, of course, be raised regarding our interpretation of Freud's relation to the Helmholtz program. One refers to our extrapolation of the "forces equal in dignity" phrase beyond what du Bois-Reymond himself may have intended. We can only reply that Freud's course seems to have followed such a line of development. The second is that we have perhaps made Freud's identification with the program appear too explicit and deliberate. In point of fact it may not even have been *implicit* except in the earliest days. We nevertheless would not go so far as to agree with Rieff (1959, p. 20 ff.) who actually interprets Freud's use of Helmholtzian language as gradually becoming "metaphoric."

Actually we do not see Freud making a clean break with the physiological; rather, we see a gradually increasing interest in the psychological from the 1882 period on, and a diminishing interest in the physiological, with the last major effort in this direction in the 1895 "Project," a production which he largely repudiated only a month and a half later (Freud, 1887-1902, p. 134). This does not mean that Freud ever gave up the *thought* of the place of physical and chemical factors (see, for instance, Freud, 1940, p. 79). Rather, we are referring to his preoccupation in his theorizing with the psychological rather than the physiological. Kris (1950, p. 8) states that "Freud's [was a] search for the appropriate degree of separation between physiology and psychology [which] had started during those [Fliess] years." Schoenwald (1952) takes a somewhat similar view, but seems to believe more like Stoodley (1959) that Freud's theory became psychological after 1895.

Amacher (1962), in a fairly detailed examination of the influence of Freud's teachers in neuroanatomy, neurophysiology, and psychiatry, tends, it appears to us, to overemphasize the role played in the building of his theories by what Freud learned on the physiological side from his teachers. He does not give enough credit to what a creative mind makes of the "building-stones" which a *Zeitgeist* leaves around. He does not recognize that originality lies more in the creative combination of old blocks than in the actual creation of new blocks. (The section on Freud in Hoff and Seitelberger [1952] is also pertinent.)

concepts, Freud's system had much to recommend it" (Freud, 1891, p. xi).

After the Fliess period, Freud was on his own. He stood his ground, emphasizing the psychological—the *motivational* psychological—with occasional backward glances toward the physiological, such as in *Three Essays on the Theory of Sexuality* (1905b) and in wistful statements like the one he made to Marie Bonaparte (see footnote 30, Chapter 2).[22]

[22] Iago Galdston (1956a) in his forthright and heterodox article has taken quite a different point of view with respect to Freud's commitment. His exposition is worth examining because it clearly presents many of the issues. In line with his own frankly positive identification with Romantic Medicine, Galdston holds that Freud was strongly influenced by Fliess in an anti-Helmholtzian direction. (Galdston [1956b] makes a similar argument in "Freud's Influence in Contemporary Culture," this time in relation to the conflict between the nineteenth century realistic and romantic literature. But here he appears to contradict some of the points made in the other paper, for example, on determinism and the importance of the rational for Freud. Actually, for what it may be worth, the authors Freud most liked fell into the group Galdston designates as "realistic" [see Jones, 1957, Chapter XVI, especially pp. 422-423].) Galdston's position is that Fliess was essentially a representative of the Romantic School, as evidence for which he offers the area of his interest—"intentions and purposes," a phrase taken from Freud.

Several questions may, however, be raised about Galdston's argument. It is difficult to avoid the impression that Galdston overestimates the influence of Fliess. Although he is correct in pointing out the tendency of the Freudians to protect Freud by denigrating Fliess, we believe that the Freudians (Kris, Jones, et al.) more accurately evaluate the place of Fliess in Freud's development. It is our impression that Fliess played primarily the role of a sympathetic listener, particularly suited to Freud's needs at that time. As Jones says: "So the talks were duologues rather than dialogues" (1953, p. 303). In this respect Fliess served a function, the importance of which cannot be overestimated. The function was, however, a formal rather than a contentual, substantive one; he was a friendly figure who was willing to serve as an object on whom to try out ideas and with whom to exchange abreactions about the uncomprehending world. As Kazin (1962, p. 358) indicates, the mutual attraction between Freud and Fliess was "founded on their common tendency to intellectual guesswork. But since Freud distrusted this tendency until it could be put on a scientific footing, and Fliess distrusted his own not at all, it is understandable that the relation between them broke down . . ." Freud did retain some of Fliess' notions, such as bisexuality, which was so important an idea to Freud (Freud, 1887-1902, pp. 179, 242, 247-248, 289, 334-335, 337) and a modified form of his ideas about periodicity (see Jones, 1953, pp. 317-318). Fliess appeared to be much more the pseudo observer, much more the speculator, and therefore decidedly more in the Romantic tradition than was Freud, despite Freud's having looked upon him as a Helmholtzian. (Note Kris' various comments about Freud's attitude and his mention of Fliess' gift to Freud of a two-volume set of Helmholtz' lectures in 1898 [Freud, 1887-1902, pp. 1-34].)

In his identification with Romantic underdogs, Galdston appears to overvalue their contribution. In order to strengthen the case for the Romantics he appears to us to understate the contribution from the "Enlightenment." In any case, he seems to misinterpret Cassirer's analysis of the period. He quotes the follow-

IMPLICATIONS OF COMMITMENTS

If we re-examine the Helmholtz program in the context of the oath taken by du Bois-Reymond and Brücke, we see that the spirit of the program could be fulfilled wholly or in part in three ways: by a true physicalist physiology—which was not attained during the whole Helmholtz period; by an objective experimental physiology (Ludwig, Helmholtz, Brücke, du Bois-Reymond, et al.) or an objective experimental psychology (Wundt, G. E. Müller, Ebbinghaus, et al.) which used physics and chemistry as *tools;* by a consulting-room psychology which used objective observational methods (Freud). The inclusion of the last naturally raises a question, for a consulting-room psychology utilizes neither instrumental controls nor the controls usually associated with experiment, coming closer to the naturalistic situation with which biology proper was occupying itself at the time.

There were those who were, and there are those who are, anxious to carry out the first part of the Helmholtz program (actually the second way in the restatement in the paragraph above) immediately, without vitalistic infiltration, even if it is applied in a narrow compass. To them, Freud's endeavor amounted to an abandonment of the scientific program. In point of fact, the area of psychology

---

ing from Cassirer's volume: "All the processes of nature, including those commonly called 'intellectual,' the whole physical and moral order of things, are reducible to matter and motion and are completely explicable in terms of these two concepts" (Cassirer, 1955, pp. 65-66). This statement is quoted by Galdston to serve as a summary of the "persuasions" of Condorcet, Lamettrie, and Holbach. Galdston does not mention the other philosophers of the Enlightenment, such as Diderot and Voltaire, whom Cassirer considers more truly representative of the period (Cassirer, 1955, pp. 55, 72-73). The quoted statement about the Enlightenment actually represents a point of view which Cassirer's book is directed at dispelling. Cassirer says that his actual aim is to provide a "revision of the verdict of the Romantic Movement on the Enlightenment. . . . [the] age which venerated reason and science as man's highest faculty . . ." (1955, p. xi) but at the same time looked "upon the affects not as a mere obstacle, but seeks to show that they are the original and indispensable impulse of all the operations of the mind" (pp. 105-106). (Hughes [1958] makes a similar point in his discussion of the Enlightenment, as does Peter Gay [1954].) Is it not also a semantic confusion to equate Freud's interest in motivation with the "wish, intention and purpose" of *Naturphilosophie?* Freud *was* interested in these areas, but approached them in as *deterministic* a way as possible, whereas the approach of the Romantic School to such problems was fundamentally intuitive and mystical. In this instance, content appears not to be distinguished from method. Freud's strength was that, in so far as it was possible, he applied an acceptable Helmholtzian method —observation—to the Romantic (but also Enlightenment) content.

Freud chose did not lend itself readily to experiment or to the application of physical and chemical techniques, whereas the area of the experimental psychologists in part did, and that was the part which was most impressive to the scientific public. For the period in which Freud worked, the nature of the material and the stage of development of the field necessitated an acceptance of the kind of observational technique and the kind of theory which he developed.[23] To Freud and others, his endeavor was an indirect but essential step toward the realization of a program which was to include obviously significant and even apparently trivial facets of ordered and disordered human behavior.

As we have said, the experimental psychologists were so imbued with the narrower interpretation of the Helmholtz philosophy and its resultant method that they limited themselves to areas of psychology in which the method was applicable, that is, to sensation and perception, the fields closest to physiology. This meant that they worked in the laboratory where they could choose their problems, and consequently could apply the method without much difficulty. Freud, on the other hand, working in the consulting room, had to deal with the problems which came to him. Careful analysis convinced him that these were affective ones. To these he tried to apply the Helmholtz philosophy as far as possible, but obviously he could not do so as rigorously as could the experimental psychologists with their more limited segmental problems. Nevertheless, he held strongly to the antivitalist position of the Helmholtz school, and to the use of observation, if not experiment. The essence of the program, common to all of its parts, was an exceptionless determinism. For Freud the "equal in dignity" part of the program took the form of the postulate of thoroughgoing *psychic* determinism. It is true that in a number of places (for example, 1913, p. 182; 1925b, pp. 25-26) Freud indicated the hope for, eventually, a "physicalist"

---

[23] Boring, in his review of Jones' first volume of the biography (Boring, 1954b), makes an analysis of Freud's scientific method. He concludes that "Freud's technic lay somewhere between that of the experimental psychologist . . . and the philosopher-psychologist . . . He had, however, no control, either in the sense of the rigorous constraint of contributing factors or in the sense of adding the method of difference to the method of agreement. Indeed he seems to have been restricted to Mill's method of agreement, pure and simple, a method which by itself is clearly unsafe" (p. 436). Also see Skinner (1954) for another critical view of Freud's approach to psychology.

explanation. S. Bernfeld (1944, pp. 359-360) makes this point with some force in relation to Freud's presentation of theory. It is nevertheless clear from other statements (for example, 1913, p. 166) that he was not willing to accept superficial and easy biological hypotheses—for instance Jung's simplistic theory of a toxic cause for dementia praecox—when he felt that psychological ones were much more relevant and meaningful.[24]

The "new forces" which Freud postulated were not "reducible to the forces of attraction and repulsion" by the means he had at his disposal.[25] His methods did serve, however, to encompass in the scope of the scientific program a broad range of phenomena which "exact" academic psychology could not at that time, nor even now, deal with adequately. It was, then, the equivalent of a psychological extension of the "equal in dignity" part of the Helmholtz program that Freud pursued for the rest of his life. As an example of his many formulations of these psychological forces, we will quote from "Instincts and Their Vicissitudes" (1915a, p. 123): "By the source [*Quelle*] of an instinct is meant the somatic process . . . whose stimulus is represented in mental life by an instinct. We do not know whether this process is invariably of a chemical nature or whether it may also correspond to the release of other, e.g. mechanical, forces. . . . An exact knowledge of the sources of an instinct is not invariably necessary for purposes of psychological investigation . . ." A detailed discussion of these psychological forces presumably "equal in dignity" which Freud found would involve a survey of the full structure of Freud's theory (see Rapaport, 1959, 1960a). In the present context it suffices to say that by assuming the existence of such forces, he made *psychological reality* a subject matter of psychological study having for many psychologists the same dignity as did the *impingements of external reality* for psychophysicists and behaviorists.

An examination of the difference in makeup of the men on either side of this methodological fence would be most fascinating. Here,

---

[24] Jones (1955, p. 138) and Jung (1907, pp. 36-37, 97-98). See also Freud on Spielrein (Jones, 1955, p. 452).

[25] Freud's positing of two opposing drives, Eros and Thanatos, may be a form of expression of "attraction and repulsion." See Freud (1940, pp. 20-23) and Strachey's discussion (Freud, 1930a, pp. 59-63).

however, we can only describe them in general terms. On the one hand we have those (Wundt and G. E. Müller; Pavlov, from a slightly different tradition,[26] also belongs here) who sought out the experimental laboratory, who chose their subject matter to conform to the narrow interpretation of the Helmholtz program, who were highly ingenious in the framework of rigorous experiment, whose interest centered on the more limited psychophysical-perceptual relationship, whose epistemology was Hume's empiricism centering on the question: what repetitions of impingements from the outside provide the basis for the veridical perception of external reality? On the other side, there were those (Freud, and in some respects James) who had little predilection for experimentation (S. Bernfeld, 1949; Perry, 1935, pp. 24, 112 ff., 139, 178, 195), but were keen and bold in observation, powerful in speculation and insight, whose ingenuity worked best on the apparently intractable intricacies of subjective and clinical reality,[27] who chose to deal with the subject matter life brought to them and persevered until somehow they could make sense of it in terms of the spirit of the Helmholtz program, and whose epistemology was Kantian,[28] centering on the question: what are the factors inherent in man's nature which organize his experience of and relation to the external world?

[26] Actually, the "three greats" of the Russian "objectivist" school, Sechenov, Pavlov, Bechterev, had close associations with the Helmholtz group (Boring, 1950b, pp. 635-638). Since we are here mentioning Pavlov, it is of interest to note, in relation to our discussion in Chapter 2, that Eysenck in his Guildhall Lecture (Eysenck, 1961b) places Pavlov instead of Freud with Copernicus and Darwin among his "three greats." Although Pavlov undoubtedly made a substantial contribution to psychology, it is difficult to see him in this role. However, he is the obvious choice for a person who is as heavily committed as Eysenck to experimental design and statistical treatment.

[27] Freud wrote to Jones: "As regards your call to write on character formation, I must confess that I feel myself not competent to the task. Jung could do it better, as he is studying men from the superficial layers downwards, while I am progressing in the opposite direction. *Besides, any kind of systematic work is inconsistent with my gifts and inclinations. I expect all my impulses from the impressions in the intercourse with the patients*" (Jones, 1955, p. 65). (Italics ours.) With regard to James, the earlier quotation (p. 39) and other sections of the chapter, "The Stream of Thought" (1890, Vol. 1, pp. 224-290), are relevant.

[28] Freud (1915b, p. 171) wrote: "Just as Kant warned us not to overlook the fact that our perceptions are subjectively conditioned and must not be regarded as identical with what is perceived though unknowable, so psycho-analysis warns us not to equate perceptions by means of consciousness with the unconscious mental processes which are their object. Like the physical, the psychical is not necessarily in reality what it appears to us to be." See Rapaport (1947, 1959).

Freud and Dynamic Psychology

In any case, the course Freud followed was in some respects similar to that of the functionalists who rebelled against the narrow interpretation of the Helmholtz program and concentrated on areas foreign to the dominant behavioristic group, such as instinctual drives[29] and emotions. As we have seen, functionalism helped to prepare the ground for Freud's influence on psychology and became the area of psychology open to his influence. Together Freudism and functionalism came to serve as the main sources of nourishment for dynamic psychology. In the long run, however, Freud, not functionalism, was decisive for the survival and growth of dynamic psychology, so much so that at present dynamic psychology and Freud are often considered synonymous. This formulation might well be questioned: it could be argued that James was the source and ultimate rallying point of all functional psychology and thus also of the dynamic psychology which sprang from it. Such a view is supported by the history of applied and clinical psychology. Both stemmed from functionalism and have become, particularly in the last two decades, the matrix for the growth of interest in motivation.

Woodworth's *Dynamic Psychology* (1918) is perhaps good evidence for the view that James is the principal source of dynamic psychology, for this volume derived from James' and Cattell's functionalism. Boring (1950b) wrote: "This book has presented Woodworth as a functional psychologist, perhaps the best representative of the broad functionalism that is characteristic of American psychology" (p. 722).

It must be realized, however, that Freud systematically pursued what James, because of his much greater catholicity, only glimpsed and noted.[30] It is likely that only Freud's adherence to such a plan made it possible for him to forge a relatively *cohesive* and meaningful theory out of his clinical observations. James, who made some of the same observations but did not (or perhaps, would not)

---

[29] We shall use "instinctual drive" rather than "instinct" for Freud's *"Trieb"* (see Rapaport's note, Hartmann, 1939, p. 29; Schur, 1958; Waelder, 1960, pp. 97-103).

[30] See also Lasswell's (1960) "Approaches to Human Personality: William James and Sigmund Freud" which brings out points of similarity and difference between these two men.

adhere to such a plan, could not (or would not) cast his insights into a cohesive theory. James' vacillation between a theory of psychophysical parallelism and one of body-mind interaction well illustrates his lack of the kind of cohesiveness that Freud achieved in building his theory. To paraphrase Freud's (1914a, p. 15) words in another but similar context, we might say that James flirted with the idea, while Freud married it.[31]

It is true that one trend in clinical psychology, that represented by Witmer (see Chapter 4), can be said to derive from Wundt and the structuralist point of view. However, this was not the trend which prevailed. Rather, it was the trend initiated by Healy, largely influenced by Freudian psychology, which became the dominant one (Shakow, 1948). The relation to Freud of many prominent dynamic psychologists, is, as we shall see later, beyond question: McDougall, E. B. Holt, Tolman, Lewin, Henry Murray, and Hull's group. All in all, it is understandable that Boring should conclude: "The principal source of dynamic psychology is, of course, Freud" (1950b, p. 693).

Overview

As we have noted previously, the dynamic trend was alien to and combatted by the main stream of development in psychology. For a very long while the commitment of the main stream to "exact

---

[31] See Jones (1955, p. 427) for a description of Freud's ego qualities which enabled him to take this stand. Or, in attributing Freud's contribution to his personal qualities, are we, as Boring puts it, missing another factor—the effect of the stream of the *Zeitgeist?* In a personal communication (December 24, 1962) he writes: ". . . Külpe said (I think posthumously in his *Vorlesungen*) that psychology had had three periods: (1) Sensation and perception—Helmholtz, Fechner, Wundt, et seq., for these keep on forever once started; (2) Learning and memory, Ebbinghaus, G. E. Müller, et seq.; (3) Thought, the Würzburg School, et seq. I think he is right. But Würzburg established the *Einstellung* (*Aufgabe*, determining tendency, set, attitude, etc.) and found thought to be what others later could see (Woodworth as early as 1914), that thought is unconscious. Külpe never knew the full significance of Würzburg's findings. But the crazy thing is that Külpe and Freud were working along the same lines synchronously and presumably without any knowledge of each other. Why? Because they were both agents of the *Zeitgeist* . . . And this current comes from way back. The anticipators of Külpe are Ludwig Lange, and then the experimental evidence of the effects of attitude on perception, perhaps including *unbewusster Schluss* (*unbewusster*, note). The antecedents of Freud have been listed by Lancelot Whyte [1960] . . . You see I use Külpe as the evidence that Freud was not original in the sense that his original ideas were completely spontaneous."

science," and the skipping by academic psychology of the naturalistic phase which had been so well represented in biology, did not encourage interest in naturalistic observation, let alone in the "rough and ready" observations and theorizing characteristic of psychoanalysis.

Woodworth clearly saw the intrinsic contrast between Freudism and the main trend in psychology: "As a movement within psychiatry, psychoanalysis was a revolt against the dominant 'somatic' tendency of the nineteenth century, and a springing into new life of the 'psychic' tendency. Just when psychology was becoming more somatic, psychiatry started in earnest to be psychic" (1931, p. 126).

It is obvious that the choice of subject matter and explanatory level, which Woodworth stresses, was important. But there is perhaps something even more crucial in the methods used in psychology and psychoanalysis. Freud resorted to methods which we still do not know how to describe precisely. The "exact science" of psychology, on the other hand, adhered to exact methods which were not easily, if at all, applied to the subject matter on which Freud developed his theories. Psychology did not have the means to prove or disprove Freud's theories.

While James' commitment was to face unflinchingly "life in the raw," and Freud's was to carry out, implicitly if not explicitly, the Helmholtz program as well as clinical reality permitted, the main stream of psychology uncompromisingly stuck to the narrower aspects of the Helmholtz program. But as we saw earlier, the originators of the program were not able to carry this out even in physiology (Cranefield, 1957). One of the present writers (Shakow, 1953) once speculated how much further developed and more widely applicable our exact scientific methods might now be, if all of psychology had initially committed itself to carrying out the Helmholtz program on the subject matter of and within the limitations of clinical reality. If nothing else, the question does identify this problem as the age-old one of the difference between working inductively from the material of naturalistic observation and working inductively from narrow premises. It would seem that major scientific advances arise from the interplay of these two quite separate approaches, and it was precisely this interplay that was prevented for a long time by the differing commitments of the main stream of psychology and psychoanalysis. In such interplay, apparently, methods develop which increasingly fulfill both the demands of the material and the demands of the criteria for relevant levels of rigorous proof. It seems that the different commitments of academic psychology and psychoanalysis not only interfered with their taking note of each other's methods, but also resulted in their focusing on different subject matters. Because of these events, the development of rigorous methods applicable to the data of psychoanalysis was prevented.

We have surveyed the differing commitments of psychology and psychoanalysis and some causes of psychology's reluctance to recognize Freud. Later we shall consider some of psychology's ambivalent feelings at greater length, but at the moment we are faced with another problem. Assuming the accuracy of this description of the relationship between academic psychology and psychoanalysis, it would not be surprising if a stalemate prohibiting any interaction had resulted, with little or no Freudian influence on psychology. The fact that there *has* been a profound Freudian influence calls for an explanation.

4

GENERAL ASPECTS OF TWENTIETH CENTURY DEVELOPMENTS: INFLUENCE AND OBSTACLES TO INFLUENCE AND UNDERSTANDING

In analyzing the way in which psychoanalysis came to affect psychology, two mutually supporting lines of influence, one indirect and one direct, seem to emerge. Although they cannot be completely separated, the indirect influence seems to be that which came predominantly from the surrounding culture, from that part of the *Zeitgeist* which was itself greatly shaped by Freudism. The direct influence appears to be that which came along natural professional lines, from sources more immediately related to psychology and psychoanalysis. We turn, then, from our analysis of the various forms of commitment to a particular phase of the scientific *Zeitgeist* to an examination of some features of the early twentieth century culture, and to a more detailed account of the reactions of psychologists to Freud's theory, reactions which were in considerable part determined by the interaction of various components of the *Zeitgeist*. In examining what we have called the direct influences, we shall sample the reactions of a range of psychologists and consider some of the obstacles which originated in the professional sources.

INDIRECT INFLUENCES

SOURCES

Freudian ideas appeared in the United States during the first and second decades of this century. At that time, although Puritan and Victorian attitudes dominated the intellectual scene, a change had already been prepared for by the muckrakers (for example, Ida Tarbell, Frank Norris, Upton Sinclair, and Lincoln Steffens) and by the literary realists (for example, Stephen Crane, Theodore Dreiser, Jack London).[1] These rebels against the "genteel tradition," as Curti (1943, p. 710 ff.) has described the literary realists, were soon joined by social protesters and socialists (Max Eastman, Emma Goldman, Floyd Dell, Eugene Debs), feminists (Olive Schreiner), and Greenwich Village Bohemians (Mabel Dodge).[2] In some ways Mabel Dodge's "salon" became the symbol of the confluence of these trends and of championship of Freud's teachings. Brill (1939), in describing his work with lay groups, wrote: ". . . I spoke during the winter of 1913 . . . at Mable Dodge's salon. The person who invited me to speak there was a young man named Walter Lippmann, a recent Harvard graduate working with Lincoln Steffens. There I met radicals, littérateurs, artists, and philosophers, some of whom have influenced the trends of our times in no small way" (p. 322).

The effect of all these trends is perhaps most succinctly summarized by Mark Sullivan (1932, pp. 165-174):

> Conventions which had been respected, traditions that had been revered, codes that had been obeyed almost as precepts of religion, had been undermined or had disappeared. In their place had come new ways, new attitudes of mind, new manners. . . .
> The largest single group of new ideas, and the ones that were most fundamental in the changes they wrought, appeared in America between 1909 and 1914. They . . . [were] originated . . . in Vienna, [by] a physician named Sigmund Freud . . . By 1910, allusions to the new concept of psychology began to appear in the lay press, usually with angry disapproval. . . . That was the average normal layman's reaction to initial acquaintance with a theory which was utterly contrary to religion and subversive of every existing conception of romantic love. To the average American of about 1910, it would be difficult to imagine anything more repellent. . . .
> . . . the average man, indeed, rarely heard the name Freud . . .
> The medium through which Freud's ideas were impressed upon the

---

[1] See May (1959, pp. 68 ff., 188-192), Hofstadter (1955, pp. 196-212), and Hacker and Kendrick (1949, pp. 353-355).

[2] See Van Wyck Brooks (1952, pp. 371-389, 475-490). For some interesting accounts of personal contacts with Freud by literary persons, see Goldman (1934, pp. 173, 455-456) and Eastman (1942), and particularly that gem of H. D.'s, *Tribute to Freud* (H. D., 1956).

country and altered its standards, consisted mainly of the novelists, dramatists, poets, critics, college teachers . . .

Chatter of all that stirred the air wherever intellectuals met; by the 1920's there were more than two hundred books dealing with Freudianism. . . .

. . . Hardly any intellectual revolution in history was more complete than the transition from reverence for Emersonian Puritanism up to about 1910, to fierce jibing at it subsequently. It was a denial, by American authors, of the most American standard, almost the only American standard, we had—a rejection of the austere morality of a New England philosopher to make way for the biological theory of an Austrian physician to diseased minds. . . .

. . . By 1915, William Marion Reedy was moved to remark, "It's sex o'clock."[3]

Although Sullivan's views are a good example of the pervasiveness of Freud's influence, it is not necessary to accept his estimate of the role of Freud's influence in relation to Emersonian ethics. Specifically, we need not accept the implication that it was in fact *Emersonian* Puritanism which was involved, that this was the generally accepted ethic, that Freud's influence was the major factor in its passing, or that Freudian thinking was intrinsically inimical to Emersonian views.[4] We have quoted Sullivan chiefly to indicate that there was a clash between two ideologies and that the ideology that won out was in part shaped by Freud's ideas. But the other died hard and in fact is still with us today in one form or another.

The victorious ideology turned Freud's theory mainly into a tool for the rebellious, so that Freud's influence on sexual morality was by no means a simple effect of his actual theory.[5] Those who be-

[3] F. L. Wells, however, indicates that he "saw this expression in the summer of 1905, in a rather 'leftish' magazine whose name I cannot now recall, in Saranac Lake, N. Y." (personal communication, January 31, 1963).

[4] Burnham (1958, especially pp. 318-320), for instance, has shown how much the "social hygiene" movement prepared for the decline of Puritanism.

[5] Freud's theory was more truly reflected in the story of the flapper who went to be analyzed by Freud only to be told to go back to the United States to pick up some inhibitions and then to return for an analysis. "Where no repressions (or analogous psychical processes) can be undone, our therapy has nothing to expect" (Freud, 1916-1917, p. 435). This is not the place to discuss the moral implications of Freud's theory (see, however, Shakow, 1964), or to pinpoint the distortions in what has come to be accepted as the theory's role in the change of morality in our time. The history of morality seems to offer evidence that such shifts occur periodically and are at least in part a natural phenomenon (see Brinton, 1959, pp. 421-426). The influence of Freudian theories in precipitating the change must surely have been a complex process.

lieved in the rebellion, whose ranks were swelled by the inveterate band wagoners, tended to accept uncritically what was presented to them as Freud's teaching. Those who understood human nature too well to accept the oversimplifications of the theory which were presented, as well as those whose emotional and socioeconomic investment in the older ideology was great, tended to join the battle on the other side. What naturally resulted in both camps was a combination of investments, convictions, and honest devotion to what was considered mankind's best interests, with shams, exploitations, and *ex parte* interests.

The process by which these contrary interests were combined is described dramatically by Allen (1931), Luhan (1936), Sullivan (1932), Cargill (1941), Kazin (1942), Curti (1943), Hoffman (1957), Hacker and Kendrick (1949), Hofstadter (1955, especially pp. 173-212), Brooks (1952), May (1959), and other literary and cultural historians.[6]

Books of the nature of Robinson's *The Mind in the Making* (1921), Lippmann's *A Preface to Politics* (1913),[7] and Martin's *The Behavior of Crowds* (1920), give a picture of the extent to which intellectual public consciousness, as well as the social and historical sciences, absorbed or reacted to Freud's conceptions.

Thus Freud's earliest impact came as a contribution to the changing *Zeitgeist* of the first decades of the twentieth century. It was not until later, however, as this Freud-flavored *Zeitgeist* resulted

[6] Some statistical data which are available make possible an assessment of popular interest in psychoanalysis. For instance the President's Research Committee on Social Trends (Ogburn, 1933), in analyzing the articles from seven mass circulation periodicals, pointed up the ebb and flow of discussions of psychoanalysis. The number of articles on psychoanalysis between 1905 and 1932 was

1905	1910	1915	1919	1922	1925	1929	1930	1931
-09	-14	-18	-21	-24	-28	-30	-31	-32
0.00	.12	.34	.29	.28	.38	.21	.07	.12

for every thousand published. Other statistics presented by the report of this committee show with equal clarity the general ideological trends.

Nathan G. Hale, Jr. (personal communication, April 16, 1963) suggests that these figures by themselves may be somewhat misleading, as they do not include the attitudes expressed in the articles. His own analysis of selected magazine articles, made in relation to his dissertation under H. F. May (Hale, 1964), indicated a most favorable attitude during the 1915 to 1919 period, followed by a much higher proportion of unfavorable articles after the 1920's.

[7] Jones (1913b) reviewed the volume for *Imago*, not Freud, as Lippmann indicated in a letter to Hoffman (1957, p. 54). See Forcey (1954, especially p. 227 ff.) for a discussion of Lippmann and Freudism.

in nonprofessional pressures in various psychological quarters, that psychology began to react to and absorb Freudian conceptions. As we shall see, this reaction was beset with conflicts, and the absorption accomplished by means of varied compromises.

In the educational sphere, the Freudian impact was also being felt. Students and teachers of psychology were continuously exposed to mass and select media, to popularizations, and to the public debate aroused by them. Teachers were under additional pressure from their students who wanted to learn about the "new psychology" in the expectation of being instructed about real life problems.

One of us was an undergraduate at Harvard in the early twenties. It was obvious that high among the reasons students chose to come to psychology was a desire to understand themselves and other human beings, to learn something about the "new psychology." But relatively little of it was forthcoming. Lippmann, a Harvard undergraduate a decade or so earlier, described a similar experience: "I read the translation [of Freud's *The Interpretation of Dreams*] as he [Kuttner] worked on it and discussed it with him and began to see how much Freud had to contribute to the psychology which I had learned at college" (Hoffman, 1957, p. 54).[8] In the period immediately after Lippmann, Tolman was at Harvard as a graduate student following a Massachusetts Institute of Technology bachelor's degree. He expressed his disappointment more directly: ". . . [the course] proved a terrible letdown from the really humanly important problems which I had supposed psychology was to be concerned with . . ." (E. C. Tolman, 1952, p. 325). And Harvard was probably more open to new developments than the majority of universities.

Student pressure, combined with the more general pressures impinging on the world of psychology, seems to have led to a new type of course offering in the colleges. These were courses on human adjustment which included discussions, if not of Freud and his work,

---

[8] Lippmann, while writing his *A Preface to Politics* (1913), shared a cabin in the Maine woods with Kuttner (Hoffman, 1957, p. 54; Eulau, 1951, pp. 299-300). Kuttner, who was associated with *Seven Arts*, the influential literary magazine of the period, was at that time translating Freud's *The Interpretation of Dreams* for his psychoanalyst, A. A. Brill. However, Brill, in the introduction to his translation, gave credit only to Professor F. C. Prescott. See Lippmann's (1915) "Freud and the Layman" for a clear presentation of Lippmann's views on Freud at this period.

at least of "Freudian themes." They were, however, usually isolated from courses in the science of psychology.

Psychologists, in addition to being pressured by ideological trends and by developments in the educational field, were feeling the demand from colleagues from other disciplines who expected them at least to elucidate if not to refute the "new psychology." Tansley (see S. M. Payne, 1956), who was one of the first reputable and established men to publish a broad-scale presentation of the "new psychology" (1920), was a botanist. Wheeler, the great authority on social insects who has been referred to as "the last of the great naturalists," was one of the first men to give a penetrating appraisal of psychology's deficiencies in relation to psychoanalysis. In "On Instincts" he wrote, in the pungent style to be expected from the author of "The Dry-Rot of Our Academic Biology" (1923), as follows:

> After perusing during the past twenty years a small library of rose-water psychologies of the academic type and noticing how their authors ignore or merely hint at the existence of such stupendous and fundamental biological phenomena as those of hunger, sex and fear, I should not disagree with, let us say, an imaginary critic recently arrived from Mars, who should express the opinion that many of these works read as if they had been composed by beings that had been born and bred in a belfry, castrated in early infancy and fed continually for fifty years through a tube with a stream of liquid nutriment of constant chemical composition. To put it drastically, most of our traditional psychologies are about as useful for purposes of understanding the human mind as an equal number of dissertations on Greek statuary would be to a student eager for a knowledge of anatomy. Such a student at once learns that the object of his investigation, the human and animal body, is very largely composed of parts offensive to the aesthetic sense, but this does not deter him from studying them as thoroughly as other parts. The typical psychologist, who might be expected to study his material in the same scientific spirit, does nothing of the kind, but confines his attention to the head and the upper extremities and drapes or ignores the other parts.
>
> Now I believe that the psychoanalysts are getting down to brass tacks. They have discovered that the psychologists' game which seems to consist in sitting down together or with the philosophers and seeing who can hallucinate fastest or most subtly and clothe the results in the best English, is not helping us very much in solving the terribly insistent problems of life. They have had the courage to dig up the subconscious, that hotbed of all the egotism, greed,

TWENTIETH CENTURY DEVELOPMENTS 61

lust, pugnacity, cowardice, sloth, hate, and envy which every single one of us carries about as his inheritance from the animal world. These are all ethically and aesthetically very unpleasant phenomena but they are just as real and fundamental as our entrails, blood and reproductive organs. In this matter, I am glad to admit, the theologians, with their doctrine of total depravity, seem to me to be nearer the truth than the psychologists. I should say, however, that our depravity is only about 85 to 90% [1921, pp. 316-317].

Even if the psychologists whose works fitted Wheeler's description were not born and raised in belfries, nor castrated as infants, nor tube-fed throughout life, the fact that the conditions deplored by Wheeler could exist shows how much conventionally accepted professional commitments can influence the workers in a particular field. As we shall see later, however, some psychologists did manage to break through the various barriers. No commitment could insulate all of them from the impact of the *Zeitgeist*.

The literature of the period which dealt with psychoanalysis was, of course, another source of influence. The part of this literature which might be considered as an indirect influence on psychology includes the extreme end of the distribution of "secondary sources," and what we shall call the "tertiary sources" of psychoanalysis. It ranges from popular material to texts meant for classroom use. The tertiary sources include material written for mass magazines, the semipopular books of such popularizers as Severn, Fielding, and Ralph, and the similar writings of those persons, such as Tridon, Van Teslaar, Jastrow, and Calvin Hall, more closely allied with the psychoanalytic and psychological professions. The group of secondary sources we refer to here are the textbooks of psychology which contain sections on psychoanalytic topics and were prepared by such persons as Gates and Shaffer who are not identified with psychoanalysis. The line between these sources and the remaining portion of the secondary sources, which we shall discuss as a direct influence, is not uniformly sharp, but is usually readily drawn in an individual case. In general, the secondary sources we shall discuss later are the more scholarly books written by psychoanalysts (for example, Fenichel, Hendrick, Hitschmann, Pfister, Waelder), and by psychologists having a strong identification with psychoanalysis (for example, Hart, Holt, Symonds, Wells). The primary sources are, of course, those coming from Freud himself.

We can get some idea of the kind of texts which came into use—and also a better notion of the nature of the "adjustment" courses which developed—from Hilgard's (1949) presidential address, the fifty-seventh annual, to the American Psychological Association. This was the first such address to be devoted largely to a Freudian topic. It expresses both psychology's interest in and reluctance to accept psychoanalysis, and states the compromise which "solved" this conflict. Hilgard said:

> The mechanisms of adjustment were the features of Freudian theory that we earliest domesticated within American academic psychology. They now have a respectable place in our textbooks, regardless of the theoretical biases of our textbook writers.
> ... we took over the mechanisms when as a profession we were hostile to other aspects of psychoanalytic teaching. ... we often gave only halting recognition to their psychoanalytic origins. Nearly all the mechanisms do in fact derive from Freud, Jung, Adler, and their followers. ... Yet Gates' [whose text Hilgard considered one of the first to mention the mechanisms[9]] only mention of psychoanalysis was in some disparaging remarks about the "alleged adjustment by repression to the unconscious," an explanation of adjustment which he rejected as neither true nor useful [1949, pp. 374-375].

The hostility and hesitancy to give recognition which Hilgard speaks of is, however, only part of the story. As part of the tertiary sources that developed in the literature, we find a semipopular literature which straddled the range between the secondary sources, to which Hilgard refers, and the articles for mass magazines. The lines are not sharply drawn in either direction: some of this literature was written by psychologists, some by medical men, and some even by psychiatrists; some of it was issued by reputable publishing houses and paraded in the garments of respectability. For the most part, however, it was a mass of oversimplification and distortion, catering to or combating the up-and-coming "new ideology." It served, therefore, as a source of misunderstanding and confusion for psychologists. It is partly to this literature that Humphrey

---

[9] The priority of having introduced these into a textbook probably goes to R. C. Givler's 1915 volume *The "Conscious Cross-Section": A Realistic Psychology* (see Burnham, 1958, pp. 232-233), although Gates' books were more widely used. According to Hilgard's characterization of his texts, Gates, at least initially, had "dynamic" leanings. Wells, in *Mental Adjustments* (1917a), had an extensive discussion of defense mechanisms.

(1922b) referred, saying that Freud would not recognize himself in it. Van Teslaar (1924) among psychiatrists, and Jastrow among psychologists, at the time he wrote *The House That Freud Built* (1932), were popularizers who seem to mark the more respectable end of this continuum. Tridon's[10] (1921) unauthorized popular version of *The Interpretation of Dreams,* and his other writings, are somewhere in the middle of this range. The continuum includes such books as E. Severn's (1917), W. J. Fielding's (1923), J. Ralph's (1921), and uncounted others. Since standards were nonexistent for distinguishing *bona fide* psychoanalytic contributions from popularizations and crude vulgarizations, it is no wonder that the psychologist-reader and -reviewer felt unbounded contempt for these publications, a contempt often carried over to psychoanalysis itself. On the other hand, in extenuation of the popularizers, it is not surprising that their presentations of psychoanalysis were oversimplified and distorted, for, as we shall see later, they had no systematic account of the theory to work with. In such circumstances, and given the complexity of the material, it was almost inevitable that the more popular[11] sources be inaccurate and incomplete.

RESPONSE TO INFLUENCE

What should be examined at greater length is the way in which psychologists responded to this mode of communication. They, as well as the general public, learned about psychoanalysis more often from the popularizations than from the primary sources, or even the more professional secondary sources. At best they acquired some such simplified view of Freud's observations, concepts, and theories before they studied the primary sources. It is this state of affairs which was acutely perceived by Heidbreder (1940) when she said that the psychologist was influenced by Freud in his role as man in the street, rather than on the basis of his special knowl-

---

[10] Tridon represented the political as well as the psychological radicalism of the period (see May, 1959, pp. 305-307).

[11] For the most part, our use of the terms "popular" and "semipopular" refers to the literature or trends likely to affect the educated layman. In this case our concern lies mostly with those whose reading ranged over the authors we have mentioned. It is this group, rather than those more likely to be influenced by such literature as the McFadden publications or S. Parkes Cadman's column, that is in a position to influence the academic world. Ordinarily social changes are initiated in this group, and only gradually percolate down to other levels.

edge. Essentially she argued that since Freud's theories were presented in a form unsuitable to scientific verification, the psychologist had no means of verifying or refuting them. The traditions and equipment of psychology were as irrelevant to Freud's theory as Freud's theory was to them. For this reason, many psychologists, including some of the leaders in the field, were kept immune to Freud's influence by the inapplicability of their methods to psychoanalytic theory. Although Heidbreder's notion of the "man in the street" has considerable validity, it does not quite describe the full problem that existed. The situation for the academic psychologist had another facet.

Being a psychologist in itself involves certain implicit demands from within as well as explicit ones from without. These demands center on studying and explaining "human nature." Even if the overriding effect of one's disciplinary training and the support of colleagues enable one to devote oneself to areas (basic or applied) quite remote from this "expected" area, there still remains, perhaps at a deeper psychological level, some residual guilt for not meeting "obligations" of the more immediate and obvious kind. There is also probably some lingering regret for one's impotence in the magical area of control of mind and behavior that a true knowledge of psychology presumably confers, and which the novice psychologist in his utmost depths hopes to achieve. This professional guilt for having "failed" both in respect to one's own and others' naïve expectations was probably mobilized when the pressure for dynamic psychology came so strongly from the surrounding culture. Psychologists found it difficult to remain aloof from "real" problems. It was apparently the fate of the psychologist to be sporadically haunted by the ghosts of life's problems which he tried to avoid by means of his commitment to the laboratory.

Thus a conflict developed within psychologists between these various pressures on the one hand and the discipline's scientific tradition on the other. The relative youth of the scientific tradition in psychology, with its concomitant self-consciousness and unavoidable defensiveness, could do nothing but exacerbate the problem. This conflict was handled in a variety of ways. Many outstanding psychologists recognized the inadequacy of the existing psychology and accepted Freudian ideas with greater or lesser degrees of ambivalence. A very few resolved the conflict by wholly accepting Freudian ideas. There were many, of course, who did not accept them at all, and still others who even claimed that what Freud talked about was already common knowledge.

Direct Influences

We have been discussing the pressures on psychologists coming from nonprofessional sources. But, as we have indicated, Freud's influence on psychology was not alone determined by the stampeding public consciousness, student dissatisfactions, colleagues' pressures, and the more popular literature on psychoanalysis. There were strong determinants deriving from strictly professional sources. These consisted largely of Freud's books, general articles, and lectures, in the original language and in translation. There were also the more scholarly secondary sources of psychoanalytic theory that were written by psychoanalysts or by psychologists who were rather strongly identified with psychoanalysis. To these "literary" sources of professional influence must be added various general effects of the different professional settings of psychoanalysis and psychology.

Again, we find the wide range of responses, from complete acceptance to complete rejection, as well as many intermediate levels of partial acceptance and ambivalence.

The Responses of Selected Psychologists

To provide some idea of the variety of response to Freud, we will give a sample of opinions of representative American psychologists[12] during the crucial four decades of 1909-1950. We shall, however, have occasion to discuss some of these persons again in other contexts in this volume.

A natural starting point for such a sampling would be Stanley Hall's reasons for inviting Freud and a relatively large number of his psychoanalytic colleagues to the celebration of the twentieth

---

[12] For the reaction of psychiatrists, which was much earlier and stronger than that of psychologists, see Burnham (1958, especially pp. 121-170). This question will be considered at greater length in Burnham (unpublished manuscript). We will not deal with psychiatrists here except as they have special relevance for psychology—as did Healy, Prince, and Sidis. We might mention here that the reaction of psychiatry was actually in part responsible for much that was published in the *Psychological Bulletin* and the *Journal of Abnormal and Social Psychology* (see Burnham, 1958, pp. 31-34). Burnham (1958) has also given a factual, detailed survey of the response of sociology and psychology to Freud's theory up to 1917.

anniversary of Clark University. Unfortunately, no statement from Hall on the subject appears to be available.[13] We do, however, have his "anonymous" write-up of the celebration published in *The Nation*[14] ([Hall] 1909a, pp. 284-285). In this article he says of Freud:

> ... he has developed what may now almost be called a new system of psychology, which seems to a growing number of workers in this field, of whom the writer is one, to be the best word yet spoken there. His views are now beginning to be talked of in Germany as the psychology of the future ... And yet, partly because so much that he taught was new and revolutionary, he has until lately had but scant recognition; and because he attempts to do justice to sex in his scheme, he was for years socially ostracized. Happily, however, he is now coming to his own and a growing circle of very vigorous young men in all civilized countries are giving him due recognition and working out his ideas. It is difficult to give, in brief and lucid phrase, any adequate conception of a system that has so many details and even technicalities. It seems certainly to go distinctly beyond Janet; and if it be confirmed, it plays havoc with many of the systems of both philosophical and of laboratory psychology.

With such an attitude toward psychoanalysis it is not surprising that Hall, wishing to make the anniversary celebration outstanding, particularly in his own area of study, should have brought not only Freud but Jung, Ferenczi, and Jones from abroad and Brill from New York—a proportionately large number of analysts in a group that was primarily a stellar array of American psychologists.[15]

On January 1, 1909, Hall (1909b) gave an address on "Evolution and Psychology" at the meeting of the American Association

---

[13] Inquiry at Clark University revealed no record. Reports of contacts with Dr. R. G. Hall, the son of Stanley Hall, now living in Portland, Oregon, indicate that practically all of Hall's residual papers have been destroyed. Dorothy Ross (1965) at Columbia University, in her forthcoming doctoral dissertation under R. Hofstadter on Stanley Hall, may have something to add about this matter. Virginia Payne (1950) was able to obtain letters with a few reminiscences of the conference from Jones (who refers to Ferenczi and Brill as the other psychoanalysts present, leaving out Jung!) and from Jung. Neither letter has truly substantive interest. See Jones (1955, pp. 53-60) for an account from the psychoanalytic side.

[14] For evidence that the article was written by Hall, see Wilson's (1914, p. 142, Item 294) *G. Stanley Hall: A Sketch*.

[15] See the famous group portrait which probably represents the most distinguished group of psychologists "exposed" at one time (Hall, 1923, facing p. 334).

for the Advancement of Science in Baltimore for the centennial celebration of Darwin's birth and the semicentennial celebration of the publication of *On the Origin of the Species*. In speaking of "The Psychology of the Future," he remarked that "the present psychological situation cries out for a new Darwin of the mind." Although he placed heavy emphasis on the unconscious, the importance of the genetic, and the need for a psychology closer to life, he mentioned Freud only once in passing. By this time, of course— in fact, about a month earlier—Hall had invited Freud to lecture at Clark and must already have been much impressed with Freud's contribution. When, toward the end of his career, he returned to the Darwin theme, he apparently accepted Freud as being the "Darwin" he had called for some fourteen years earlier. In 1923 he wrote a friendly letter to Freud: ". . . in fact history will show that you have done for us a service which you are not at all extravagant in comparing with that of Darwin for biology" (Burnham, 1960, p. 313).[16]

In some respects William James' reaction forecast the ambivalent response of even the most receptive psychologists. On the one hand, there is Jones' account of James' reaction to Freud and his pupils after the Clark Celebration. Jones (1955, p. 57) says: ". . . I shall never forget his [James'] parting words, said with his arm around my shoulder: 'The future of psychology belongs to your work'. . ." On the other hand, in a letter of the same period to Flournoy, James, while confirming his positive attitude toward psychoanalysis, wrote: ". . . I confess that he [Freud] made on me personally the impression of a man obsessed with fixed ideas" (James, 1920b, p. 328; also R. B. Perry, 1935, pp. 122-123). He expressed the same opinion in a letter to Mary Calkins: "I strongly suspect Freud, with his dream-theory, of being a regular *halluciné*. But I hope that he and his disciples will push it to its limits, as undoubtedly it covers some facts, and will add to our understand-

---

[16] We might, in passing, indicate that this letter was written in the context of a plea for a father's magnanimity to rebelling children—he was referring to Jung and Adler. If Hall does not seem to have been willing to take the full responsibility for the Darwin judgment on himself, we must recognize that this particular designation had special meaning for him. In his autobiography (Hall, 1923, p. 360) he recalled that he himself had once been introduced as the "Darwin of the mind" by an overzealous friend. He said, ". . . it gave me more inner satisfaction than any compliment ever paid me by the most perfervid friend."

ing of 'functional' psychology, which is the real psychology" (Perry, 1935, p. 123).[17]

Holt was a psychologist who was perhaps even more sympathetic toward psychoanalysis. Yet he took from the primary Freudian sources mainly what fitted his own theory and discussed in his writing only those of Freud's concepts which seemed indispensable for his purposes.

Langfeld's (1946) obituary of Holt confirms and amplifies this assessment:

> Freud was so very close to Holt's heart that he refused to write an article on him for the *Psychological Review* because there were so many 'grave defects' in Freud's theory which he did not care to describe publicly. As to the features of the theory which he liked, Holt wrote:
> "The points for which I venerate Freud are his fine empirical observations in the earlier part of his career; his substituting the dynamic 'wish' for Janet's non-dynamic and futile 'dissociations'; and lastly, his supreme integrity, in science and in everything. On the second point (where Freud helped me so greatly toward a motor psychology) I said in 'The Freudian Wish' all that I could now say.

---

[17] Aside from the points we have already made we might add the following. To judge from a letter of James to Hall dated September 8, 1909 (in the possession of Dorothy Ross), James could only spend from about 6:00 p.m. on the 9th to about the same time on the 10th attending the meetings. (This is corroborated in the letter to Flournoy mentioned in the text, where James said: "I went there for one day in order to see what Freud was like . . .") Thus, their personal contact extended over a day, and James heard only the fourth lecture on Friday morning. (The five lectures seem to have extended from Tuesday to Saturday, and were given at 11:00 on each of these mornings.)

In addition, from various sources close to Hall in his later years, one gets the impression that Hall talked about an incompatibility which had existed between James and Freud. It is hard to judge how much of this incompatibility was real, growing out of personality differences, and how much created by Hall's projecting his own long-standing difficult relationship with James. The latter conflict apparently began approximately a year after the founding of the *American Journal of Psychology* in 1888, and Hall's review of James' *Principles* in the same journal in 1891. This was followed by the 1895 controversy about Hall's (1895a) rather boastful editorial announcement in the first issue of the *Journal* for that year, which raised a stir over the matter of the beginnings of experimental psychology in America (see James et al., 1895; G. S. Hall, 1895b). As an aside, a James letter in the possession of one of us (Shakow), dated March 13 (no year) to Col. Higginson explains that James could not attend a Stanley Hall lecture because of another engagement but "I dare say the learned Hall will talk all the more freely and easily without the sense of my critical ear."

In any case, the evaluation of the Freud-James relationship cannot depend too heavily on reports of what Hall might have said. The forthcoming dissertation of Dorothy Ross (1965) should provide some information on this and other matters relating to Hall.

And I think that few readers understood or cared; since so few have been led on to a motor psychology" (November 14, 1939) [p. 256].

John B. Watson was one of the extreme exponents of the commitment to the exact science program. But contrary to the usual assumption that his attitude toward psychoanalysis was a negative one, there is evidence that he took a stand on its behalf. According to Woodworth, Watson was one of the psychologists who accepted Freudian teaching to some extent (Woodworth, 1917, p. 174). Watson's (1916) article in *The Scientific Monthly* provided sufficient ground for this view (see also his autobiography, 1936). As we shall see later, other behaviorists attempted to tame the wild horse of Freudian theory (wish, pleasure-pain principle, etc.) by the "exact science" methods and concepts available to them (for example, those of association and conditioning). If they failed to penetrate the network of the theory more than superficially, it was their program and methods more than their personal "resistance" that prevented them from doing so. In many instances it seems obvious that an interest was there.

We turn now to an outstanding dynamic psychologist, Woodworth. He appraised the situation in 1917 as follows:

> A number of psychologists, as Holt, Watson, Wells and Lay, have espoused the Freudian teaching to a greater or less extent . . . The majority . . . are probably to be counted as skeptics. For myself I am very skeptical. I admit that a good deal of stimulus can be derived from the work of the psychoanalysts towards a study of neglected topics in psychology; and I rather expect that many germs of truth will . . . be found in the teachings of this school; but their methods . . . seem to me excessively rough and ready, and their conclusions one-sided and exaggerated [1917, p. 174].

But fourteen years later Woodworth wrote: ". . . the atmosphere has cleared somewhat; both adherents and opponents have become more discriminating; and the Freudian psychology is now generally regarded, we may safely say, as an important contribution to our growing science . . ." (1931, p. 133). And in 1948, he wrote: "Freud himself was a man of marvelous energy and enterprise . . . a keen observer, a fearless and original thinker. . . . and however his theories may be finally evaluated, he was a stimulating pioneer whose important place in the history of psychology is amply assured" (1948, p. 192).

In 1921 George Humphrey (1921, pp. 385-386), wrote: "The service of the Freudians lies, indeed, in their fact, not their theory. That the whole movement will have a far reaching effect upon the psychology of the future is beyond question. . . . As it stands today, the doctrine is rather a viewpoint of which progressive science should take account than a system which it should regard very seriously."

Thurstone, one of the exponents of the quantitative method in psychology, was among the first to appreciate the importance of the phenomena and relationships Freud studied. In 1924, he wrote: "The content of psychoanalysis . . . is much more important than the content with which we have busied ourselves as scientific psychologists. . . .

"Let us . . . apply to these phenomena the methods of controlled scientific experimentation" (1924, p. 183).

In personal conversation, Thurstone told one of us (Shakow) that his period at Ardmore, where he had the opportunity to become acquainted with psychopathology, was the most profitable psychological three months that he had ever spent. In his autobiography in *A History of Psychology in Autobiography* (1952) he said: "One of my principal interests in psychology to which I have returned several times has been the study of personality. Soon after completing the doctorate, I turned my attention seriously to the study of abnormal psychology, and I read Freud and a good deal of the psychoanalytical literature. My conflict here was that, on the one hand, the center of psychology probably was the study of personality, but, on the other hand, I was unable to invent any experimental leverage in this field" (p. 318).

In 1926 McDougall, who will be discussed at greater length below, wrote: "Unlike many of my academic colleagues, I do not regard the psychoanalytic movement with indifference, still less with hostility. I believe that Prof. Freud has done more for the advancement of psychology than any student since Aristotle. At the same time, I by no means accept all of his teachings; I regard much of the current psychoanalytic doctrines as ill-founded and somewhat fantastic" (1926, p. viii).

Terman, whose opinions about Freud over a range of approximately fifty years are available to us, wrote in a personal communication (February 24, 1956): "My first interest in Freud was aroused by some lectures given by Stanley Hall at Clark University in 1904-05. However, the first reading I did on psychoanalysis was when the lectures were published that were given at Clark University in 1909 by Freud and others. . . . I read and reread them. From that time until perhaps 1935 or so, I read a good many books on psychoanalysis, at least one magazine, and comments and articles by psychologists who ranged from favorable to most unfavorable in their attitude toward Freudianism." In his autobiography (1932), written in 1930, Terman said: ". . . the Freudian concepts, even when their validity has been discounted about 90 per cent, nevertheless, constitute one of the two most important contributions to modern psychology, mental tests being the other" (p. 330). Neal Miller (personal communication, January, 1956) reports that while he was at Stanford in 1931-1932, Terman made him aware of the importance of Freud's theory. Terman himself, in the letter already referred to (February 24, 1956), indicates that he subsequently took an even stronger position. He discovered evidence for and a method of corroborating Freudian observations and theories:

> My estimate now would be that Freudian psychology does not have to be discounted to the extent of 90%. In fact I think that Freud and other analysts, however much they may have differed on specific points, have left a terrific imprint upon modern psychology. What seemed 50 years ago so speculative regarding the part played by the subconscious has now become generally accepted and commonplace—the concepts of repression, the Oedipus complex in the broad sense of that term, overcompensation, and the subconscious factors in human motivation. The hundreds of projective techniques that have been devised or at least many of them are based on concepts that Freud and his associates developed 50 or more years ago. I may add that I have been much interested in biographies which draw upon psychoanalytic concepts. Such biographers have probably gone too far in applying psychoanalytic concepts, but in my opinion the lives of many great men cannot be understood without some knowledge of the Freudian School. There are a good many persons in my large group of gifted subjects whose lives I have followed from childhood who could serve as good examples of early subconscious influences.

Dorothy G. Park, in 1931, made the first study of Freudian influence on academic psychology, using the texts published between 1910 and 1930. She concluded: ". . . Freudian influence has been quite steadily increasing since 1910 and is consistently holding its own at the present time despite opposition and controversy" (1931, p. 85).[18]

Heidbreder (1933) was one of the first psychologists to present a systematic appraisal of psychoanalysis. At that time she said that some psychoanalytic concepts had been extremely hospitably received by behaviorism. Psychoanalysis had influenced both abnormal and social psychology "tremendously," and even found its way into elementary texts. Its "seemingly inexhaustible curiosity" gave a vitality to its observations which worked with its "first-hand contact with its material" and its "scope" to give it an impact upon psychology in general. Many psychologists found the psychoanalytic concepts of conflict, repression, rationalization, and indirect wish-fulfillment to be "fruitful hypotheses . . . abundantly illustrated in everyday life." They also recognized as valuable Freud's stress on the problems of the "personality as a whole" and on the "conative and affective" as against the "rational." Further, his emphasis on infancy and childhood, though often not the sexual aspect, was in accord with their findings, and it was generally recognized that Freud promoted "a more naturalistic view of man." Finally, his concept of the unconscious raised "fundamental problems concerning the methodology and the basic structure of the whole science of psychology" (1933, pp. 409-412). In 1940 Heidbreder wrote an obituary of Freud in which she said: his "theories found their way into psychology without the backing of accepted, or acceptable, scientific evidence" (1940, p. 192), and, as we mentioned earlier, have influenced the psychologist "in his role as man in the

---

[18] The question of courses devoted to psychoanalysis in the early days is shrouded in some mystery. Although Ofiesh's (1959) dissertation throws some light on introductory psychology courses, it contains only some casual remarks about the relationship of psychoanalysis to these courses. Stanley Hall appears to have been the earliest psychologist to deal with Freud in courses, as is witnessed by a communication to us from Terman (February 24, 1956) which we mention in the text. This gives a date of 1904-1905. The Clark University Catalogue, for at least the years immediately following this date, lists Hall as giving courses which included discussion of Freud, Jung, Janet, and Adler. It is difficult, however, to determine how systematic these were, since Hall did not necessarily follow a promised pattern. Murphy (1956, p. 667) mentions Elliott Frost's reference to Freud's concept of dreams in a course at Yale in 1914.

Rosvold (1955, p. 327), in his obituary of Calvin Stone, believes that Stone's course at Stanford in Freudian psychology in 1923 was "the first formal course on this subject offered as a regular part of the curriculum in an American university."

street, not on the basis of his special knowledge [as a psychologist] . . ." (p. 192). "Like Copernicus and Darwin . . . he put the facts of common observation in a setting which profoundly altered their meaning, and which introduced into both science and common knowledge radically new perspectives" (1940, p. 195). Unlike the other two, however, ". . . Freud presented his theories in a form unsuitable to scientific verification and use" (p. 195).

Boring, who made only passing mention of Freud in the 1929 edition of his history of psychology, in the 1950 edition lists him among the four great men of psychology, along with Darwin, Helmholtz, and James, and indeed places him with Darwin ahead of the other two.[19] He characterizes Freud as the man who reawakened psychology's interest in "human nature" (Boring, 1950b, p. 713), who "accomplished the invasion of psychology by the principle of the unconscious process" (p. 743), who gave to psychology the concept of motivation to replace the "will" it had exorcised (p. 713), and was "The principal source of dynamic psychology . . ." (p. 693).

Finally, we must mention John Dewey. Although Dewey was not primarily a psychologist, he was a philosopher of great influence known especially for his writings on psychology[20] and his great contribution to education. After an initially positive attitude, in his major psychological work, *Human Nature and Conduct,* Dewey (1922, pp. 86-87) expressed himself as only moderately favorable to psychoanalysis:[21]

> The rise at the present time of a clinical psychology which revolts at traditional and orthodox psychology is a symptom of ethical import. It is a protest against the futility, as a tool of understanding and dealing with human nature in the concrete, of the psychology of conscious sensations, images and ideas. It exhibits a sense for reality in its insistence upon the profound importance of unconscious forces

---

[19] A quantitative reflection of this change in opinion among psychologists in general is shown by a comparison of the Tinker-Thuma-Farnsworth (1927) study and the Coan-Zagona (1962) study.

[20] See particularly *Human Nature and Conduct* (1922) and *Reconstruction in Philosophy* (1920).

[21] G. W. Allport (1951, p. 270) has pointed out that Dewey shifted from an instinct to a habit point of view between 1917 and 1922. By 1922, the date of *Human Nature and Conduct,* Dewey had become acquainted with F. M. Alexander, who Levitt (1960, p. 154) feels was likely to have been instrumental in Dewey's change of opinion about psychoanalysis.

> in determining not only overt conduct but desire, judgment, belief, idealization.
>
> Every movement of reaction and protest, however, usually accepts some of the basic ideas of the position against which it rebels. So the most popular forms of the clinical psychology, those associated with the founders of psycho-analysis, retain the notion of a separate psychic realm or force. . . . Their elaborate artificial explanations, like the mystic collective mind, consciousness, over-soul, of social psychology, are due to failure to begin with the facts of habit and custom.

But in general he came to deplore the "oversimplifications" that psychoanalysis represented.

As is so clearly (perhaps too clearly) brought out by Feuer (1960),[22] Dewey was an optimist, oriented toward the future,[23] a reformer, a believer in "unlimited total peace," an interventionist, an acceptor of the therapies of action and love, and, finally, a monist attempting to bring dualism to a higher unity. Freud, on the other hand, was concerned with the tragic virtues,[24] oriented more toward the past, more of a spectator, skeptical about "unlimited total peace," a necessitarian, an acceptor of the therapies of consciousness and love, and a dualist in his emphasis on polarities—Eros and Thanatos, pleasure and reality, conscious and unconscious (see Jones, 1955, pp. 422-423). Though these sketches are too sharply drawn, they are essentially accurate.

We have been discussing psychologists who have had mixed attitudes to psychoanalysis. We will now turn to a small group of psychologists who, during the twenties and thirties, could on the whole be considered as acceptors of psychoanalysis. Among these were Raymond R. Willoughby, Phyllis Blanchard, P. M. Symonds, Gardner Murphy, H. A. Murray, J. F. Brown, Else Frenkel-Brunswik, and several others. From this group we shall single out Willoughby and Murphy for brief discussion, and we shall consider Murray later.

[22] Although Feuer's distinctions may be too sharp, his perceptions are much keener than those of Morton Levitt in *Freud and Dewey on the Nature of Man* (1960).
[23] See his attitude on instinct, the importance of which he tended to denigrate, in *Human Nature and Conduct* (1922, pp. 150-151).
[24] See Kaufmann, *The Faith of a Heretic* (1961, Chapter XI), for a discussion of Freud and the tragic virtues.

Although Willoughby[25] died at the age of forty-eight, he managed to make a substantial contribution by joining his own brand of psychoanalysis with academic psychology. Willoughby was at Clark University, 1926-1936, and at Brown University, 1936-1940. These major periods of professional activity provided him with a number of different channels through which to work. He was at first Assistant and then Associate Editor of the newly established *Psychological Abstracts,* the only journal which was being distributed to all members of the American Psychological Association at the time. The journal was under the editorship of Walter S. Hunter, but Willoughby was the sole professional person devoting full time to it. In this capacity he had an unusual opportunity to make a broad range of psychological material available to psychologists. Because of his interest in psychoanalysis, which grew in part out of his own analysis obtained during his graduate years at Stanford, he provided substantial space for psychoanalytic authors and writings. His catholic view of psychology (which included the genetic, statistical, psychoanalytic, and personality fields) enabled him to recognize the relative neglect of psychoanalysis by psychologists and the importance of clinical as well as experimental evidence. From the very first volume, Willoughby was largely responsible for the high standards achieved by the *Abstracts.* During his tenure the number of annual abstracts increased from 2730 in Volume 1 to 6557 in Volume 12. His deep lexicographic interests led him to establish a cross-referenced index which is a model of its kind and has been most useful to more than a generation of psychologists.

Although he was not actually on the faculties of Clark and Brown Universities, where *Psychological Abstracts* was edited during the two periods, he carried out extensive informal teaching in both places, holding seminars for faculty and graduate students on his own individualistic interpretation of psychoanalytic topics. In addition, he engaged in a heavy program of psychoanalytically oriented psychotherapy for students and others, and in his late years carried out a similarly oriented program of teaching and therapy for ministers. Through these contacts he greatly influenced

---

[25] See Willoughby's obituary (Hunt, Hunter, and Schlosberg, 1945).

a large group of persons, many of whom subsequently held important university positions.[26]

His own publications along psychoanalytic lines fall into four categories. He wrote a few short papers on dreams (1929, 1933b), and in an extensive paper made a substantial contribution on "Magic and Cognate Phenomena" (1935). His work on the emotional maturity scale (1932) combined his psychometric and personality interests; in conception and development it is probably the most sophisticated instrument of its kind, with a strong psychoanalytic orientation. In addition he wrote on psychoanalysis proper. An early report on work done between 1928 and 1930 (1931) describes an experiment with brief psychoanalysis. This anticipation of the work of Alexander and French (1946) reflects Willoughby's characteristic inquiring and unorthodox attitude and his need to test new approaches. His other paper dealing directly with psychoanalysis (1940) is the one contributed to "Psychoanalysis as Seen by Analyzed Psychologists," a symposium which we shall discuss immediately below.

Willoughby is perhaps outstanding because his influence, though effected largely through informal channels, helped substantially to keep psychoanalysis before groups of students in psychology.

Generally belonging in the group of persons early favorable to psychoanalysis is Gardner Murphy. His eclecticism and Jamesian catholicity, combined with his special interest in the fields of personality and social psychology, made him receptive to Freudian influence. Though he cannot easily be typed, he has perhaps done as much as any one psychologist to bring Freudian ideas into psychology. His contribution is reflected mainly in his *Historical Introduction* (1929a, 1949), in his monumental work on *Personality* (1947), and in his book with Jensen (Murphy and Jensen, 1932). It also appears in other volumes: the two editions of *Experimental Social Psychology* (Murphy and Murphy, 1931; Murphy, Murphy, and Newcomb, 1937), and *Outline of Abnormal Psychology* (1929b; Murphy and Bachrach, 1954), as well as in his *General Psychology* (1933). Always overlapping psychoanalytic psychology, but never quite of it, Murphy's teaching at Columbia University and at the City College of New York, as well as his

---

[26] Robert Leeper, Mason and Dorothea Crook, Norman Munn, and C. H. Graham are examples.

writing, laid a strong foundation for students' interest in psychoanalysis. He is continuing actively along the same lines in his present work as Director of Research at the Menninger Clinic, as can be seen in one of his latest works on the perceptual world, in which he collaborated with Solley (Solley and Murphy, 1960).

In closing this section, we turn to a somewhat different example of the response of psychologists to immediate experience with psychoanalysis.

Gordon Allport, the Editor of the *Journal of Abnormal and Social Psychology,* published in the first three issues of Volume 35, for 1940, a symposium of eleven articles (nine by psychologists and two by psychoanalysts) dealing with psychoanalysis. This series of papers shows not only psychology's growing notice of, and tendency to deal directly with, psychoanalysis, but also the potential for reciprocity between psychology and psychoanalysis. In his letter to prospective participants Allport said: "Since it is of the utmost importance to encourage open discussion concerning the principles and practices of psychoanalysis among well-informed psychologists, it would, I think, be timely and profitable to publish a symposium written by psychologists who have completed a standard psychoanalysis with an authorized analyst."

The psychologists who finally participated were Boring, Landis, J. F. Brown, Willoughby, P. M. Symonds, H. A. Murray, Else Frenkel-Brunswik, Shakow, and McGranahan. The Symposium also included a comment on Boring's paper by his psychoanalyst, Hanns Sachs, and a final review of the series, as well as a report of his own psychoanalysis, by Franz Alexander.[27]

By its very nature the Symposium could not provide systematic data. It did, however, offer a forum for the presentation by psychologists of a wide variety of material, ranging from views about the psychoanalytic process itself, through reports of actual experiments on psychoanalytic themes, to suggestions for revision of psychoanalytic theory. Even the most impersonal of the reports were sufficiently detailed to give some indication of the effects of the analytic process on the participants. The Symposium leaves one

---

[27] The next year the *Journal* published an article by Austin Wood (1941) on the same theme.

with the distinct impression of important contributions to psychology from psychoanalysis.

That this series of articles has created some interest among psychologists is evidenced by its republication as a separate volume (G. W. Allport, 1941), five thousand copies of which were sold by September, 1962. The ending note of the psychoanalyst judge, Alexander, "that we are approaching a time which is ripe for the systematic introduction of experimental methods in the study of personality" (Alexander, 1940, p. 323), seems to indicate that much progress had been made toward a convergence of psychology and psychoanalysis.

OBSTACLES TO INFLUENCE AND UNDERSTANDING

The presentation of the views of the above group of psychologists serves to illustrate well our contention that there was no uniformity in psychology's reaction to Freudian theory. The related uneven development of psychoanalysis within psychology is due to certain characteristics of the professional sources of influence which came to serve as obstacles. It now becomes our task to try to examine some of these in detail. We see them as falling into three main categories: general causes of conflict and incompatibility, the nature of the primary sources, and the nature of the secondary sources.

General Causes of Conflict

In reporting the results of his studies, the investigator usually tries to relate his own findings to past and contemporary work in the field. By showing the continuity between the old and the new, he cushions the sharp impact of new ideas and facilitates the reader's understanding. For the the most part, Freud was not in a position to provide such continuity and cushioning.[28] His work has virtually no precedent in the history of psychology: he was both an

---

[28] In *The Interpretation of Dreams* Freud did provide an introductory survey of the literature of dreams and referred to this later in the work. But not even this review served the purpose of facilitating communication, for dream literature was itself in a no-man's land with which no audience was familiar. (In this connection note Brill's decision to leave out all but a small part of the literature section in the *Basic Writings* edition [1900c].) Quite late in his career, however, Freud used another method of relating his views to those of others outside psychoanalysis—criticism of them. The theory in *Group Psychology and the Analysis of the Ego* (1921) was presented in the context of extensive arguments with Le Bon and McDougall.

TWENTIETH CENTURY DEVELOPMENTS

innovator and an outsider. The communication of radically novel observations and theories may also be facilitated if the investigator's implied or explicit frame of reference is derived from a familiar philosophical tradition.[29] Here, too, Freud was at a disadvantage, since he offered no such frame of reference. Although he did study philosophy with Brentano and translated J. S. Mill (Gomperz, 1880) at Brentano's request, he seems to have studiously avoided reference[30] to philosophers and upon occasion even to have deliberately neglected their writings.

Since Freud opened up a new realm for psychological study without relating his work to what psychologists considered already established, the negative reactions of psychologists are understandable. Some thought the area and the method of exploration unfit to be dignified with the name psychology; others resented Freud's disregard of psychology. It took a James not to feel this resentment. But James died before his attitude could become clearly formulated and widely expressed. J. R. Angell accepted the importance of some Freudian ideas, but also expressed his impatience at what he felt was Freud's ignoring of psychology.[31] Even a man of the stature

---

[29] See L. L. Whyte (1960, especially p. 169), *The Unconscious before Freud*, for Freud's neglect of the historical background of the unconscious. However, Whyte does not indicate the many ways in which Freud's concept of the unconscious was different from those of his precursors. See also Gill (1963) on the history of the topographic theory.

[30] Of the few exceptions to this, perhaps his reference to Kant (Freud, 1915b, p. 171) is the most important, though his indirect reference to the Anglo-Saxon empiricists is also revelant (1923, p. 23). In his *On the History of the Psycho-Analytic Movement* (1914a, pp. 15-16) Freud acknowledged that Schopenhauer had the same concept of repression as he had, though he said he did not realize it until Rank brought it to his attention. A systematic study of Freud's relationship to schools of philosophy and his reference to philosophers and philosophies does not yet exist. Some beginnings have been made, however, by Wisdom (1943), Kaplan (1957), and some of the contributors to Hook (1960). On the relationship of psychoanalysis to Kant's philosophy, see Rapaport (1947). Although it might be argued that other theories, such as those of Herbart and Lipps, are only distantly related to Freud's theory of the unconscious, he did occasionally refer to some of them, e.g., to Lipps (Freud, 1900a, p. 614; 1905a, p. 155). Bakan (1958) has suggested the Jewish mystical tradition as the background for some of Freud's theories. Although Bakan develops his argument ingeniously, as Kaufman (1959, p. 190) says, "... the book quite fails to establish even a probability in its favor." Dr. Gershom Sholem (personal communication, July, 1960) of the Hebrew University, the leading scholar of Jewish mystical tradition, has also raised many doubts about this thesis.

[31] In his autobiography, Angell (1936, p. 37) said: "... it has unquestionably constituted one of the major movements in twentieth-century psychology and one whose impress upon subsequent theory and technique is bound to be of first-rate importance. My impatience was always stirred by the failure of the expounders

of Woodworth could not avoid feeling antagonistic.[32] Such resentment was intensified by Freud's own sharp criticism[33] directed at those who limited themselves to "the psychology of consciousness" (1900a, pp. 610-621; 1915b), and by the even more antagonizing tone in which Freud's early followers criticized psychology (see Wells, 1912).

Morton Prince (Taylor, 1928, pp. 100-101) spelled out the issues in some detail:

> ... 'one of the most astounding things in the Freudian philosophy is that it either totally disregards everything that has been written by capable students of psychology upon the emotions, or, when it recognizes these important innate dispositions, it does so in a most superficial and inadequate way and subordinates them all to the use of one instinct, the sexual.... One hardly knows whether to ascribe this attitude on the part of the psychoanalysts to an amazing ignorance of psychology or to that Freudian mechanism which represses from consciousness disagreeable and intolerable facts.... to dismiss without discussion well-known facts and plausible interpretation ... is not calculated to render Freudian interpretations acceptable to those who have a wider or different culture.... Considerable complaint is made (and with justice) by psychoanalysts that their critics have not made themselves acquainted with Freudian data and conceptions. Is not the boot on the other leg, or at least on both legs?'

Prince's statement can be accepted as a fair description of the situation as it existed and the obstacles to the influence we are tracing. Perhaps the only deficiency in the statement is Prince's failure to

---

of . . . [psychoanalysis] to acknowledge adequately the achievements of their predecessors in the psychiatric and psychological field upon whose foundations they were actually building."

[32] Woodworth expressed the point most poignantly: "As a psychologist, I probably do have a certain prejudice against the Freudians, since they have been very contemptuous of our modest efforts to throw some light on the intricate processes of mental activity and development, disregarding what we may have found that would bear on their problems, characterizing our efforts as barren and superficial, and even going so far as to accuse us—since we must often admit ourselves unable to explain a mental occurrence except in a summary way—of holding that such occurrences are events without a cause. In short, they treat us rather shabbily, and I am willing to admit a certain feeling of irritation against them" (Woodworth, 1917, p. 175).

[33] Freud's negative attitude toward academic psychology is clearly reflected in his exchange of letters with Magnes relating to psychoanalysis and psychology at the Hebrew University. In this, Magnes, the President of the University, indicated the university's preference for first establishing a professorship in general psychology, in this case for Kurt Lewin (Rosenbaum, 1954).

note that the "wider or different culture" he claimed for psychologists was also claimed by the other side.

It is perhaps not unfair to ask for a tolerant understanding of Freud's disregard for academic psychology amidst his labors to master his material and build his theoretical edifice. But can one ask for the same tolerant understanding for his followers, even if it is admitted that zealotry for a newly discovered "truth" is only human? It is equally human to be repelled by zealotry. Psychoanalysts applied the technical term "repression-resistance" rather indiscriminately to all who did not agree; as we shall see, an equivalent of this in the form of an accusation of overpreoccupation with sex was soon adopted by the other side. We might point out that the resistance argument could also have been used, although it was not, with equal justification for those of Freud's followers who produced secondary sources which obscured the essence of his theory.

While Freud's use of "resistance" as an explanation of the non-acceptance of his views was a keen, if no more than an offhand, perception of the commonality between clinical resistance and ordinary conservatism in the face of innovation, there is much reason to consider the formulation an oversimplification. It certainly aroused negative reactions, often to the extent of ire, especially when Freud's disciples used it as a weapon in debates. While the irritation was in part defensive, it was also in part justified by the loose, *ad hominem* nature of the arguments of the supporters of psychoanalysis. The same arguments were raised not only against those who were flippant about psychoanalysis, but even against psychologists who were objectively interested enough to ask the most searching questions.

Freud's followers too frequently disregarded, or at least obscured, what clinical psychoanalysis (and particularly ego psychology) has come to heed along with the mechanism and motives of resistance. These are the *occasions* for and *means* of resistance, the circumstances and conditions which are conducive to the production of the resistance reaction. To elucidate the role of unconscious motives in parapraxes, Freud (1901, p. 21) once used the following example: "Let us suppose that I have been imprudent enough to go for a walk at night in a deserted quarter of the city, and have been attacked and robbed of my watch and purse. I report the matter at the nearest police station in the following words: 'I was in such and such a street, and there *loneliness* and *darkness* took away my watch and purse.' " Freud commented that a man who blames alcohol, tiredness, etc., for his parapraxis acts like this complainer: his slip is no more caused by the tiredness than the loss of the wallet was caused by darkness. These are merely occasions and means used by the motive and the robbers. Present-day psychoanalysis, however, is interested not only in the drive motivation which causes the slip but also in the state of the ego which explains the loss of control over that motivation. The occasions and means which facilitated psychology's "resistance" to Freud's influence are analogous to the state of the ego. The overtime use of the resistance explanation prohibited attention, as it so frequently does in therapy, being directed to its occasions and means as well as to what was valid in its rationalizations. It is quite probable that such factors as the differences in interpretation of the Helmholtz program between psychology and psychoanalysis, the differences in subject matter and methods, psychoanalysis' own primary sources and formulations, the inadequacies of the secondary sources, are all parts of the actual material out of which the resistance was built, that provided the occasion for resistance—or better, that the resistance used. As resistance is wont to do, it resulted in only a very attenuated form of Freud's theory becoming influential.

That most of Freud's followers were medical men, schooled in a tradition different from that of academic psychologists, augmented misunderstanding and antagonism. Instead of making available the psychopathological material from which their concepts developed, psychoanalysts strongly tended to deny psychologists access to this material. Freud's followers were partly defensive and partly disdainful toward "scholarship," and certainly unfamiliar with its canons and prejudices. An abyss also existed between the academician whose work on a problem and championship of a theory were independent of his livelihood, and the private medical practitioner whose advocacy of a theory could always be explained as mere propaganda for and defense of a lucrative practice. In the United States, there were still other conditions involved. These included the complex social and cultural issues unique to this country: the doubtful belongingness of "the professions" among the intellectuals; the attitudes of intellectuals toward the sciences; the relationship of the professions in general, and of the medical profession in particular, to the public and to the intellectuals.

A first glimpse of these issues may be gained from a comment James (1920b, p. 328) made about Freud in September, 1909: "A newspaper report of the [Worcester] congress said that Freud had condemned the American religious therapy (which has such extensive results) as very 'dangerous' because so 'unscientific.' Bah!" James, the author of *The Varieties of Religious Experience* (1902), must have felt that Freud, the advocate of the study of the irrational in man, was contradicting himself when he reacted so negatively to "religious therapy." Likewise he must have found Freud's emphasis and reliance on reason, rather than faith, strange in this instance.[34] James, like many American intellectuals, was far more pragmatic than his European counterparts about such problems as the arts of healing. The European intellectual had a rationalist's reverence for science engendered by the Enlightenment; his American colleague was by and large a far less dogmatic rationalist. The American, by his Anglo-Saxon tradition, had always been more inclined to orient himself to reality than to trust blindly in the powers of reason. He had seen how much the technician could achieve that science could not yet achieve or sometimes even understand. Moreover, in the United States, the professions, for instance the medical profession, had certainly not been regarded as the representatives of intellect and of science, as they so frequently were in Europe at that time.

Additionally, when the psychoanalytic institutes and societies became clearly professional associations,[35] psychoanalysts were to discover that on the American scene a professional association cannot remain a scientific group in the eyes of the public: it will be treated as, and tend to become, an interest organization.[36] Some-

---

[34] It is indeed strange, in some respects, considering Freud's attitude toward psychical research and the occult (see Jones, 1957, pp. 375-407). One sees here how much more consistent in his open-mindedness James was.

[35] See Lewin and Ross (1961), who discuss institutes as graduate schools. In our opinion, however, they fail to make their case in this respect.

[36] Freud's preface to a 1930 special issue of *The Medical Review of Reviews* on psychopathology may overstate the issues, but does point them up:

"Dr. Feigenbaum has asked me to write a few words for the [number of the] Review of which he is in charge, and I take the opportunity of wishing the best success to his undertaking.

"I often hear that psycho-analysis is very popular in the United States and that it does not come up against the same stubborn resistance there as it does

what later, further difficulties were caused by the extra-academic and exclusively medical character of the psychoanalytic training provided by American psychoanalytic institutes (see Shakow, 1962). When clinical psychology followed its own path toward professionalization, it did not significantly bridge the gap between psychology and psychoanalysis; rather, it tended to add another gap—one between clinical and academic psychology.

We might mention at this point a barrier to Freud's influence that existed within one segment of early clinical psychology. J. E. Wallace Wallin and Lightner Witmer are two who apparently took little cognizance of Freud's theories, even though, as clinicians, they were directly in the path of Freudian developments and were less hampered by the problem of methodology than were more academic psychologists.

Wallin's position is somewhat more difficult to define than that of Witmer. Because of his concentration on educational disabilities and his consequent association with educational rather than mental

---

in Europe. My satisfaction over this is, however, clouded by several circumstances. It seems to me that the popularity of the name of psycho-analysis in America signifies neither a friendly attitude to the thing itself nor any specially wide or deep knowledge of it. As evidence of the former fact I may point out that, although financial support is to be had easily and in plenty for every kind of scientific and pseudo-scientific enterprise, we have never succeeded in obtaining a backing for our psycho-analytic institutions. Nor is it hard to find evidence for my second assertion. Although America possesses several excellent analysts and, in Dr. A. A. Brill, at least one authority, the contributions to our science from that vast country are exiguous and provide little that is new. Psychiatrists and neurologists make frequent use of psycho-analysis as a therapeutic method, but as a rule they show little interest in its scientific problems and its cultural significance. Quite particularly often we find in American physicians and writers a very insufficient familiarity with psycho-analysis, so that they know only its terms and a few catch-words—though this does not shake them in the certainty of their judgement. And these same men lump psycho-analysis with other systems of thought, which may have developed out of it but are incompatible with it to-day. Or they make a hotch-potch out of psycho-analysis and other elements and quote this procedure as evidence of their *broad-mindedness,* whereas it only proves their *lack of judgement.* [The words in italics are in English in the original.]

"Many of these evils which I have mentioned with regret no doubt arise from the fact that there is a general tendency in America to shorten study and preparation and to proceed as fast as possible to practical application. There is a preference, too, for studying a subject like psycho-analysis not from the original sources but from second-hand and often inferior accounts. Thoroughness is bound to suffer from this.

"It is to be hoped that works of the kind that Dr. Feigenbaum intends to publish in his Review will be a powerful encouragement to the interest in psycho-analysis in America" (Freud, 1930b).

health institutions, occasions for expressing himself on psychoanalysis were perhaps limited. The most extensive expression of his opinion of Freud is in his textbook, *Clinical and Abnormal Psychology* (Wallin, 1927), and that appears to be generally negative. From a cursory survey of his articles, books, and autobiography, *The Odyssey of a Psychologist* (1955), it appears that he was never greatly concerned with Freud. This attitude may have stemmed from his predilection for the educational rather than the psychopathological function of clinics, and his contention that such facilities might best be established in association with departments of education (1914).

Witmer's situation is clearer, but still somewhat different. Despite the fact that he was a pioneer in a field which had natural affinities for Freudian thinking, Witmer was too much concerned with the cognitive-intellectual functions to be readily influenced by a psychology which emphasized the conative-affective. Like Wallin, he was predominantly interested in educational problems, primarily in those of the mentally defective. But even more important than the nature of Witmer's material (or perhaps inextricably woven into the material) was his approach, which was essentially segmental and static. He tended to identify himself with the decidedly less imaginative and less "dynamic" Wundtian-Kraepelinian approach, rather than with the functional point of view. A systematic skimming of the full run of *The Psychological Clinic* leaves one with the impression that Witmer was burdened by a conservatism which temperamentally set him in opposition to what he considered the "unscientific" nature of the new, radical, dynamic psychology.[37]

---

[37] This may seem a peculiar statement to make about a person who is considered a pioneer. But careful examination of Witmer's career suggests that his pioneering was not really in new thinking but rather in the application of old thinking to new material. This judgment is further supported by the violent attacks which he made on James as a psychologist and scientist. (For his attack on James and Münsterberg in the context of his own strong identification with Wundtian psychology, see L. Witmer, 1909.) Although he may have been correct in some aspects of his criticism, he revealed little grasp of the spirit and total significance of James. The vehemence of his attack makes one doubt its objectivity as well. Witmer, we must conclude, undoubtedly missed out in his estimate of the future. One would guess that he suffered from what James would have called a "certain blindness" which prevented him from choosing the more promising and meaningful leads. However that may be, Witmer failed to make the contributions which he was in such a strategic position to make, with the result that clinical psychology passed him by (see Shakow, 1948, p. 234).

Primary Sources of Psychoanalysis

We turn now to a major obstacle to Freud's influence more directly related to psychoanalysis itself: the written sources through which psychoanalysis became available.

Among various failings of the primary psychoanalytic sources, the most outstanding was that there was (and is) virtually no systematic account of the various aspects of Freud's theory. The fact that the theory underwent major changes during the course of Freud's life, and that terms which continued to represent his concepts had different meanings in various phases of the development of his theory, made the situation even more difficult. For example, the term "ego" meant something different before and after 1923;[38] the term "affect" had one meaning before 1900,[39] another meaning between 1900 and 1926,[40] and still a third after 1926. Freud's *On the History of the Psycho-Analytic Movement* (1914a), *Introductory Lectures on Psycho-Analysis* (1916-1917), and *An Autobiographical Study* (1925b), together with the meager discussion in Jones' (1953, 1955, 1957) biography, do provide a framework and some of the raw material for tracing the history of Freud's clinical theories. Fenichel did, of course, give a systematic presentation of the clinical theories. But we have only the beginnings of a history of Freud's concepts,[41] and no really systematic treatment of his general psychoanalytic theory,[42] or of his general psychological

---

[38] The publication date of *The Ego and the Id* in which the ego concept was first clearly coined. See Hartmann (1950a) and Rapaport (1958a).

[39] The publication date of *The Interpretation of Dreams*, the real beginning of Freud's psychoanalytic theory.

[40] The publication date of *Inhibitions, Symptoms and Anxiety*, the first detailed application of ego psychology.

[41] For instance, Bibring (1936) on the concept of instinct; Hartmann (1948) on instinctual drives; Schur (1953, 1958) on anxiety; Jacobson (1953) and Rapaport (1942a, 1953b) on affects; Lewy and Rapaport (1944) on memory; Rapaport (1950a, 1951) on thinking; Hartmann (1956b) on the ego concept; Rapaport (1959) on the general theory; and Kris (Freud, 1887-1902, pp. 1-47) on the origins of psychoanalytic theory.

[42] Nunberg (1955) and Waelder (1960) have made important beginnings in this direction. Several elementary textbooks have attempted to fill this need, but by their very nature they fall far short of it. Brenner's (1955) *An Elementary Textbook of Psychoanalysis* comes closest, but is inadequate because of its simplification and limited scope. C. S. Hall's (1954) *A Primer of Freudian Psychology* has pretensions to being systematic, but is not. Though certainly well-intentioned, the *Primer* illustrates the point we have been making about the broad gap between psychoanalysis and psychology.

theory, which he called metapsychology.[43]

Thus it was difficult for the psychologist to be sure what psychoanalysis was. This confusion among psychologists acted as a major obstacle to the effective spread of Freud's theory in psychology. One can only speculate to what extent the confusion was also responsible for the ambivalence in psychologists' attitudes toward psychoanalysis. It is certain, however, that the situation increases the difficulties of our assessment, for we are trying to trace the influence of something which itself cannot be defined in definite terms.

The difficulties created by unsystematic presentation were aggravated by another characteristic of the primary sources: Freud's writing is characterized by subtlety and power of language rather than precision and organization of propositions. While his case histories and clinical discussions are unrivaled to this day, his theoretical formulations still leave very much for the reader to unravel. This became an insurmountable obstacle to the reader who was not a master of the German language, and the evidence indicates that few were. In addition, Freud's writings presented so formidable a task for the translator that even such outstanding students of his work as Riviere, Strachey, and Jones, or such an excellent translator as Mosbacher, often failed to convey crucial nuances of Freud's meaning in their translations (see Erikson, 1955). The Brill translations, which for a long time were the only ones available, failed in much more than nuances.[44]

Secondary Sources

In view of the inadequacies of the direct presentations of the theory, the secondary sources require careful analysis, especially

[43] For attempts in this direction, see Hartmann (1939, 1950a, 1950b, 1952), Hartmann, Kris, and Loewenstein (1946, 1949, 1953), Rapaport (1957b, 1957-1959, 1959), Rapaport and Gill (1959), and Colby's (1955) quite original contribution centering on what he thinks metapsychology *should be* rather than what it *is*. See also Gill (1963).

[44] F. L. Wells, in reviewing Brill's translation of *The Interpretation of Dreams* (1900b), underscored this point, although tempering it by his urbanity: "The literary excellence of the original is known to many of us, and it is unfortunate that the translator should not combine his accurate knowledge of the material with the ability to preserve better the former quality. One must take the charitable view that what is very well worth doing, may be worth doing not so very well; there are some lapses, however, that careful editorship should have guarded against" (Wells, 1913c, p. 551). However, B. D. Lewin's (1962, pp. 40-41) report of Brill's comments about his translations should be kept in mind. The early translators *did* have particular difficulties which the later ones did not. For the third English edition, an improved translation was provided (Freud, 1900c).

because most psychologists seem to have preferred these sources. Even when a good primary source was available, psychologists made little use of it.[45] For example, relatively little reference is made to Freud's 1909 Clark University lectures (Freud, 1910), the earliest *primary* source and summary of the theory available in English.[46]

Psychologists' preference for secondary sources was in part a result of their traditional adherence to the laboratory method; the psychoanalytic method made little sense to them.[47] As a result, Freud's method was of little interest to psychologists. Consequently they would not discipline themselves to study the extensive and often circuitous derivation and documentation of his theories. One's efforts to discipline oneself to follow and assimilate the abstractions which are part of any theory are usually sustained by interest in the method. Without an interest in the method, one may resort to "skimming" the results, or relying on summaries and popularizations. Instead of the highways and byways of search, which are so necessary for an appreciation of a theory, one has only its terminals. It seems probable that this happened to the majority of psychologists in their relationship to Freud's writings. As we shall see, the nature of these "terminals," particularly the early secondary sources, both psychoanalytic and nonpsychoanalytic, provided another area of difficulty for psychoanalysis.

The earliest group of popular secondary sources in English are Hitschmann (1911), Brill (1912), Hart (1912), Jones (1913a),

---

[45] It is of interest that a lay writer such as Brophy (1962, pp. 140-141) also recommends going back to the primary sources.

[46] One person, however, who actually "read and reread" this material was Terman (see pp. 70-71).

[47] To this day the principles of the psychoanalytic situation as employed in psychoanalytic therapy have not been systematically stated, though several attempts to disentangle them have been made, e.g., Hermann (1934), Gill and Brenman (1947), Brenman and Gill (1948), Benjamin (1950), Rapaport (1959; 1944, especially lectures 3, 4, and 5). At the present state of psychoanalysis we can make the following comments. The salient characteristic of the method is that it cannot elicit the phenomena it studies, but must await their appearance. By the same token it cannot manipulate variables to test its hypotheses. The user of this method can, however, amass data, organize them intuitively, and attribute validity to propositions consistent with an available set of such data, if the propositions are internally consistent with the other propositions of the theory. This procedure is in its essence similar to that of other sciences. The difference lies in the fact that whereas in other sciences the data gathering and proposition testing follow well-established rules, in psychoanalysis they are dependent on the individual investigator's intuition, insight, and ability to command a wide range of observations and theoretical relations.

and Pfister (1913). Of these, Hart's is the most frequently quoted—understandably, for within the compass of its 176 small pages, it gives the most simple and lucid account. Hart is informative without any pretense at precision, giving some idea of Freud's observations and terms, but none of the nature of his concepts or of his theory. We might point out that in some respects the material is derived more from Jung than from Freud. (Hart and Pfister were in part responsible for the role that the term "complex"—usually associated with Jung, and having no conceptual status in Freud's theory[48]—came to play in the psychological literature. However, the major reason for the term's currency appears to have been the importance of the "association experiments" in experimental psychology [see Burnham, 1958, pp. 199-200, 230-231].) Jones' volume, parts of which come closest of the early sources to being systematic, is but a collection of independent essays. Hitschmann's volume is hurried, unsystematic, and strangely lacking in critical reflection, resembling a "believer's" *ex cathedra* presentation.

Brill's volume, evaluated by Wells (1913b) in his review as being "without the violence of Ernest Jones, or the superciliousness of Hitschmann," consists of loosely connected chapters, and is mainly a collection of illustrations. Statements of clinical relationships are presented instead of theoretical analysis or explanation. All in all, it is what one would expect from a man who planted his feet solidly on the clinical ground of psychoanalysis, but who lacked interest in its general theory. In this connection, Brill's translation of *The Interpretation of Dreams* (Freud, 1900b) is of interest.

Pfister's (1913) volume is more scholarly, and the only one which attempted to establish a continuity between psychology and psychoanalysis, particularly in the chapter on the unconscious. Unfortunately it is overambitious, attempting to bridge not only this gap but the one between Jung and Freud as well. Moreover, it becomes labyrinthine in its massing of clinical detail and literary parallels. Thus, Freud's theory does not emerge distinctly even here. It can be uncovered only by a rather determined search.

In the context of a combined review of Freud's *Introductory Lectures on Psycho-Analysis* and Tansley's *The New Psychology*,

---

[48] Freud used the term "complex" in his *Five Lectures* (Freud, 1910) a number of times, but as a term introduced by the Zurich school (p. 31). See also Freud (1906, p. 104; 1912a, p. 103 ff.).

Humphrey (1922b, p. 224) criticized the publications popularizing psychoanalysis: "In days to come . . . Professor Freud will perhaps come across some of these early pictures taken of him by admiring friends, and wonder whether he ever really looked like that. Certain it is, that in much of the Freudian literature it is difficult to recognize Freud." Though Humphrey's criticism was primarily directed at the popularizations, the line between them and some of the secondary sources, for instance Hitschmann (1911), is sometimes very thin.

Even more enlightening on the nature of the secondary sources are the books by Holt, the psychologist, and Tansley, the botanist. Holt's (1915) *Freudian Wish and Its Place in Ethics* summarizes the arguments of *The Interpretation of Dreams, Jokes and Their Relation to the Unconscious,* and *The Psychopathology of Everyday Life.* His account is as acute and accurate as can be expected within the limited space of forty-six pages, and considering his aim of reducing the whole theory to the "wish" and the "censor." This focus probably stemmed in part from Holt's interest in the ethical implications of Freud's theory. It can also be attributed to his tendency to deal only with those aspects of psychoanalytic theory which had special relevance for his own "motor theory." Nevertheless, Holt's volume became one of the most important secondary sources.

Tansley's (1920) volume was considered to be one of the best presentations of the "new psychology" in the 1920's. The work cannot be thought of as a systematic presentation of Freud's ideas, however, for it was eclectic in intent. Tansley refers frequently to Holt, McDougall, Jung, and Trotter in this volume. While his greatest number of references is to Freud, one cannot be sure that some of these references are not from secondary sources.

In the more recent period, the frequently used secondary sources have been Healy, Bronner, and Bowers, Hendrick, and Fenichel.[49] *The Structure and Meaning of Psychoanalysis,* by Healy, Bronner, and Bowers (1930), is clearly a heroic effort at a clear presentation of the crucial concepts of psychoanalysis. Their attempt to give

---

[49] There were two relatively short presentations of psychoanalytic theory in the early 1930's which reached psychologists in volumes which had wide circulation. One was Flugel's (1930) contribution to *Psychologies of 1930,* and the other Anna Freud's (1931) chapter in Murchison's *Handbook of Child Psychology.*

definitions of these concepts and to state what Freud and other analysts had to say about each of them is impressive. Yet for a number of reasons they failed to present Freud's theory adequately. Part of the difficulty lies in the very attempt to give definitions, for Freud did not usually give clear-cut and consistent definitions. The authors, apparently reluctant to derive definitions from Freud's various statements about particular topics, simply let one or several of his statements stand for definitions. Even when the statements chosen are the crucial ones, they are usually not complete. The reader who wants more than easily read statements is left dissatisfied. In addition, the arbitrary isolation of concepts, which resulted from the attempt to be "systematic," and the lack of specific page references to the sources from which the quotations were taken, do not invite the reader to study the context of the quotations so that he may form his own definitions. In summary, the book provides the reader with a glossary of isolated ingredients of psychoanalysis without a meaningful way to bring them together. To a large extent, the book presents what Freud "says," without giving the grounds for the statements. Nevertheless, some psychologists quoted Freud from this book and proceeded to "verify" or "refute" the isolated assertions they found in it.

Regardless of the outcome of their effort, Healy, Bronner, and Bowers did try to meet the serious need for a systematic account of Freud's theory. Although they did not achieve their goal, they deserve much credit for being the only ones who attempted this necessary and overwhelming task. We might point out here that Healy himself made outstanding contributions in the history of psychiatry. He established the first child guidance clinic oriented toward psychoanalytic dynamics,[50] initiating a trend that has had a revolutionary effect on developments in child guidance (Shakow, 1948). His writings include *The Individual Delinquent* (1915), one of the earliest books to take a psychoanalytically oriented view of juvenile offenders, and *Roots of Crime,* written with Alexander twenty years later (Alexander and Healy, 1935), which took a similar view of adult criminals.

Perhaps Jastrow's rather intemperate and superficial *The House that Freud Built* (1932) should also be mentioned here since some

[50] See Helen Witmer (1940), and J. D. Hunter (1925).

psychologists gained their first introduction to Freud from it.[51] It is based on Healy, Bronner, and Bowers, and contains no direct references to any of Freud's writings.[52]

It has not been until comparatively recently that anything approaching adequacy has appeared. Hendrick's (1934, 1939, 1958) successively expanded three editions, and Fenichel's (1934, 1945)[53] volumes are careful and systematic presentations centered for the most part on clinical relationships. Fenichel's 1945 volume treats the subject matter of his 1934 *Outline*—the characteristic features of the individual neuroses—"in a more systematized and up-to-date form," and also takes up questions of "general" theory. While we might say that each tries to accomplish too much—Fenichel in his broad, Hendrick in his narrower, compass—their presentations are more satisfactory, precise, and systematic than any of the other sources mentioned thus far, and Fenichel's coverage is really encyclopedic. But the very superiority of these volumes points up a characteristic of Freud's theory which made these sources of little

[51] A comment by Hull (1952, p. 147) on Jastrow may be relevant here: "Professor Jastrow had a remarkable linguistic fluency. He would sometimes lecture for five minutes at a time in perfectly good sentences, yet hardly say a thing. Naturally it was difficult to quiz on the basis of such lectures. When the students would complain about their inability to understand the lectures I used to reply with the true formula: 'Professor Jastrow has genius of a kind but it is not of the pedagogical variety.'"

[52] R. R. Willoughby commented in a review (1933a, p. 257): "The recent animadversions of Jastrow (*The House that Freud Built*) . . . [suggest that he] has not troubled to inform himself regarding the subject matter of his discourse though he has displayed his characteristic acumen in discussing what he inferred from other discussions to be this subject matter."

[53] We have already mentioned Nunberg's and Waelder's presentations (see footnote 42, p. 86).

We might also mention Munroe's (1955) *Schools of Psychoanalytic Thought* which provides a balanced, but brief and less intensive presentation of Freudian theory than either of the above volumes, largely because of the general level at which it is aimed and the range it is attempting to cover.

In a very recent volume, Fine (1962) "undertakes to examine the whole body of Freud's thought, to clarify what he said, and to review his ideas critically in the light of the best available existing knowledge" (p. vii). This is indeed a tall order and it is unnecessary to say that Fine falls far short of accomplishing it. In certain contexts, however, it may be useful to have his chronological ordering of Freud's views despite his superficiality.

Mention should be made here in passing of a series of books intended as texts in either abnormal psychology or personality theory which have relatively substantial sections devoted to psychoanalytic theory: Symonds (1931; but particularly, 1946), Brown (1940), Maslow and Mittelmann (1941, 1951), Murphy (1947), White (1948, 1956), Blum (1953), Shaffer and Shoben (1956), Hall and Lindzey (1957). They are examples of the important way in which psychoanalytic thinking has affected these areas.

use for purposes of theoretical examination. Since the clinical psychological theory of psychoanalysis and the metapsychological theory of psychoanalysis are radically different, volumes which provide an excellent general clinical orientation to psychoanalysis are not likely to serve the psychologist who seeks to grasp the metapsychological theory of psychoanalysis.[54]

A special claim of psychoanalysis also contributed to neglect of systematization. This claim was a proposition that seemed self-explanatory to psychoanalysts but not to other people: only a person who has submitted to the psychoanalytic procedure can fully understand psychoanalysis.[55] Here was the resistance argument in its most concrete form: the understanding of psychoanalysis is opposed by resistances, and only the analysis of these can free a person for a full understanding of the theory. To the academician, this smacked of the attitude of initiates of lodges, religious orders, and mystical sects. And in one respect the psychologists certainly had a point.

It is true that the requirement of a personal analysis has great validity for the understanding of psychoanalytic *therapy*. Anyone who wishes to use psychoanalysis effectively as a therapeutic tool must himself undergo an analysis in order to become familiar with, and if possible, get rid of, blind spots which would otherwise prevent him from understanding and helping the patient. When generalized, however, the argument is questionable and even dangerous. Psychoanalysis is not only a therapeutic procedure but also a method of investigation, a body of observations, and a theory. Granted that the investigative method and the therapeutic process

[54] We are making a distinction between the "special clinical psychological" (psychological) theory of psychoanalysis and the "general psychological" (metapsychological) theory of psychoanalysis. By the first, we mean those aspects of the theory which are highly dependent upon the primary data and the method by which they were derived—the psychoanalytic method. It includes such areas as free association, types of resistance, distorting devices, interpretation, transference, and the characteristic features of the individual neuroses.

Those aspects of psychoanalysis which are called the metapsychological theory of psychoanalysis, on the other hand, are not highly dependent on the psychoanalytic method, or on the primary data. They are more abstract and deal with the propositions which center on the various conceptual models which underlie psychoanalysis: the dynamic (e.g., affect-force and drive-force), the economic (e.g., cathexis, neutralization, binding), structural (e.g., id, ego, superego; "apparatuses," "modes"), genetic (e.g., libido development, psychosocial stages, autonomous ego), and adaptive (e.g., pleasure/pain, average expectable environment) (see Rapaport and Gill, 1959).

[55] Note what the sympathetic F. L. Wells had to say on this score (see p. 155).

cannot be separated, that they have to be learned in the one way they can be learned. Nobody would expect to be a microbiologist without learning to work with a microscope. Nevertheless, the data and the theory should be so presented that they are intellectually understandable even to the unanalyzed, and they must stand or fall on this basis. Unfortunately, the theory was not so stated, and few people, analyzed or nonanalyzed, could rectify this failing. It would appear that psychoanalysis was not only too new and too strange, but also had many internal inconsistencies which were difficult to reconcile (and which probably accounted for Freud's own frequent changes). It was also too complicated in its fourfold role as therapy, method of investigation, body of observations, and theory, for either friend or foe to be able to separate and define its various implications in the early stages of contact with psychoanalysis.

It becomes clear, then, from this survey of the status of the primary and secondary sources, that a clear-cut statement of definitions and relationships which could be used by the psychologist to test the theory directly and to develop further psychoanalytic propositions was not really available.[56] When these inadequacies are added to the general background of incompatibility between psychology and psychoanalysis, we can see that there were substantial obstacles to Freudian influence.

Despite these obstacles, some psychologists did establish contact with psychoanalysis. Heidbreder (1933, p. 411) well described academic psychology's response: "It is as if academic psychology, confronted with a theory which it could neither prove nor disprove, but which it could not ignore, matched intuition with intuition and risked a judgment. Its collective verdict has been something like 'two-fifths genius and three-fifths sheer fudge'. . ."[57] If the assertions of psychoanalysis have observational validity, why then were they not put into a form that allowed for quantifiable tests or for other tests of agreed-upon validity? The question is essentially, why could not psychology prove or disprove the theory?

The complex intertwining of the difficulties psychology encountered in attempting to examine psychoanalytic propositions is most

---

[56] See Hartmann and Kris' (1945) discussion of this issue, also Rapaport (1959).

[57] Apparently Heidbreder did not feel that psychology was ready to grant as much to Freud as did James Russell Lowell to Poe (*Fable for Critics*) in his characterization of Poe as "three fifths of him genius and two fifths sheer fudge"!

strikingly illustrated in the activities of the Hull Seminars at the Yale Institute of Human Relations, conducted over several years beginning in 1936 (Hull, 1936-1942). We shall discuss these seminars in detail in Chapter 5. Suffice it to say here that for most psychologists interest in and intuitive perception of Freudian theories were not accompanied by familiarity either with systematic data about them or with methods by which such data could be gathered. Many psychologists have not come around to such data and methods until late in their professional lives.

Summary

The American atmosphere of the first decades of the 1900's was a peculiarly favorable one for Freudian ideas. The muckrakers and early realists of the last decades of the nineteenth century had already laid the foundations for breaking down the "genteel" tradition of a primarily Puritan and Victorian culture. This trend was markedly accelerated by the literary realists, the social protesters, the feminists, and the Bohemians, all of whom were influential in the period surrounding the First World War. Freudian ideas were welcomed with open arms by these rebellious forces, and relationships developed among them in which the Freudian influence became paramount. In fact, Freudian ideas became so integral a part of the *Zeitgeist* that this *Zeitgeist* became an indirect but major channel for Freud's influence on professional psychology. The impact of the new ideology led to the development of a simplified and distorting popular and semipopular literature dealing with Freud. This in turn contributed to the public consciousness of psychoanalysis which led students and members of other disciplines to expect psychologists to deal with dynamic aspects of human behavior. By the nature of the ideas it dealt with, Freudism rearoused dormant "guilts" among psychologists for not having met a reasonable obligation—the greater understanding and control of the forces of human nature.

Concurrent with these "indirect" factors which played varying roles in Freud's influence, more directly professional influences were at work. But in spite of the combined pressures of public consciousness, impatient colleagues and students, and professional influences, psychoanalysis did not immediately become a part of American psychology. It had first to overcome many difficulties, some of which were actually created by the very vehicles that carried it.

There were, of course, many general professional factors which no doubt worked against psychology's receptiveness to psychoanalysis. Freud was a stranger and an "outsider," one whose unconventional methods were suspect, whose air of condescension to academic psychology was repugnant, and whose use of the doubtfully defensible "resistance" argument was particularly antagonizing. A further obstacle was probably the professional medical orientation of psychoanalysis, whose students were trained in independent and nonacademic settings, in contrast to the conventional academic setting of the education and work of the psychologist.

But such factors were in the end probably only accessory to the major obstacles. Most of the difficulties grew out of particular qualities of the material provided by psychoanalysis, material which is the usual means of transmitting new theories and ideas. The language barrier, confounded by the circuitous course of psychoanalytic development, made it difficult for the psychologist to be sure what psychoanalysis really was. The subtlety of Freud's writing made understanding of the original German difficult even for those who knew German fairly well, and it was a rare psychologist who could do better than this. Those who went to whatever translations were available were hindered by their general inadequacy. Further, psychologists seemed preponderantly to prefer secondary sources. But it was difficult to find a reliable secondary source which covered even a portion of psychoanalytic theory. Until fairly recently the secondary sources made no pretense of providing any systematic presentation of psychoanalysis. At the very best, they presented only parts of the theory, frequently emphasizing the clinical rather than the general theory; at the worst they were misleading.

To the general lack of familiarity with psychoanalysis was added the misinformation provided by the oversimplifications and distortions of the more popular sources.

The opinions of outstanding psychologists from James and Hall to Murphy provide a glimpse of the academic reaction to Freud. Whether the responses were made as a "man in the street" or as a psychologist, the result of dormant professional "guilt" or of the particular quality of the written sources, they ranged from the violently negative, through the indifferent, to the generally positive.

At all these levels, however, reactions were characterized by conflict and hesitancy.

Thus while Freud's influence was being inescapably forced upon psychology by various public and professional pressures in a period of great social and moral upheaval in the United States, particularly during the years surrounding the First World War, concrete and practical factors joined cultural and social trends to complicate and obstruct the course of this influence. Clashing philosophical and professional commitments, language and methodological barriers, and mutual defensiveness and misunderstanding, prevented any semblance of continuous integration of psychoanalysis into American psychology, leading instead to complex interactions that resulted in a fitful, though steadily increasing, growth.

5

THE UNCONSCIOUS AND MOTIVATION

Of the many major contributions of Freud to psychological theory we shall single out two of especial importance—*the unconscious* and *motivation*—and attempt to trace the course of their influence on psychology. These are areas central to the interests of psychologists and lend themselves more readily to specific examination than do other areas to which Freud contributed, such as dynamic psychology and the understanding of human nature. Actually, in different parts of this study we have already touched upon specific aspects of these latter areas.

We shall organize our discussion of these two topics largely by a consideration of particular persons important in the history of each concept. Although the discussion will center mainly on these concepts, we shall also occasionally consider the person in respect to the broader question of his relation to Freud.

The Unconscious

FREUD'S OWN CONCEPT

Before considering predecessors, contemporaries, and descendants, let us first be clear about Freud's own concept of the unconscious. The most detailed presentation of the history and nature of Freud's concept is to be found in the recent publication of Gill (1963, particularly pp. 9-10, 12, 21, 23-24, 64, 78-79, and Chapter 7), although it has been presented before in many places.[1] Gill has elucidated many aspects of Freud's theory hitherto not clearly

---

[1] For instance, Strachey gives a very much briefer, but still helpful, account in his Introduction to *The Ego and the Id* (Freud, 1923, pp. 3-11).

recognized. He has traced the history of the development of Freud's concept from the December 6, 1896 letter to Fliess (Freud, 1887-1902, pp. 173-181) through the writing of *An Outline of Psychoanalysis* (1940) in 1938.[2] Here we can merely sketch Gill's presentation of the unconscious, but we urge our readers to refer to the original monograph for the fuller scholarly account.

Freud's theory of the unconscious includes two different kinds of unconscious (not including the *pre*conscious): a nonrepressed unconscious and a repressed unconscious. Both function according to the primary process, the hallmark of Freud's concept of the unconscious. The *nonrepressed unconscious* is the matrix and beginning point of all mental activity, with two exceptions: (1) mental activity can be initiated by stimulation from the outside, and (2) mental processes can be considered to arise in the preconscious (ego). When nonrepressed unconscious material becomes preconscious, the only change it undergoes is inhibition of energy, that is, it then functions according to the secondary process; it does not undergo distortion of content.

The other unconscious is a *repressed unconscious,* which Freud, somewhat confusingly, often called the "dynamic unconscious." It too operates by the laws of the primary process. Except in pathological or certain other special conditions, material from this unconscious can gain access to consciousness only if it first undergoes distortion through defense (also called censorship, repression). One way this distortion occurs is by "transference" to preconscious material. There has been no inhibition of energy of the unconscious impulse and the preconscious material to which it has been transferred becomes subject to the laws of the primary process. As Freud put it, ". . . the preconscious thoughts which have reinforced themselves with an unconscious instinctual impulse are reduced to the unconscious condition" (Freud, 1940, p. 50). One of the reasons this point has not been clearer heretofore is terminological. When transference of the repressed unconscious contents to preconscious material has taken place, should the psychic contents be referred to as "preconscious" or "unconscious"? The issue comes down to whether "preconscious" and "unconscious" should be defined in terms of the relationship to consciousness, or in terms of the mode

[2] After the Fliess letter the history appears to run as follows: Freud (1900a, Chapter 7; 1912b, 1915b, 1915c, 1916-1917, 1920, 1923, 1932, 1940).

of functioning of the psychic contents and the nature of the energy with which they are invested.

In its passage through the psychic apparatus, then, nonrepressed unconscious material undergoes inhibition of energy but no distortion of content, while repressed unconscious material undergoes distortion of content but no inhibition of energy. Freud (1900a, p. 607) says:

> ... we must recognize that the psychical mechanism employed by neuroses is not created by the impact of a pathological disturbance upon the mind but is present already in the normal structure of the mental apparatus. The two psychical systems, the censorship upon the passage from one of them to the other, the inhibition and overlaying of one activity by the other, the relations of both of them to consciousness—or whatever more correct interpretations of the observed facts may take their place—all of these form part of the normal structure of our mental instrument . . .

PRECURSORS AND CONTEMPORARIES

There were, of course, conceptions of the unconscious—those of Leibnitz, Herbart, Carpenter, von Hartmann, Helmholtz, Hering,[3] O. W. Holmes,[4] and others before them—which antedated Freud's (see L. L. Whyte, 1960). This historical fact seems to have had several consequences for the way psychology related itself to Freud's concept. While it made the general conception of the unconscious familiar and prepared the ground for acceptance of Freud's *conception,* it obscured the unique character of Freud's *concept* and permitted its by-pass in favor of one or another of these earlier conceptions. It also permitted the claim that Freud's concept was derived from Herbart's or from von Hartmann's, and even occasionally the superficial assessment that what was good about Freud's concept was not new, and what was new was not good.

As pointed out in our introductory remarks, Freud does not seem to have been very directly affected by these early conceptions of the unconscious in the development of his own concept. He was probably somewhat familiar with them—for the general idea of the

---

[3] For Hering, see Freud (1915b, p. 205), and the personal communication from Kris in Rapaport (1959, p. 61, note).

[4] See Holmes (1871, pp. 48-50). This is also the Address which contains that exquisite deflator: *"A strong smell of turpentine prevails throughout"* (p. 47).

unconscious was a part of the European *Zeitgeist* by the 1880's.[5] Freud surely knew something about Helmholtz' "unconscious inference," and he may have learned about Leibnitz' and other philosophic conceptions of the unconscious from Brentano's course. He referred to Herbart (1900a, p. 76), and we know from Dorer (1932, pp. 148 ff., 160 ff.) that Freud became familiar with Herbart's ideas through Meynert and Griesinger (also see Sidis, 1914, p. 199 ff.). In a footnote added in 1914 to *The Interpretation of Dreams* Freud (1900a, pp. 528-529) commented that he learned about his theory's general kinship to von Hartmann's from Pohorilles' 1913 paper.[6] There is no evidence, as far as we know, that he was familiar with Carpenter's concept of unconscious ideas. Freud referred only to Carpenter's paper on "Dreaming" in the bibliography of *The Interpretation of Dreams* (1900a, p. 708). In any case, it does appear that Freud was not very deeply acquainted with earlier views of the unconscious and that any influence they had upon him very likely came, as we have indicated, through the *Zeitgeist*.

While they may prove fruitless, the tasks of tracking the affinities of Freud's concept to its precursors, and of showing which of them Freud was or was not familiar with, are, in the long run, unavoidable. They are not, however, tasks for our study. Although it is not likely that new light will be shed on Freud's concept by such studies,

[5] See Whyte (1960, p. 169). Boring (1961) points out the evidence in Whyte for the historical continuity of the idea of the unconscious and for the workings of the *Zeitgeist*. Also see Northridge's (1924) volume which deals mainly with theories contemporary to Freud, but has an introductory section on precursors. For a scholarly discussion of the cultural matrix in which Freud's ideas of the unconscious developed, see Rosenzweig (1956; see also 1963).

[6] However, we know (Jones, 1955, p. 64) that in 1910 Freud had read a paper by Hart (1910) which included a discussion of von Hartmann. It is unsafe to state flatly on any matter that Freud was not aware of it, because he himself and others have turned up instances of his "forgetting" of earlier "awarenesses," for example, the bisexuality notion of Fliess (Freud, 1901, pp. 143-144).

Freud (1900a, p. 134) had already referred to von Hartmann regarding dreams in *The Interpretation of Dreams*. It is likely that he had been hearing about von Hartmann since early adolescence. At that time von Hartmann's name and theories, as well as the general idea of the unconscious, were very popular and apparently the subject of table conversation in educated circles, very much as Freud and his theories were to be many decades later (see Whyte, 1960, pp. 163-170; Braun, 1909, pp. 18-19). Flugel (1951, p. 292) says that "Freud's work may perhaps even be looked upon as a scientification of von Hartmann's philosophy of the unconscious." It is in this sense that Jones' remark (1953, p. 379) about the "tiny atom of truth" should be taken.

the place of Freud's thinking in the history of thought will probably be better elucidated with this knowledge.

Whatever general influence these earlier conceptions had on Freud's idea of the unconscious, we know from Breuer and Freud (1893) that Charcot's *condition seconde* of hysteria was its direct predecessor.[7] In hysterics, the primary and secondary states were not conscious of each other. It is possible, of course, that Charcot's *condition seconde* was for Freud in relation to his precursors' views what the "precipitating event" in a clinical case is to the antecedent life experience. Nevertheless, we know that the Charcot *condition seconde* did not actually crystallize Freud's conception of the unconscious.[8] Rather, his concept was derived from observations in hypnotic and nonhypnotic cathartic therapy, from the analysis of dreams, and perhaps most important, from his self-analysis.[9] The material for a detailed historical tracing of this crystallization is to be found in Freud's letters to Fliess, especially those of 1896, 1897, and 1898 (Freud, 1887-1902).

An important role in the fate of the concept of the unconscious in psychology was played by Freud's contemporaries, Janet, Prince, and Sidis, with their conceptions of subconscious and coconscious.[10] Janet derived his conception of the subconscious from Charcot. His publications on it in the period 1886-1892 (particularly his *L'Automatisme Psychologique,* 1889) definitely antedate Freud's, though Breuer's observations—the ones which actually influenced Freud—in turn probably antedate Janet's.[11] Janet (1914) claimed

[7] Breuer, in his theoretical chapter, wrote: "She oscillated between her *'conditions primes'* and *'secondes',* between the conscious and the unconscious ideational complexes" (1895, p. 238). Freud himself also referred to this point, even as late as 1923 (pp. 30-31).

[8] See the obituary Freud (1893, particularly pp. 18-19, and 22) wrote on Charcot, also "The Unconscious" (1915b, pp. 170-171).

[9] Actually the concept of unconscious did not become clarified until Chapter 7 of *The Interpretation of Dreams;* before that, usage is infrequent and mostly adjectival rather than substantive.

[10] Prince is generally credited with the invention of the term "coconscious" (see Prince, 1939, p. 34). In any case, he was the one who used "coconscious" most consistently.

[11] Strachey's comments on these relationships, in his introduction to the 1955 translation of *Studies on Hysteria,* show some of the relevant facts: "At the International Medical Congress held in London in 1913, Pierre Janet had distinguished himself by making an absurdly ignorant and unfair attack on Freud and pyscho-

priority for the concept of subconscious, as well as for the concept of traumatic origin of neuroses. By that time Freud had long discarded the traumatic theory of the 1890's for which Janet claimed priority. As for his other claim, Janet's conception of the subconscious in reality has but a vague resemblance to Freud's unconscious. His 1889 terms, still similarly expressed even in 1914, were: "subconsciousness through psychological disintegration." Ordinarily, however, he used the term "dissociation." Nevertheless, even some psychoanalysts failed at the time to recognize the difference between Janet's and Freud's views.[12] Jung's (1907) introductory chapter in *The Psychology of Dementia Praecox* is a good illustration of this.

---

analysis. A reply was published by Ernest Jones in the *Journal of Abnormal Psychology, 9* (1915), 400; and a German translation of this appeared in the *Int. Z. Psychoanal., 4* (1916), 34. In the course of his diatribe Janet had said that whatever was of the slightest value in psycho-analysis was entirely derived from his own early writings, and in traversing this assertion Jones had remarked that, though it was true that the actual publication of Breuer and Freud's findings was later than that of Janet's (which were published in 1889), the work on which their first paper was based preceded Janet's by several years. 'The cooperation of the two authors', he went on, 'antedated their first communication by as much as ten years, and it is expressly stated in the *Studien* that one of the cases there reported was treated by the cathartic method more than fourteen years before the date of the publication.' At this point in the German translation (ibid., 42) there is a footnote signed 'Freud', which runs as follows: 'I am obliged to correct Dr. Jones on a point which is inessential so far as his argument is concerned but which is of importance to me. All that he says on the priority and independence of what was later named psycho-analytic work remains accurate, but it applies only to *Breuer's* achievements. My own collaboration began only in 1891-2. What I took over I derived not from Janet but from Breuer, as has often been publicly affirmed.' The date given here by Freud is a puzzling one. 1891 is two or three years too late for the beginning of the case of Frau Emmy and a year too early for that of Fräulein Elisabeth" (Breuer and Freud, 1893-1895, pp. xii-xiii, note).

Cranefield (1958) makes some relevant comments about the relationship between Breuer and Freud.

[12] A careful study of Silberer's (1912) paper on symbolism indicates that he made a distinction between the two views of symbolization—one that it stems from conflictual material and the other that it stems from "apperceptive insufficiency." The latter may be due to either intellectual or affective causes, almost always both, with one preponderating. Silberer shows that one aspect of Janet's, his predecessors', and his successors' views had observational validity. They also had some significance for the understanding of normal and pathological cognitive processes, but were not a *general* explanation of neuroses and psychoses. This did not become obvious, however, until after the development of psychoanalytic ego psychology (see Rapaport, 1957a). Janet himself does not seem to have seen it and Silberer's reward for an early glimpse of it was Freud's limited recognition (1900a, p. 524; 1916-1917, p. 237; 1932, pp. 37-38) and a sharp attack by Jones (1948, pp. 117-137). See also Rapaport (1951, pp. 283-284).

It is worth noting, however, that Woodworth[13] recognized that Janet's conception is descriptive, while Freud's concept is causal-explanatory, that Janet's subconscious is within the framework of the organic conception of degeneration, inferiority, and weakness of synthesis, while Freud's is within the framework of a thoroughgoing psychological determinism.[14]

We now come to Prince and Sidis, whose respective conceptions of the subconscious seem to have been derived from Charcot and Janet, or at least from observations of the same dramatic type of material: multiple personalities, fugues, automatic writing, and hypnosis. But even though Prince's indebtedness to Janet is obvious, the precise relation of the conceptions of these two Americans to those of the two Frenchmen could be made clear only by detailed analysis. It seems likely, though this requires verification, that in the long run the very dramatic character of the empirical material used by all of them will prove to have been one of the major factors which prevented them from going beyond a descriptive level and arriving at a conception of unconscious motivation. It is only since the development of psychoanalytic ego psychology that it has been possible to attempt an explanation of the dramatic phenomena they dealt with (see Gill and Brenman, 1959; Rapaport, 1942a).

Prince (1891) arrived at his conception of the subconscious rather late, as is clear from its absence in his paper on "Association

---

[13] "His predecessors, and even his contemporary, Janet, had spoken of the neurosis as an expression of the subject's weakness. Janet spoke of 'low mental tension' as the fundamental weakness of the neurotic, a weakness which was experienced by the subject as a 'feeling of inadequacy,' and out of which the particular phobia or obsession grew as a sort of interpretation by the subject of his own weakness. But Freud interpreted the neuroses as due to desires and their repression" (Woodworth, 1931, p. 143). It should perhaps be indicated that Hart (1910) in "The Conception of the Subconscious" had pointed out this difference a long time before, even before his *Psychology of Insanity* (1912) appeared. This article led Freud to write to Jones: "Have you read the article of Bernard Hart on the Unconscious [sic]? The first clever word upon the matter" (Jones, 1955, p. 64). In this article Hart also gave an important discussion of the problem of psychological as opposed to physiological conceptualizing with which Freud apparently agreed.

[14] McDougall, though he continued to regard Janet's concept of dissociation as a valid one, saw this distinction clearly, at least toward the end of his career. He wrote (1938, p. 149): "Dissociation then is failure or imperfection of the associative mechanism or structure. Conflict and repression are affairs of the dynamic or moral relations between units." Hart (1926) and Prince in 1913, according to McDougall (1938), were also concerned with the distinction.

Neuroses."[15] His observations and conception lacked a concept of unconscious motivation, just as Breuer and Freud's did. Breuer and Freud together did not arrive at one. Freud, himself, finally did around 1897. Prince seems never to have arrived at one. He explained his observations by using the associationists' concept of "coupling." In contrast, in Freud's concept the associative link is established by an unconscious instinctual drive: the energy of the instinctual drive is displaced along the associative pathway. That Janet too lacked such a dynamic and economic[16] conception of association is clear from his discussion of Jung's association experiments in the 1914 paper we referred to above.

In sum, Freud may or may not have known Janet's work (a point of some historical interest which could probably be decided by investigation), but certainly did not know Prince's before his own crucial discoveries. If we try to make a balance sheet of Janet and Prince in relation to Freud, we find that they did have priority over Freud in certain respects. But they cannot be said to have influenced Freud in a specific way, because the essential part of his discoveries lies in precisely the place where he went beyond them.[17] It might be said that by the time their priority was well established, the substance of their claims had vanished.

Sidis based his primarily cognitive conception of the subcon-

---

[15] It seems that in this paper he anticipated the Freudian discovery of somatic compliance. He described somatic symptoms which are triggered into action by a percept or idea which had been incidentally associated with the somatic state. Prince (1891, p. 259) wrote: "Inasmuch as all nervous processes are fundamentally alike in their nature, it is to be presumed that if brain processes, with their correlated mental states, can be welded together into an automatic mechanism, it is similarly true that the pure physical activities of the spinal cord, although not correlated with subjective states, may also be welded together by association in the same manner; and that this is true whether these neural activities are simply physiological and normal or pathological in their nature. This is the thesis which I hope to establish, and I believe that with this [association] law so extended, we shall find that many so-called hysterical affections, many neuroses and psychoses, which otherwise are unintelligible, may be readily explained. They may be termed *association neuroses and psychoses.*" Prince (1885) first mentioned this conception of automatic mechanism as created by associations in *The Nature of Mind and Human Automatism*. See also Prince's *The Unconscious* (1914 and subsequent editions).

[16] For a definition of these terms, see Rapaport and Gill (1959).

[17] With regard to Prince, Freud emphasized this in his 1911 emendation to *The Interpretation of Dreams* (1900a, pp. 520-521). As for Janet, we have already seen Freud's 1916 comment (see footnote 11, pp. 102-103). See Freud (1911, p. 218) for an interesting sidelight on his attitude toward Janet.

scious on his hypnotic experiments. In many respects his conception was similar to Janet's, although he held that the subconscious was important for the normal as well as the abnormal person. Sidis developed his ideas about the subconscious in *The Psychology of Suggestion* (1898), and in *Multiple Personality* (Sidis and Goodhart, 1904). His general view is expressed in this quotation from *The Foundations of Normal and Abnormal Psychology* (1914, p. 175).

> The subconscious may be briefly defined as mental processes of which the individual is not directly conscious. Such knowledge is all the more requisite as *psychopathic disturbances with which psychopathology proper deals are essentially affections of subconscious life activity.* The general drift of my *Psychology of Suggestion* is the description of the subconscious as a diffused consciousness below the margin of personal consciousness. I sometimes use the term "subconscious self." I designate by "self" not personal consciousness, but mere consciousness. In *Multiple Personality,* in which I develop the theory of thresholds in regard to the phenomena of normal and abnormal mental life, I define the subconscious as consciousness below the threshold of attentive personal consciousness. I find that my clinical and psychological investigations more and more confirm me in the view of the subconscious advanced by me in *The Psychology of Suggestion.*

There is clear evidence that Sidis was one of the first in the United States to refer to Freud's studies (see Burnham, 1958, pp. 53, 131), although he was silent about Freud later in his career. Sidis was under the impression that he alone had a theory which was the key to all psychopathology; nevertheless, he seems to have profited from Freud's studies. Freud's influence on Sidis is perhaps best described in "The Present Position in Clinical Psychology" by McDougall (1918, p. 7): "Dr. Boris Sidis has, by applying the Freudian method, sought to show that *fear* is the source of all the psychoneuroses, all those troubles of thought and conduct which Freud attributes to the sex-impulse, and Adler to the self-assertive tendency and its opposite." We cannot refrain from a brief discussion of fear despite its only indirect relation to the unconscious.

The role of anxiety in neuroses was not underestimated by Freud himself, as his two papers (1895a, 1895b) on anxiety neurosis clearly show, although his earlier, so-called toxic, theory of anxiety for a long time prevented him from making a systematic evaluation of this role. As early as 1900 he wrote thus about a phobic patient: "If we remove this symptom by compelling him to carry out the act of which he believes himself incapable, the consequence will be an attack of anxiety; and indeed the occurrence of an anxiety-attack in the street is often the precipitating cause of the onset of an agoraphobia. We see, therefore, that the symptom has been constructed in order to avoid an outbreak of anxiety; the phobia is erected like a frontier fortification against the anxiety" (1900a, p. 581). However, it was not until Freud introduced the danger concept and the concept of signal anxiety in *Inhibitions, Symptoms and Anxiety* (1926a) that the role of anxiety in normal and abnormal development could be clarified.

It would be interesting to trace the part Sidis' theory played in the central position of fear in early American dynamic psychology. From McDougall's statement above it seems that Sidis was one of the forerunners of the neo-Freudians, Horney and Sullivan, who likewise put anxiety in the center of psychopathology. If this is so, the customary view of Sidis as an isolated oddity in the development of American psychology and psychiatry may have underestimated his importance in the spread of Freud's influence; for without question the neo-Freudian version of the central role of fear was one of the major vehicles of the spread of that influence. The curiously great receptiveness of the American lay and professional public to this idea awaits exploration and explanation.

The conceptions of subconscious and association neuroses of Janet, Prince, and Sidis affected psychology in two ways: they were often regarded as having priority over and superior exactness to Freud's unconscious dynamics of neuroses; they also prepared the ground for the acceptance of the Freudian *conceptions* of the unconscious and of the psychological origin of neuroses and psychoses. Janet, Prince, and Sidis could not, however, prepare the ground for Freud's *concepts,* since they did not have such concepts.

Janet, Prince, and Sidis had initially partially accepted Freud's ideas, but this recognition was withdrawn when they later encountered the disregard and acrimony of Freud's pupils. Priority issues came to the fore, disregard was matched by disregard, and argument took the place of any earlier wish for understanding. In 1914 Janet referred only to Freud's pre-1900 writings. Prince, when he learned that Jones was to come to the United States to speak about

Freud, told Putnam that he "would teach Jones about conflicts and show him examples such as he knew nothing of" (Taylor, 1928, p. 102).

What were the consequences of this complicated interaction of predecessors, coeval rivals who were probably influenced by Freud, various would-be "successors" of Freud (for instance, Jung), and antagonism aroused by psychoanalysts and psychoanalytic theory? What did this combination contribute to the fate of the concept of the unconscious?

THREE SYMPOSIA

In 1918 a symposium, "Why is the 'Unconscious' Unconscious?" (Nicoll, Rivers, and Jones, 1918), was presented before the Joint Session of the British Psychological Society, the Aristotelian Society, and the Mind Association. It was followed in 1919 by a second similar symposium, "Instinct and the Unconscious" (Rivers et al., 1919). The two symposia reflect the consequences of this complex interaction fairly accurately.

Captain Nicoll began the discussion: "The original teaching of Freud was that the unconscious part of the human psyche contained only what had once belonged to the conscious personal life. It became unconscious because it was repressed. . . . I do not know exactly what the Freudian school believe at the present moment, over and above this original view. I do not think it is possible to find very clear formulations in the modern Freudian writings" (Nicoll, Rivers, and Jones, 1918, p. 230). Thus Nicoll limited the unconscious to what is repressed, ignoring both the primally repressed and the nonrepressed active unconscious which so clearly became the matrix of the impulse-drive life in Freud's definition of the id. But it is irrelevant for our purposes that the ignorance implied in the first statement was an ill-fitting introduction to the sweeping criticism of the second. What is relevant is that both statements reflected existing and rather widespread attitudes, and that Nicoll went on to propound Jung's view, the valid core of which is in fact Freud's concept, although this core is almost unrecognizable among the Jungian modifications. In Nicoll's hands Freud became a philosophical empiricist, just as in the hands of the empiricists he became a theorist of nature, blind to any effects of life experience.

The next speaker was the venerable and open-minded Rivers. In a neurologizing paper, he rediscovered the intimate relation between the unconscious and instincts, and the antagonism between instinct and intellect, without making a single reference to Freud. He explained: "Whenever instinct tends to interfere unduly with reason, Nature has ready to her hand the process of dissociation which is instinct's peculiar instrument" (p. 245). While Nicoll changed Freud's concept into a Jungian conception, Rivers fell back on Janet's conception, although he significantly modified it by linking it with instinctual drive as Freud had done, but as Janet of course had not.

The last speaker was Ernest Jones, who tried to explain and to correct. But his usual cohesiveness and organization were absent from this presentation. His contribution leaves the impression of a man trying to find solid ground in common with the other two, but failing to do so.

The situation was hardly different in the second symposium (Rivers et al., 1919) a year later. Instinct and the unconscious were brought together, but with barely a mention of Freud. If one were not aware that Freud *was* well-known to the group, one might think that the topic of discussion was a psychological version of von Hartmann's ideas, and that Freud's influence consisted of no more than keeping von Hartmann's ideas alive. Rivers opened the discussion. If his paper of the previous year had contained a great deal of neurologizing, his new one contained even more. Myers followed him both in sequence and in suit. Jung was next. Although it is difficult if not impossible to follow his line of thought, he seems to have been repeating and embroidering what Nicoll said the year before. Graham Wallas was as usual clear and simple, but it is not easy to divine the relevance of what he said. Drever was the first to refer to Freud—indirectly, through Jones' paper of the previous year. But he tended to explain everything in terms of his own most recent book, *Instinct in Man* (1917). Nonetheless, Drever's central theses have some resemblance to Freud's:

> I take it that 'psychical' includes facts of at least two distinct kinds, those of the order of 'dispositions,' and those of the order of 'experiences' [Rivers et al., 1919, p. 28].

In its wider sense, as inclusive of both disposition and experience, the unconscious covers a group of psychical facts of which the facts of instinct constitute a part [p. 29].

The unconscious or subpersonal consciousness underlies at all times the conscious or personal consciousness, just as the instinctive propensities underlie the ends and purposes of our rational activities, and it is unconscious because it represents either a stage of psychical evolution beyond which we have passed by normal development, or a mass of experience upon which we have, as it were, tried to turn our backs by some more or less abnormal process of dissociation, repression, or substitution, but instinct has precisely the same psychological position and function in subpersonal as in personal consciousness [p. 33].

The last speaker was McDougall, who dealt with dissociation and repression. Though critical of Janet on the issue of dynamics we discussed earlier in this chapter, he sided with Janet against Freud: ". . . [In the] question to what extent such dissociation occurs in the normal person, or whether it is confined to neurotics, . . . Janet is more nearly right than Freud, though Janet made the great mistake of ignoring wellnigh completely the conative factors in the production of the *amnesias* with which he has dealt in so masterly, but too intellectual, a fashion" (p. 42).

To complete the "series" of symposia on the unconscious, mention should be made of the group of papers presented under the auspices of the Illinois Society for Mental Hygiene in 1927 (Dummer, 1927). The orientation of this symposium, organized by W. I. Thomas, apparently under the stimulus of Ethel S. Dummer, was different from that of the two previously mentioned. The participants were asked not to consider the regressive aspects of the unconscious, but to discuss its integrative and synthetic aspects—its relation to imagination, hypothesis, the inspiration of the poet, and human intuition in everyday life.

With this assignment, it is not surprising that not even the psychoanalysts present (Marion Kenworthy and William A. White) discussed Freud at any length, for what they were being asked to do was to extrapolate beyond any theory of the unconscious, Freudian or otherwise, that existed at that time. Kenworthy actually said nothing about Freud's concept. White, who gave the most systematic presentation of psychoanalytic developments, did point out: "While it is true that Professor Freud early recognized the ego aspect of the personality, it is also true that this aspect did not come

in for anything like adequate consideration until after the war. . . .
The recognition of the importance of the ego aspects of the personality and the constitution of the ego-ideal . . . are matters of only the past few years" (Dummer, 1927, p. 254). The symposium seems to have involved an early consideration of a topic which was not fully developed until much later in ego psychology (see Rapaport, 1958a).

Of the other participants, Koffka referred directly to Freud's theory of the unconscious to argue one particular facet of it. John B. Watson, on the other hand, made no specific reference to the theory, even though his discussion dealt most directly with Freud. Among other things, he said: "The scientific level of Freud's concept of the unconscious is exactly on a par with the miracles of Jesus. I say this despite my reverence for Freud and my admiration of his courage in insisting upon the role sex plays in the lives of all" (Dummer, 1927, p. 93).

KNIGHT DUNLAP

In view of these symposia, it should not surprise us that Knight Dunlap, in *Psychologies of 1930,* wrote:

> There has been evident an increasing tendency among psychologists to use the term "unconscious" in the loose explanatory way which was introduced by the Freudians, a tendency against which scientific psychology must resolutely set itself if it is to avoid the quagmire of merely verbal explanations which is fatal to further progress [1930, p. 321].
>
> What I have done, perceived, thought, felt, in preceding days and years, of course, has entered into the determination of what I do, perceive, think, and feel now. This is no Freudian discovery, but a fundamental postulate of psychology for many years. The Freudian discovery (analogous to someone's going out and discovering the moon) was that in some cases, in responding consciously, we are not conscious of the vast stretches of past life which have contributed to the present response. The real joke in the situation is that psychology has long recognized that not only in these apparently peculiar cases but *in all cases except certain special ones* one is unconscious, during a specific response, of the antecedent conditions: The exceptions are those thought responses in which one thinks of the past, and these occur relatively seldom [pp. 321-322].

Dunlap informs us in his autobiography (1932, p. 59) that "There are not many further propagandist efforts in which I am interested.

The abolition of 'emotions' and the attempt to get American psychologists generally to understand the concept of the 'unconscious' and its implications, I shall probably continue . . ."

Nor should it surprise us that in the late 1940's, unconscious perception came into the psychological literature under the name of "subception," without any reference to Freud's theory—for that matter, without reference to any theory at all.

SUMMARY

To sum up briefly what this all-too-hasty survey of the unconscious reveals: the long history of the conception of the unconscious laid the foundations for receptiveness to the idea of an unconscious when this was proposed by Freud; on the other hand, it made true appreciation of his *concept* of the unconscious much more difficult. In fact, psychologists often acted as if they did not know it existed.

MOTIVATION

Let us now turn to the other Freudian contribution to psychology we have selected for special consideration—motivation. After reviewing Freud's concept of instinctual drive, we shall consider its part in the general controversies that surrounded theoretical discussions of motivation. Following a discussion of the relationships of Freud's theory to the theories of motivation of his predecessors, contemporaries, and those who came after him, we shall turn more specifically to the role of his concept in what has been termed "the instinct controversy." Our section on motivation will close with a consideration of Freud's influence on several of the group of dynamic psychologists for whom motivation was a central theme.

FREUD'S CONCEPT OF INSTINCTUAL DRIVE

We might best introduce our discussion of motivation with Freud's own major statements of the concept of instinctual drive, the theory which is central to the problem of motivation.[18]

Freud's initial theories were empiricist. It was not until about 1897 that he came to the first glimpse of his nativist concept of the instinctual drive, and even in *The Interpretation of Dreams*

---

[18] For a detailed consideration of the relationship of instinctual drive to motivation, see Rapaport (1960a, pp. 193-213).

(1900a) there are few references to it. The two major statements of the concept, of which we quote small sections, are in *Three Essays on the Theory of Sexuality* (1905b) and "Instincts and Their Vicissitudes" (1915a). The 1905 statement says: "By an 'instinct' [*Trieb*] is provisionally to be understood the psychical representative of an endosomatic, continuously flowing source of stimulation, as contrasted with a 'stimulus', which is set up by *single* excitations coming from *without*. The concept of instinct is thus one of those lying on the frontier between the mental and the physical" (1905b, p. 168). In 1915, Freud defined instinctual drive similarly, as "a concept on the frontier between the mental and the somatic, as the psychical representative of the stimuli originating from within the organism and reaching the mind, as a measure of the demand made upon the mind for work [*Mass der Arbeitsanforderung*] in consequence of its connection with the body" (1915a, pp. 121-122).

Rapaport (1960a, pp. 193-208) further clarified the definition of "instinctual drive," largely on the basis of Freud's writings, in terms of the categories of pressure, aim, object, and source. *Pressure* involves energy—psychological energy expended in the initiation, regulation, and termination of behavior. The *aim* of the instinctual drive is discharge: "satisfaction" if the discharge takes place in action, "wish fulfillment" if the discharge takes the cognitive form of fantasy, dream, delusion, etc. This satisfaction, the psychological counterpart of the physical principle of entropy, is termed the pleasure principle, which we shall discuss shortly. The *object* is postulated by Freud as a defining characteristic of the instinctual drive; it includes a limited range of objects which are peculiarly fitted to make satisfaction of a particular instinctual drive possible. The *source* of the instinctual drive is the somatic process which occurs in the organ. An exact knowledge of the source is not invariably necessary for purposes of psychological study. Thus Freud's concept of instinctual drive is fundamentally a *psychological* concept whose "psychical representatives" are behaviors—both idea and affect—originating within the organism.

GENERAL BACKGROUND: THE POLARITIES

The immediate paradox of motivation concepts is that they are called upon to bridge the gap between the apparent teleological character of human behavior and science's demand for deterministic explanations. (As we shall see, psychoanalysis was also brought into the other dichotomous controversies—mechanism-vitalism, hedonism-antihedonism, nature-nurture—which were involved in theoretical discussions of motivation.) Psychology, in keeping with its commitment to exact science, had limited its explorations to areas where the goal-directed character of behavior did not have to be considered. It hoped that goal-directedness could eventually be understood in terms of elementary mechanical relations, such as association and conditioning. Freud, on the other hand, insisted on the immediate causal explanation of all behavior, whether elementary or complex, whether apparently aimless or apparently goal-directed.

Freud's answer to the motivation paradox was to postulate a concept of instinctual drive which avoided the extremes of both mechanism and vitalism. The strict mechanist disregards goal-directedness and attempts to construct an explanation of behavior from elemental deterministic relations. The vitalist disregards mechanistic causes and assumes that behavior is controlled by goals. As we have seen, Freud conceived of his instinctual drives as forces which originate in the biological organism but are triggered into action by objects specific to them. His theory implies that these internal forces and their external objects are innately coordinated and that experience only modifies and amplifies this coordination during the developmental process.

Freud did not shy away from apparent teleology. Rather, it prompted him to assume that the goal toward which a behavior is directed should readily reveal the cause, that is, the driving force of that behavior. Thus, just as had some of the functionalists (Ladd, for example), he made himself liable to the accusation that he was a vitalist, rather than a scientist exploring determinants. To this day this argument has hounded Freud's theory and obscured it in the eyes of many psychologists. Freud's exposition in *The Psychopathology of Everyday Life* (1901) of his view of thoroughgoing determinism (pp. 1-2, 240), and of the relation between conjunction and cause (pp. 21-22), was either unnoticed or misunderstood.

On the other hand, the genetic, evolutionary, and "force" character of Freud's motivation concept made it equally vulnerable to the charge of being totally mechanistic. This misunderstanding was furthered by Freud's labeling as "mechanisms" the characteristic operations of the instinctual drives. The more opposed a psychologist was to the exact science program, the more susceptible was he to this misapprehension. Not only psychologists, but also the so-called neopsychoanalysts like Rank and particularly Sullivan, adopted this view. Even persons favorable to classical psychoanalysis like Healy, Bronner, and Bowers (1930, especially pp. 192-261) felt uncomfortable with Freud's "mechanisms," and rechristened them "dynamisms."

But mechanistic vs. vitalistic, deterministic vs. teleological explanations, were not the only force-fields which seem to have obstructed the psychologist's grasp of Freud's motivation theory. To this ancient debate was joined the equally ancient one of pro- and antihedonism. Besides Freud's general penchant for anthropomorphic language, the main reason for his having so often been mistaken for a vitalist, or at the very least a hedonist, was his use of the term "pleasure principle." The pleasure principle is the principle by which the energy expended by the instinctual drive is regulated. It represents the common implication of the energy concept, the tendency of energy toward discharge (tension reduction). It is clearly a causal principle. But its name—derived from the frequent though by no means invariable concomitance of energy discharge and subjectively experienced pleasure—gave, and still often gives, the impression that the workings of the mental apparatus are regulated by a striving for subjective pleasure. Such misunderstandings are part of the history of Freud's influence on psychology. This particular confusion was augmented by a somewhat more specific outgrowth of the conjunction of libido and pleasure principle in Freud's theory. The obvious conjunction of libido and pleasure in personal experience naturally led many to believe that this particular conjunction was the basis for Freud's pleasure principle. Freud was thus indicted as a hedonist (see Rapaport, 1960a, pp. 200-202). The closer a psychologist was to the program of exact science, the more susceptible he was, in general, to this misconception.

Through Bentham, the Mills, Spencer, and Bain, the hedonism of English philosophy had become a potent factor in Anglo-American psychology at the turn of the century. Later on, through Thorndike's law of effect, hedonism also became an important part of the exact science program. Whereas people like McDougall (1918, 1925) fought hedonism, and decried Freud as a hedonist, those representing the exact science program avowed a "hedonism of the past" (a striving for what was pleasurable in the past), and decried Freud as a teleological "hedonist of the future." This was the clash of the empiricist conception of "the burnt child dreads fire" and the nativistic conception of the instincts striving for gratification. Freud's theory therefore became involved not only in the hedonist-antihedonist debate, but also in the nature-nurture controversy. While it became embroiled in the former adventitiously, it fell into the midst of the latter by its very character, just as it did into the determinism-teleology controversy (Weber and Rapaport, 1941)—although entanglement in the nature-nurture controversy was even more inevitable. The appearance of Freud's answer to the motivational paradox was deceptive. On the one hand his answer was only apparently teleological and, on the other, obscured by the word "pleasure" not used in a hedonistic sense. However, in relation to the nature-nurture controversy, *both* nature and nurture conceptions were clearly central to it.

Two opposite kinds of misunderstanding developed: psychoanalysis was taken to be either a pure nature or a pure nurture theory. Gordon Allport's (1947) treatment of it as a genetic reductionist early nurture theory[19] is a good example of one such misunderstanding. Nativist Gestalt psychology classes psychoanalysis with the behaviorist theories as a nurture theory. Behaviorist theories, on the other hand, especially in pure forms such as the late Watsonian, were nurture theories which rejected psychoanalysis as being nativist. The neo-Freudians did the same. Organically-minded psychiatrists rejected psychoanalysis because they took it for a nurture theory. The neobehaviorist learning theorists—Dollard, Miller, and Mowrer—embraced psychoanalysis because of what they considered its nurture aspects.

[19] "Odd as it may appear, Freud resembles the mechanical and phylogenetic psychologists in wanting his doctrine of motivation anchored to neuro-anatomy. I assume that this is his desire because of his refusal to see anything at all in the coöperative, socialized, affiliative, undertakings of mankind excepting goal-inhibited sexuality. . . . The trouble lies chiefly in the excessive emphasis upon infantile experience. We are asked to believe that an individual's character-structure is, in all essentials, determined by the time his last diaper is changed" (Allport, 1947, p. 185; see also Allport, 1946, particularly pp. 57-58).

Nevertheless, Freud was simultaneously neither and both a nativist and nurturist. Freud wrote:

> No other influences on the course of sexual development can compare in importance with releases of sexuality, waves of repression and sublimations—the two latter being processes of which the inner causes are quite unknown to us. It might be possible to include repressions and sublimations as a part of the constitutional disposition, by regarding them as manifestations of it in life; and anyone who does so is justified in asserting that the final shape taken by sexual life is principally the outcome of the innate constitution. No one with perception will, however, dispute that an interplay of factors such as this also leaves room for the modifying effects of accidental events experienced in childhood and later. It is not easy to estimate the relative efficacy of the constitutional and accidental factors. In theory one is always inclined to overestimate the former; therapeutic practice emphasizes the importance of the latter. It should, however, on no account be forgotten that the relation between the two is a co-operative and not a mutually exclusive one. The constitutional factor must await experiences before it can make itself felt; the accidental factor must have a constitutional basis in order to come into operation. To cover the majority of cases we can picture what has been described as a 'complemental series', in which the diminishing intensity of one factor is balanced by the increasing intensity of the other; there is, however, no reason to deny the existence of extreme cases at the two ends of the series.
>
> We shall be in even closer harmony with psycho-analytic research if we give a place of preference among the accidental factors to the experiences of early childhood. The single aetiological series then falls into two, which may be called the dispositional and the definitive. In the first the constitution and the accidental experiences of childhood interact in the same manner as do the disposition and later traumatic experiences in the second. All the factors that impair sexual development show their effects by bringing about a regression, a return to an earlier phase of development [1905b, pp. 239-240].

On the one hand, Freud insisted on the genetic-experiential origins of mental disease, in the face of contemporary theories of mental disease centered on constitution, degeneration, and inferiority. On the other hand, in the face of the purely empiricist association theory, he insisted on an explanatory principle rooted in the organism: the instinctual drive. Woodworth recognized both characteristics of Freud's theory, though he did not bring them together.

The controversies surrounding Freud's theories of both motivation and the unconscious obstructed the penetration of his concepts, yet seem to have promoted the spread of his conceptions. Psychologists brought Freud's conception of motivation into the center of debate, partly in attempts to debunk it,[20] and partly in hailing those aspects of it which seemed to fit their own views.[21] Perhaps the most significant indication of Freudian influence was the "anonymous" acceptance (of which Herma, Kris, and Shor spoke) among psychologists of some of his observations and conceptions, and even some of his concepts. Outstanding examples among behaviorists are Watson and Tolman.

This concatenation of debunking, praising, and silent adoption leads into the very heart of the struggle of Freud's theories within

---

[20] For instance, Knight Dunlap (1920).

[21] For instance, McDougall (1936, p. vi) wrote: "If from among all the rival systems of psychology I have singled out as the object of my critical attack the system of Freud, it is not that I regard his views as more in need of criticism than any other, it is rather because I hold Freud's system to be the most deserving of honest criticism, to have the essential foundations of truth that are lacking in most other contemporary systems, to be, in short, nearer than any other to the system elaborated by myself . . ."

At the very end of his life McDougall stated explicitly his view of the relation between his theory and Freud's: "The most essential features of my own system were sketched in my *Introduction to Social Psychology* (written in 1907, before I had made acquaintance with Professor Freud's writings, and first published in 1908)" (1936, p. vi). Further, in addition to his comparison of Freud with Aristotle, quoted earlier (p. 70), he went on in a footnote as follows: "In order that there may be no mistake about my attitude to Professor Freud, I add that in my judgement he is a great man, both morally and intellectually; I esteem and admire him greatly" (p. 17).

Nonetheless, he then criticized the way Freud handled his concept of suggestion. "He makes a brief and very inadequate statement of my views, and having brushed aside my theory of suggestion, without examination, he proceeds to restate it as his own, mixing it wellnigh inextricably with a highly fanciful history of the supposed differentiation from the sex instinct in primitive man of that submissive propensity which he and I agree in postulating and in regarding as the source of the conative energy at work in all suggestion. Now I am sure that Professor Freud did not mean to steal my theory; I feel sure that he is not aware of having done so. I am delighted that he should agree with me; I would be still more pleased if he would acknowledge the fact of agreement. I refer to this instance as illustrating the great difficulty in the way of fruitful discussion between psycho-analysts and psychologists" (pp. 21-22). And in a footnote he adds: "In his *Group Psychology* Freud refers specifically to my 'Note on Suggestion' (loc. cit.) in which my theory is very explicitly restated. He refers to the article as though it were merely an attempt to define the proper usage of the word, an attempt which he seems to accept; but since his remarks make it clear that he has read the article, I cannot see that he can be acquitted of the venial error of subconscious plagiarism. The incident illustrates one drawback of my now abandoned policy of modesty, of abstention from all claims of priority and independence. If my article had been entitled 'A New Theory of Suggestion,' Freud could hardly have fallen into this error" (p. 22).

psychology. Further elucidation of these controversies and of the conjectures we have thus far made cannot be attempted here. Yet we wish to risk one further conjecture. The very monumentality of Freud's contribution made inevitable its becoming a frequent center of contention for many of the major trends within the theoretical climate of psychology. Not only was there the pressure of the general intellectual and public climate on the psychologist, so that wherever he went and whatever he read he was likely to come up against Freud; there was also the fact that, whatever trend or theory he adopted or combatted in his psychological thinking, he was likely to bump into Freud either as a presumed protagonist of the same trend, or as a horrible example of the opposing one. The lasting influence of Freud's theories is probably rooted in this same monumental character.

RELATION TO OTHER THEORIES OF MOTIVATION

Up to this point we have been discussing the general background of Freud's motivation theory. The survey of the more specific background of Freud's theory and its relationship to contemporary theories and to theories descending from these is still ahead of us. We shall first briefly consider the possible roots of Freud's theory in association and act psychology. We shall then consider those contemporary and subsequent theories which have similarities to Freudian thinking, and try to determine to what extent they may have been influenced by Freud.

Predecessors' Theories

Late in the nineteenth century, a primitive conception of the motivated character of ideation was already implicit in some trends of association and act psychology. Some associationists, Herbart for instance, felt that associations are not simply couplings of inert ideas by the glue of frequency or contiguity. Boring has labeled their views "active ideas." Somewhat later, act psychology, particularly Brentano's "intentionalism" (1874), spoke for an "internal active principle," directing not only the coupling but also the very "perception" and "presentation" of ideas. The character of the first of these trends was mechanistic-deterministic, that of the latter vitalistic-teleological. The likelihood was that Freud knew a little about "active ideas" through Mill (just as he probably knew about the hedonistic view of motivation from him) and through Meynert and Griesinger (see p. 101). Study of Freud's pre-1897 writings suggests that his treatment of ideas and groups of ideas may be related to the "active ideas" conception. However, the Breuer-Freud conceptual discovery attributing the "activity" of ideas to their "affect charge" overshadows the earlier conception of "active ideas." Similarly, Freud's rather persistent use of the term "purposive ideas" in *The Interpretation of Dreams* may be related to the conception of active ideas, although this relationship, too, is overshadowed by the more important fact that the ideas he dealt with represent instinctual drives. These relationships can be understood completely only through a thorough study of the texts involved. It is even more difficult to trace the influence of act psychology, with which Freud was no doubt familiar through his courses under Brentano himself. The particular influence of Brentano's concept of intention seems traceable throughout the so-called "Papers on Metapsychology";[22] nevertheless, traceability is one thing and obviousness is another. G. W. Allport (1947), advocating a psychology of intention, seems to have had an inkling of the influence of Brentano on Freud's theory.

Contemporaries' Theories

There can be no doubt that motivation conceptions in general, some of which were formally if not contentually quite similar to the one Freud propounded, were being advanced around the turn of the century. Thorndike's may be the most striking example. In 1898, at a time when Freud's concept was taking shape in his letters to Fliess, Thorndike, summarizing his experiments, wrote: "The groundwork of animal associations is not the association of *ideas*, but the association of idea or sense-impression with *impulse*" (1898, p. 71). In spite of the marked similarity of this concept to Freud's, there is a difference between them. Thorndike spoke of association *between* idea and impulse, while in Freud's theory (1900a, 1915a, 1915b) the idea is a *representation* of the impulse, and the impulse is the *organizer* of ideas. Thorndike's theory was

---

[22] We mean here all the papers of the 1911-1917 period which were included under that title in the *Collected Papers,* Vol. 4, rather than only those which are (correctly) so grouped in the *Standard Edition.* See also Barclay (1959).

not alone in resembling Freud's. Claparède (1903) emphasized the role of interests in association,[23] and Ach (1905) crystallized the conception of the "active idea" into the conception of "determining tendencies."

Two other theories of motivation which were also similar to Freud's should be mentioned. These theories had limited impact because they were not associated with experimental investigations and were subsequently of little heuristic value. One of them is McDougall's, to which we have referred repeatedly. The other is Drever's (1917), which is very much like McDougall's and also somewhat like Freud's in spirit.[24]

Descendants' Theories

The descendants of Thorndike's, Claparède's, and Ach's early conceptions were not linear continuations of them. The descendant of Thorndike's conception was his own law of effect, that of Claparède's was Piaget's sensorimotor theory of intelligence, and that of Ach's was Lewin's "action and affect psychology." We will discuss each of these because they were major theories of motivation which, although they issued in part from roots independent of Freud, were also influenced by Freud's theory and became carriers of its impact.

Piaget. Among the "descendants," Piaget offers an interesting example of varied constituents of influence. Piaget's central interest, as his autobiography and the references to pre-Socratic philosophers in his early studies show, has always been epistemology, and he considers his investigations to be an empirical approach to epistemology. To the extent to which the pursuits of his epistemological aims brought him to psychology, he was, during the beginning of his crucial studies, under the influence of Claparède (see Piaget,

---

[23] In his autobiography (1930, p. 76) Claparède quoted and summarized his argument as follows: "This fundamental property of mental activity (that of serving the biological interest of the organism) has seemed to me worthy of being called a law: the *Law of Momentary Interest.* 'At any given moment, that instinct which is of greatest importance takes precedence over the others,' or, 'at any given moment, an organism acts according to its strongest interest.' "

[24] Drever's (1917) volume contains no bibliographic references to Freud (although it does to Jones) and only a single, though significant, sentence about him: ". . . the notion of the 'unconscious'. . . has been a very fruitful one for abnormal psychology, and, through Freud and his school, by a kind of 'total reflection,' as it were, has, in recent times, affected other aspects of the psychology of Instinct" (p. 68). But we remain uninformed of what these aspects are.

1952, pp. 245-246). It was in response to Claparède's invitation that Piaget went to the Rousseau Institute in Geneva. Claparède had been familiar with, interested in, and positively inclined toward most of Freud's theories.[25] Although Piaget's own attitude toward Freud and interest in thinking and motivation were very different from Claparède's, it seems that Claparède influenced Piaget's pattern of investigation and led him to Freud's theoretical views. These studies were based on direct inquiry outside of the psychoanalytic situation. From a broad and varied set of data, he showed the existence in children of those mechanisms of motivated thought which Freud inferred from the study of the dreams, parapraxes, and neuroses of adults. Admittedly aware of and influenced by Freud, Piaget continued to publish studies preponderantly of this character until the middle of the 1930's. His studies, supplemented by the derivative studies of the psychoanalyst Susan Isaacs (1930, 1933), were the most extensive group of psychological investigations at that time to show the clear imprint of Freud's influence.[26]

In the Preface to Piaget's *The Language and Thought of the Child,* Claparède wrote:

> Our author shows us in fact that the child's mind is woven on two different looms, which are as it were placed one above the other. By far the most important during the first years is the work accomplished on the lower plane. This is the work done by the child himself, which attracts to him pell-mell and crystallizes round his

[25] Claparède was one of the out-of-town members of the "Freud Group" formed in Zurich in 1907 (see Jones, 1955, p. 29). He also attended the Salzburg Congress in 1908. In his introduction (Claparède, 1920) to Le Lay's French translation of *Five Lectures* which appeared in the *Revue de Genève* in December, 1920 and January and February, 1921, he gave a thumbnail sketch of Freud's major theories and concepts, illustrating them with lucid examples from French *belles-lettres* and scientific literature. His command of the issues seems remarkable even to today's reader. Although Claparède was by no means uncritical, he ended his review with the following appraisal: "Experimental psychology, which has tried to study the mechanism of mental processes, has almost completely forgotten to investigate the underlying basis of these mechanisms. It is these hidden springs that psychoanalysis has tried to discover and to describe.

"The work of Sigmund Freud constitutes one of the most important events in the history of the science of the mind, by the originality of the ideas which it suggests and by the fruitfulness that it has shown" (Claparède, 1920, p. 864).

[26] It should be noted, however, that his references to psychoanalysis have a Zurich cast, particularly of the Bleuler (1911) conception of psychoanalysis. Piaget thus became instrumental in the spread of the concept of autism in America (see footnote 14, Chapter 6). We find Piaget referred to most frequently in discussions of the topics of socialization (see Murphy and Murphy, 1931) and of autism (see Murphy, 1947).

wants all that is likely to satisfy these wants. It is the plane of subjectivity, of desires, games, and whims, of the *Lustprinzip* as Freud would say. The upper plane, on the contrary, is built up little by little by social environment, which presses more and more upon the child as time goes on. It is the plane of objectivity, speech, and logical ideas, in a word the plane of reality [Piaget, 1923, p. xii].

In the same volume Piaget himself writes: "Janet, Freud, Ferenczi, Jones, Spielrein, etc., have brought forward various theories on the language of savages, imbeciles, and young children, all of which are of the utmost significance for an investigation such as we propose to make of the child mind from the age of six" (1923, pp. 2-3). He goes on to summarize the views of psychoanalysis (and particularly of Spielrein) on language.

In characterizing the forms of thought that he observed during the study reported, he writes:

> ... it may be useful at this point to note that everything leads us to consider the mechanism of syncretistic thought as intermediate between logical thought and that process which the psychoanalysts have rather boldly described as the 'symbolism' of dreams. How, after all, does autistic imagination function in dreams? Freud has shown that two main factors contribute to the formation of the images or pseudoconcepts of dreaming and day-dreaming—*condensation* by which several disparate images melt into one (as different people into one person), and *transference* by which the qualities belonging to one object are transferred to another (as when someone who may bear a certain resemblance to the dreamer's mother is conceived of as his actual mother).[27] As we have suggested elsewhere[28] there must be every kind of intermediate type between these two functions and the processes of generalization (which is a sort of condensation) and abstraction (which is a sort of transference). Now syncretism is precisely the most important of these intermediate links [1923, p. 158].

Piaget goes on to explore this proposition further.[29]

---

[27] *Displacement* would be appropriate here, despite his correct use and definition of the term transference.

[28] In a footnote Piaget gives the reference: "J. Piaget, 'La psychanalyse dans ses rapports avec la psychologie de l'enfant.' *Bullet. Soc. Alf. Binet,* No. 131-133, pp. 56-7."

[29] Further substantiation of Freud's influence on Piaget can be found in various Piaget writings of the period: *Judgment and Reasoning in the Child* (1924, pp. 145, 175, 202, 204-205, 209-210, 244-245), *The Child's Conception of the World* (1927a, pp. 35, 151, 234, 245-247, 377-378).

Piaget's studies supported some of Freud's findings on motivation. Once Piaget's volumes (1923, 1924, 1927a, 1927b, 1932) reporting these investigations were translated into English, they became important and often cited sources. This was despite the fact that the attempts to replicate the studies in the United States only partially confirmed Piaget's results (Lerner, 1937; Dennis, 1942, 1943; Ugurel-Semin, 1952; MacRae, 1954). There seems to be little doubt that these works became a significant channel for the spread of a number of Freudian conceptions. They were, however, divorced from their theoretical matrix and from the concepts which could have given them precision.

Though Piaget initially had close contact with psychoanalysis, he eventually turned away from it. In his autobiography (1952) he makes the barest reference to psychoanalysis. Piaget's studies of the last twenty years have been concerned with tracing the development of thought from early infancy. In the course of these studies, his interest in empirical epistemology has become increasingly central, and his attitude toward psychoanalysis overtly and increasingly critical. Nevertheless, his theories have some relationship to Freud's. In effect, his theory, which derives abstract intelligence from sensorimotor intelligence, parallels both Freud's derivation of the ego from the body ego and Werner's sensory-tonic theory of perception, which in turn is clearly though distantly parallel to Freud's genetic theory (see Rapaport, 1960b).[30] Moreover, Piaget's theory, like Freud's, explicitly unites nature and nurture. In this respect, it is very closely related to Freud's, and is also close to Freud's in its

---

[30] About the general influence of Freudian ideas upon him, Dr. Werner, in a personal communication (November 30, 1955), wrote: "As to my own relations to psychoanalysis, I have been brought up, of course, as you know, in Vienna at a time when Freud's psychoanalysis was in a state of rapid expansion. There are probably three aspects of Freud's psychology which have been of considerable influence on my own conceptualizations: one is the genetic frame of reference itself, the insistence of Freud on theory of development rather than pure description; two, in contradistinction to the associationistic psychology within which I was brought up which has been of an entirely static nature, Freud's psychology has suggested to me that concepts have to be introduced in psychology which are of a dynamic nature. In this respect I was, and still am, immensely impressed by Freud's theory of dream, not in terms of its content aspects, but in terms of the dynamic conceptualization. My early study of the origins of metaphor I believe will bear this out. The third aspect of Freud's psychoanalysis which I am sure was of great influence on me was his opposition to the surface psychology of the academic scholars, his insistence on operations which though themselves unconscious and unreflective can be brought to light by methods created for that particular purpose."

hierarchic conception of, and in the pervasive role it gives to, motivation—however basically it differs from Freud's theory in other ways. P. H. Wolff (1960) has analyzed extensively a number of these parallels and should be referred to for the detailed elucidation of the similarities, but still great differences, between Freud and Piaget. Whether or not these later parallels should be considered evidences of Freud's influence must for the present remain a moot question. There can be no doubt, however, that they are part of the same *Zeitgeist* which determined Freud's impact and was in turn influenced by it.

Lewin. Lewin's early interests were, like Piaget's, epistemological, as his prepsychological writings attest. A trace of this interest is still obvious in his "Gesetz und Experiment in der Psychologie" (1927).[31] He began his investigations of motivation with an experimental criticism of Ach's theory of will and association. His first step was to generalize and differentiate Ach's determining tendencies into a wide variety of kinds of "action readiness." He published the preliminary report of his experiments from the trenches of the First World War (1917) and followed it with an extensive article (1922a, 1922b). After the war he began, with his students, Zeigarnik, Rickers-Ovsiankina, Dembo, and others, to publish a series of some twenty studies on "Action and Affect Psychology" (Lewin et al., 1926-1932), all of which were designed to test a theory of motivation. So pervasive was his interest in motivation that Gibson (1941) characterized his theory, much as Woodworth characterized Freud's, as having one dominant issue: motivation. But this is merely an external indication of the relationship between Lewin and Freud. From its early statement in "Intention, Will, and Need" (1926), and its elaborated form in *A Dynamic Theory of Personality* (1935), Lewin's theory can be summarized as follows: there are "genuine needs" in the organism which lend valence to objects

---

[31] It is worth pointing out that Freud's preoccupation with the relationship between unconscious processes and conscious thought substantially amounts to an epistemological interest even if Freud refrained from indicating his awareness of this fact. It may be no mere coincidence that Freud, Piaget, and Lewin, whose theories have much in common, shared epistemological interests. An inclination to a certain type of theory probably goes with a predilection for certain types of philosophical and ideological approach. If this conjecture could be empirically demonstrated, one would have a new dimension of the nature of influence and of the carriers of the *Zeitgeist*.

of the environment, making them into goal objects. The attainment of these goal objects discharges the existing need tension and eliminates the valence of the objects. From the tension systems corresponding to these "genuine needs," acts of intending segregate subordinate tension systems, the "quasi needs," as Lewin called them. These function like the genuine needs and motivate actions other than those directly motivated by "genuine needs."

The formal kinship of this motivation theory to Freud's is obvious, and the question of influence an interesting one. In personal communications Dembo, Heider, and Rickers-Ovsiankina—some of Lewin's closest friends and collaborators in his early period—agree that the starting point for Lewin was not Freud's theory. Rickers-Ovsiankina is sure that Lewin did not even know Freud. Dembo believes that he knew Freud's theories and read them—that in the 1920's "everybody read Freud"—but that this was not particularly significant because Lewin's motivation concept came from the field-force concept which physics had already used so effectively.[32] Lewin's early publications (1922c, 1923; Lewin and Sa-

---

[32] We are giving the communications in relatively complete form here. Heider (personal communication, 1955): "I don't think [the] Zeigarnik, etc. experiments 'lean directly on Freud . . .' I asked Lewin once how he got [the] idea for Zeigarnik's experiments, and he said: 'Well, we were always talking about tensions and I tried to take the concept of tension seriously and tried to derive consequences from it'—but no word of Freud, I am quite sure he did not know about day residues . . ."

Rickers-Ovsiankina (summary of a conversation): 1. Lewin never read things. He listened, but remembered only what struck him as fitting his own system of thought, and often forgot where a thought came from. She is sure that Lewin did not know Freud. 2. In the Berlin Institute of Psychology there was a comment abroad: Lewin would not be possible without Freud. To her this meant simply that the time was ripe for dynamic thinking, and so Freud and Lewin came to it independently. 3. Repression, etc., came into the Zeigarnik and Birenbaum papers through quips made in the department; this is like "repression"—and then this went into the papers. She doubts that either Zeigarnik or Birenbaum knew Freud's writings. 4. The beginnings of this work are to be found in Lewin's doctoral thesis on the role of attitudes in learning.

Dembo (summary of a conversation): 1. Lewin's interest in these experiments came from his interest in the dynamics of memory which grew out of the Würzburg school, particularly Ach. His doctoral thesis shows this. 2. His concepts of motivation, forces, and vectors were derived from the generally adaptable concept of field forces which physics used first, but which he subsequently used for psychology; the concept of tension came later. 3. She believes that Lewin knew Freud's theories, that he read Freud, that in the 1920's everybody read Freud. This was not crucial, however, because his motivation concept was in large part arrived at independently.

Compare these, however, with Cartwright's (1959, p. 41) cryptic statement: "All of these studies [the memory, the interruption and resumption studies, the

kuma, 1925) seem to corroborate this view of the origin of Lewin's concept.

Nevertheless, the experiments of Zeigarnik (1927) and Rickers-Ovsiankina (1928) on the remembering and resumption of interrupted tasks, and Birenbaum's (1930) related experiments, show a striking relationship to Freud's theory of "day residues" in the seventh chapter of *The Interpretation of Dreams* (1900a, especially pp. 555-564).[33] They also show a relationship to his theory of "forgetting of intentions," in the seventh chapter of *The Psychopathology of Everyday Life* (1901).[34] Zeigarnik alludes to the

---

substitution studies] . . . are dealing in an experimental fashion with a concept originally advanced by Freud."

(We cannot forbear, however, reporting an anecdote we have from Boring [personal communication, December 24, 1962] about the immediate origin of the Zeigarnik experiments in a long discussion in a restaurant. The crowd talked and talked and then asked the waiter to say what they owed. He knew at once and Lewin paid. Then they talked and talked and it occurred to Lewin to ask the waiter what they owed and he had no idea. Closure had apparently cleared his memory.)

[33] Freud wrote: "If we wish to classify the thought-impulses which persist in sleep, we may divide them into the following groups: (1) what has not been carried to a conclusion during the day owing to some chance hindrance; (2) what has not been dealt with owing to the insufficiency of our intellectual power —what is unsolved; (3) what has been rejected and suppressed during the daytime. To these we must add (4) a powerful group consisting of what has been set in action in our *Ucs.* by the activity of the preconscious in the course of the day; and finally (5) the group of daytime impressions which are indifferent and have for that reason not been dealt with" (1900a, p. 554).

The first of Freud's groups is the one particularly relevant here, though some of the others too have parallels in the Lewinian literature.

[34] Freud (1901, p. 152) wrote: "The *forgetting* of intentions, to which we are subject every day and in every possible situation, is *not* a thing that we are in the habit of explaining in terms of such a revision in the balance of motives. In general we leave it unexplained; or we try to find a psychological explanation by supposing that at the time when the intention was due to be carried out the attention necessary for the action was no longer at hand—attention which was, after all, an indispensable precondition for the coming into being of the intention and had therefore been available for the action at that time. Observation of our normal behaviour in regard to intentions leads us to reject this attempt at an explanation as being arbitrary. If I form an intention in the morning which is to be carried out in the evening, I may be reminded of it two or three times in the course of the day. It *need* not however become conscious at all throughout the day. When the time for its execution draws near, it suddenly springs to my mind and causes me to make the necessary preparations for the proposed action. If I am going for a walk and take a letter with me which has to be posted, it is certainly not necessary for me, as a normal individual, free from neurosis, to walk all the way with it in my hand and to be continually on the look-out for a letter-box in which to post it; on the contrary I am in the habit of putting it in my pocket, of walking along and letting my thoughts range freely, and I confidently expect that one of the first letter-boxes will catch my attention and cause me to put my hand in my pocket and take out the letter. Normal behaviour

latter volume when she uses the term "repression" (*Verdrängung*) in her paper (1927, p. 77) for the occasionally observed forgetting of interrupted tasks, although she does not refer to Freud in this context. In ordinary circumstances, her experiments demonstrated superiority in recall of interrupted tasks over the completed tasks. Birenbaum refers (1930, p. 220) to *The Psychopathology of Everyday Life* in connection with intentions, and repeatedly uses the term *fixation* (e.g., p. 265). Rickers-Ovsiankina (personal communication) explained that such terms came into Zeigarnik's and Birenbaum's papers through quips in the Berlin Department: ". . . this is like 'repression.' " But Boring (personal communication, 1957) writes: "I do remember clearly how American spies went to Berlin around 1925 (I should say; anyhow long before 1929) and came back saying that there was this Gestalt psychologist, Lewin, who was known to be combining Freud with Gestalt psychology." (Of course, this may have been merely a reflection of the sensitivity of Americans to anything Freudian.)

We see, then, that though a similarity between Lewin's and Freud's ideas is clear, the question of influence is undetermined. It is somewhat clarified, however, if a distinction is made between Lewin's early work at the Psychological Institute in Berlin, around 1925 to 1930, and his later work in the United States after 1930. In the earlier period it is not certain whether Lewin read or was acquainted with Freud's work in any real sense. His colleagues do agree, however, that Lewin's ideas did not derive from Freud. Nevertheless, Freud was "in the air" during that period, particularly after the 1926 Zeigarnik experiments. It is clear that in the later period Lewin was acquainted with Freud. In 1937, for example, he wrote a paper on the two theoretical systems (Lewin, 1937).

No matter what the direct influence of Freud may have been, the experimental work of the Lewinian group has many areas of involvement in common with Freud. Schwarz's (1927, 1933) experi-

---

after an intention has been formed coincides fully with the experimentally-produced behaviour of people to whom what is described as a 'post-hypnotic suggestion at long range' has been given under hypnosis. This phenomenon is usually described in the following way. The suggested intention slumbers on in the person concerned until the time for its execution approaches. Then it awakes and impels him to perform the action."

The parallel to Lewin's conception of intentions is striking. It should be noted, however, that the psychoanalytic exploration of the implied role of the stimulus object did not begin until recently (see Rapaport, 1958b).

ments exploring the forgetting of intentions in the course of the change of a learned habit corroborated Zeigarnik's and Rickers-Ovsiankina's findings. The experiments of such investigators as Dembo (1931) and Sliosberg (1934) demonstrated that the Lewinian type of motivation also operates by substitution of goal objects and other mechanisms similar to the so-called Freudian mechanisms. Later Barker, Dembo, and Lewin (1941) even produced and explored phenomena similar to what Freud described as regression.

Other experiments which were stimulated mainly by Freud but also by Lewin show an increased confluence of Lewinian and psychoanalytic concepts. Rosenzweig (1933, 1941, 1943, 1945; Rosenzweig and Mason, 1934) discovered that interrupted tasks which are experienced as failures are forgotten, instead of being better remembered. Rosenzweig assumed that he had found an experimental method for studying repression, and the pleasure and reality principles as well. These experiments, together with Lewinian findings which also referred to such ego-level equivalents,[35] became an important channel for the spread of Freud's influence. This is true even though Freud in a letter to Rosenzweig[36] denied

---

[35] For an early discussion of the hierarchic conception to which this phrase refers, see Rapaport (1942a, pp. 100-103); for a more recent exposition, see Rapaport (1951, Part 7, especially pp. 700-701, 703-704, 711-712).

[36] Dr. Rosenzweig wrote (personal communication, June 20, 1956): "I am enclosing a copy of Freud's letter—the original German and an English translation. Erik Erikson, during the days when he and I were both at Harvard, helped me transliterate the German and arrive at the translation.

28.2.1934
Wien IX., Berggasse 19

Sehr geehrter Herr

Ich habe Ihre experimentellen Arbeiten zur Prüfung psychoanalytischer Behauptungen mit Interesse zur Kenntnis genommen. Sehr hoch kann ich diese Bestätigungen nicht einschätzen, denn die Fülle sicherer Beobachtungen auf denen jene Behauptungen ruhen, macht sie von der experimentellen Prüfung unabhängig. Immerhin, sie kann nicht schaden.

Ihr ergebener
Freud

My dear Sir

I have examined your experimental studies for the verification of the psychoanalytic assertions with interest. I cannot put much value on these confirmations because the wealth of reliable observations on which these assertions rest make them independent of experimental verification. Still, it can do no harm.

Sincerely yours
Freud"

Dr. Max Schur, who was Freud's personal physician from 1929 to 1939 (personal communication, April 18, 1963), points out, however, "that the timing of

the need for experimental proof, contending that sufficient clinical proof of repression was available; it is true even if it is questionable that Rosenzweig's findings demonstrated more than ego-level equivalents.

this letter of February 28, 1934 must be taken into consideration. Freud, who was 78 years old, had to undergo at that time a radiotherapy because of local papillomata with intolerable pain, which made eating, speaking and smoking extremely difficult. Nevertheless, Freud did not interrupt his work, seeing about six patients daily and ... all this without any sedation. After a full day's work, he would answer his entire correspondence in longhand. That such letters were occasionally brief and somewhat perfunctory could not be surprising." Dr. Schur also points out that although Freud was not greatly in favor of the "experimental" approach to validation, he was nevertheless definitely impressed by such work as Pötzl's and Hartmann's.

Dr. Rosenzweig continued his June, 1956 communication as follows: "You may be interested in some comments that I pass on for such use as you may wish to make of them in your article.

"1. I have never published the letter in full though I did paraphrase it pretty exactly in a paper, 'The Experimental Study of Psychoanalytic Concepts,' *Character and Personality,* 1937, 6, 61-71.... Sometime between the receipt of Freud's letter to me and the writing of my article, probably in the summer of 1934 or 1935, Henry Murray had a visit with Freud in Vienna. [Actually in 1937, as S.R. has since verified. Communication February 22, 1963.] He brought back the impression that Freud's attitude toward the work of the Harvard Psychological Clinic was more favorable than that implied in the letter Freud had written me ..."

Rosenzweig goes on to make some comments about a report brought back to him by Grinker regarding a question Freud had asked him about Rosenzweig in 1934 in which Freud expressed a more negative attitude [see Grinker, 1958, p. 132]. Rosenzweig also reports Freud's negative reaction in 1937 to becoming an advisory editor of a "Journal of Experimental Psychopathology." Janet, McDougall, and Adolf Meyer, who were also invited to serve as honorary editors, accepted. Freud, according to Rosenzweig, indicated in this later letter that he "saw no need for such a separate or special organ of publication devoted to *experimental* studies."

In a later communication (February 22, 1963), Rosenzweig states in part: "The net that I should feel justified in concluding regarding Freud's attitude toward research is that: (a) Freud was favorable to research as long as research was defined in his terms as done by *analyzed* researchers and in *life situations* that preserve the totality of the personality, etc. (b) He was opposed to experimental research of the sort involved in my memory experiments and, I would guess, Jung's word-association excursions.... (c) To use a standard psychoanalytic interpretation, I think Freud was ambivalent about research on psychoanalytic concepts ..."

What shall we make of these comments of Rosenzweig's and Schur's? In addition to accepting the justice of Schur's point about the context, we tend in general to agree with the arguments presented by both. Freud was certainly not personally inclined toward experimental studies. Neither was he enthusiastic about experimental studies carried out by others. When he was "impressed" it was by the work of people he knew, either those who were psychoanalysts, such as Hartmann, or those he considered close to psychoanalysis, such as Pötzl. (See Jones, 1957, pp. 214-215; Jones, 1955, p. 193 re Pötzl.) Toward strangers (and perhaps especially toward American strangers, whom he never could quite understand!) he tended to be suspicious or negative.

Rosenzweig's chapter on "The Experimental Study of Repression" was the earliest part of the Harvard Psychological Clinic studies, which culminated in Murray's *Explorations in Personality* (1938), one of the milestones of Freudian influence. Moreover, Rosenzweig's experiments led to Rosalind Gould's (1942) and Thelma Alper's (1946a, 1946b, 1948) studies.[37] These studies, dealing with ego-involvement vs. task-involvement, linked the experiments of Freudian and Lewinian parentage to Gordon Allport's ego psychology (1937a). Allport, though avowedly an opponent of Freudian and other genetic theories, actually proved to be a stimulus to interest in psychoanalytic subjects by his encouragement of the study of personality and ego-psychological explorations (1937a, 1937b, 1940, 1943), and by his emphasis on the idiographic approach. Rosenzweig's experiments were also supported by another line of Lewinian descent, the level of aspiration studies, which began with Hoppe's (1930) and Dembo's (1931) investigations.[38]

In addition to these considerations, however, and probably underlying them, remains the more crucial one: Lewin's theory of psychological motivation was based on the concept of tension systems which, just like Freud's theory of instinctual drives, involved a concept of psychological energies. Lewin himself wrote:

> The attempt to use topological and vector concepts in psychology originated in connection with studies concerning need, will, and personality; in other words, in a field closely related to the interests of psychoanalysis. Moreover, the topological psychologists have tried for a number of years to investigate experimentally some of the basic psychoanalytical phenomena such as substitution.
>
> Indeed there are more than superficial similarities between these approaches: (1) For both, the center of interest lies in the problems

---

[37] For a criticism and partial survey of Rosenzweig's and Alper's work relevant to our discussion, see Glixman (1948). See also Caron and Wallach (1957), and Eysenck's *Handbook of Abnormal Psychology* (1961a, pp. 278-284). See particularly the discussion of this topic in the recent chapter by MacKinnon and Dukes (1962).

[38] There is a good possibility that Rosenzweig's studies also paved the way for another line of experimentation, which was to become one of the broad channels of Freudian influence—namely the frustration experiments. (For a brief summary of his work in this area see Rosenzweig [1960].) See, for example, the volume of Dollard et al. (1939) on frustration, and Rapaport (1942b) on frustration experiments. A much later series of experiments dealing with psychodynamic mechanisms which may have a remote ancestry in Rosenzweig's work is Blum's (1961) *A Model of the Mind*.

of emotions, personality structure, and personality development. (2) Both try to break down the barriers separating the different parts of psychology. (3) Both emphasize the psychological meaning of actions and objects instead of merely their physical appearance and their "superficial" properties. (4) Both are unsatisfied with descriptions and try to deal with the conditions and causal interrelations of psychological phenomena [1937, p. 202].

Thorndike Followers: General. The complex course of the relationship of Piaget's and Lewin's motivation theories to Freud's, the similarities and substantial differences, are interesting and significant. However, the most complex and, for the spread of Freud's influence, perhaps most important relationship is the one between Freud's theories and the theories which derived from Thorndike.

Although in his animal studies (1898, 1911) Thorndike made the impulse-idea association central, in his studies on human learning (see 1913) he put the stress on the law of effect. According to the law of effect, behavior which is followed by a "satisfying state of affairs" is "stamped in," and behavior which is followed by an "annoying state of affairs" is "stamped out." This law of learning is certainly a derivative of Thorndike's own 1898 theory of the association of idea and impulse (presumably instinctual). Its terminology has lent itself, however, to a theoretical interpretation which severs it from its original nativistic conception: instinct-gratifying acts become "original satisfiers," and those which fail to gratify "original annoyers"—"success" stamps in, while "failure" stamps out. This, indeed, became the accepted interpretation of the law of effect (see Postman, 1947). Thorndike's original nativistic concept, that of the impulse, was squeezed out of the picture, and his theory became an environmentalist-empiricist nurture theory.

Experimental psychologists who attempted to test Freud's repression theory and pleasure principle for a long while interpreted them to mean that the pleasant is remembered and the painful is forgotten. With this premise, they had no way of deciding whether they were testing a hedonistic hypothesis, a Freudian hypothesis, or the law of effect. Reviews of this literature by Beebe-Center (1932, especially pp. 354-384) and Rapaport (1942a) clearly demonstrate the predicament. Were these scores of experiments then wasted effort? Were hedonism and the law of effect obstacles to the understanding and adoption of Freud's theory? To answer these questions in the affirmative would be to disregard the peculiar way in which ideas are born and spread. Actually, these experiments sustained interest in Freud, and were indications of his influence. They were attempts to apply the methods that the exact program had at its disposal to Freud's motivation theory as it concerns memory. True, this spread of influence was not without cost. The theory was equated with a few haphazardly chosen formulations from various of Freud's writings which, as we have seen, were so interpreted that they were largely indistinguishable from hedonistic propositions and from the law of effect (see Henderson, 1911; Meltzer, 1930, 1931a, 1931b). But as has already been pointed out, even to this day psychoanalysis has no systematic presentation of the kind which would prevent such arbitrary selection from its formulations.

In any case, psychology did not have the methods available to test psychoanalytic propositions proper. It seems possible that the development of theoretical understanding does not usually outstrip the range of available methods for testing the theory in question. Indeed the unsystematic form of psychoanalytic theory itself may be due to the limitations of the psychoanalytic method by which the theory was arrived at. It is easy to be critical of the "piddling" quality of psychological methods; it is irritating to hear that with them psychologists have "proved," and even more that they have "disproved," what is clinically obvious. On the other hand, no matter how negative the psychoanalyst's reaction to these efforts may be, the fact remains that such experiments are signs of and serious attempts to overcome some of the problems arising from the inexact and unsystematic formulation and elucidation of Freud's method. It should be noted that psychology has made advances toward more adequate methods for tackling Freud's theories, although it does not as yet have methods alternative to those Freud used for validating his theories. The Lewin experiments and their outgrowths were far superior, both in the methods used and in the underlying grasp of the theory being tested, to the earlier ones derived from Thorndike which obscured the differences between the law of effect, hedonistic, and psychoanalytic propositions. But even the Lewinian experiments were only a step in the development of adequate methods. We shall discuss this question later.

Let us return to the law of effect. It became one of the main conceptual tools of behaviorism, matched in importance only by Bechterev's and Pavlov's theories of conditioning, until in the hands of Hull (1943) these two trends were fused to provide a new theory of behavior. To understand the significance of this fusion for Freud's influence on psychology, we must make a detour to the historical relationship of conditioning to Freud's theory.

Conditioning, like the law of effect, was used by psychologists from an early period as a method to master and "domesticate" psychoanalysis to the exact science program. We will mention only a few such attempts which centered on the use of conditioning to explain the wish. Holt tried it abortively in 1915; Kempf tried it systematically with the aid of Bechterev's concept in 1917; Humphrey in his behaviorist days tried it repeatedly (1920, 1921, 1922a); Troland (1920, 1928, 1932) tried it by turning psychoanalysis into hedonism and by using both the reflex concept and his own retroflex concept.[39] Watson's 1916 paper, which fell just short of fully embracing Freud's instinct theory, suggests that his *Psychology from the Standpoint of a Behaviorist* (1919) may be a covert attempt in the same direction. French (1933), the noted psychoanalyst, also attempted to mate conditioning with Freud. When later he became familiar with Lewin's theory, he then proposed that as still another mate for psychoanalysis (1941, 1942).

Psychologists, including Watson, were not misguided in trying to harness psychoanalysis by whatever method they had. They were remiss, however, in not studying psychoanalysis carefully and in not understanding the instinctual drive concept. They missed the essence of this concept: a somatically rooted innate world which, as Woodworth (1927) put it, prevents man from being molded like putty by environmental forces.[40]

A psychologist-psychiatrist who did combine an attempt to fit Freud's theories into a behaviorist frame with an understanding of his concepts was G. V. Hamilton. Hamilton was a pioneer both in his early acquaintance with Freudian literature and the use of the experimental approach to psychodynamic problems. He actually began his career in medicine. But after three years of neuropsy-

[39] Troland's retroflex concept is in some ways similar to J. M. Baldwin's (1915) circular reactions which Piaget (1924, p. 179) seemed to accept. Troland, it appears to us, is one of the psychologists who has never received due recognition.

[40] For surveys of this aspect of the psychoanalytic theory, see Rapaport (1958b, 1959, 1960a).

chiatric practice, he went to Harvard to work with Yerkes, and subsequently conducted research in comparative psychology in addition to the private practice of clinical psychiatry. According to his own account (1925, p. 300), Hamilton had studied Freud's writings by at least 1907—earlier than even McDougall. While he objected to Freud's "psychomorphism," he freely acknowledged Freud's "invaluable contributions to our understanding of human behavior." In the context of the influence of Yerkes, Watson, Thorndike, Adolf Meyer, Loeb, and Jennings, he devoted himself to a behavioristic translation of Freud's concepts and of the psychoanalytic theory of sexuality, trying to fit his methods into the framework of general medicine. He recognized particularly Freud's ideas with regard to prepubertal sexual tendencies and "the 'wish' as dynamic for behavior" (1925, Chapter XII). Although he carried out systematic clinical work with patients and normal subjects (1925, 1929), perhaps his most important contributions were his studies in the comparative psychology of social and sexual interaction in animals (1914, 1916, 1925).[41]

Thorndike Followers: Hull and Yale Group. Hull's attempt to integrate psychoanalysis and conditioning was different from almost all the earlier efforts (including French's), for Hull was aware that conditioning theory was in need of a concept of motivation. Mark May and Neal Miller (in personal communications) suggest that Hull's work with rats brought to his attention for the first time the importance of hunger and motivation, and that his idea of hunger

[41] Hamilton, like Troland, is a person who has not received due recognition in psychology. Although this does not seem to be entirely because he was outside of academic psychology (for we have the example of Troland who was in the stream of psychology but still seems to have suffered a similar fate), his medical identification probably played a significant role. The predictions in Yerkes' most enthusiastic Foreword to Hamilton's *An Introduction to Objective Psychopathology* (1925, pp. 13-15) about the future place of Hamilton in psychopathology and dynamic psychology have not come to pass. With the exception of *A Research in Marriage* (1929), his work is rarely referred to now, and his important role as a pioneer in dynamic psychology seems largely forgotten. Sears (1959) is an exception. Hamilton's major works are those we have referred to.

Another person with a background in both psychiatry and psychology who became strongly identified with psychoanalysis early in his career was Trigant Burrow (1958). Like Hamilton he attempted to extend psychoanalytic principles, but applied them in the social rather than the animal frame of reference. He developed a form of group analysis which he called "phyloanalysis," and a field of study he called "phylobiology." Although his interests led to his isolation from both psychoanalysis and academic psychology, he continued to emphasize the importance of Freud's ideas for his own thinking.

as a drive derived from Cannon. May also suggests that Hull's background of functionalism, with its emphasis on adaptation, may have prompted him to postulate that if the conditioning theory of behavior is true, it follows that behavior must be unadaptive and unpurposeful. It is likely that familiarity with Thorndike, too, helped Hull in his attempt to solve the motivation problem. It is rather certain that Hull introduced into his theory first a persistent stimulus [Sp] (1930) and then a drive stimulus [SD] (1931) in order to explain purposiveness. This he did even before he restudied Thorndike and before much of the psychoanalytic influence came to bear on him at Yale.

Nevertheless, it appears that Thorndike (1898, 1927, 1933) provided Hull with a principle (the law of effect) to account for the elimination of the unpurposeful and unadaptive responses and for the reinforcement of the purposeful and adaptive ones—for which conditioning seemed unable to account. Spence believes that Hull derived his motivation concept from Thorndike: "Apparently the reading of Thorndike's *The Fundamentals of Learning* (1932), which Hull reviewed for the *Psychological Bulletin* [Hull, 1935], was the decisive factor leading him to reverse the direction of his thinking and to employ the principle of reinforcement (effect) . . . Subsequent to this review Hull's writings became more and more Thorndikean in tone, although he continued to make use of many Pavlovian concepts" (Spence, 1952, p. 645).[42]

It does appear that Hull adopted Thorndike's motivation concept and coupled it with conditioning. He nonetheless stressed that while Thorndike seemed to regard motivation as primary, he himself believed that it too could be derived from principles of conditioning. Hull also extended Thorndike's concept by defining any persistent and intense stimulus, external or internal, as a drive, that is, a motivation. The distance of this from Freud's concept of instinctual drive makes it fairly certain that Hull's concept probably did not originate in Freud's conception of motivation.[43]

Having introduced a drive concept into conditioning, Hull tried to account for psychoanalytic propositions by means of his theory of

[42] There is much here that calls for detailed historical study. Hull kept extensive notes on his reading which might well provide the necessary information.

[43] McClelland's (1957) article, "Freud and Hull: Pioneers in Scientific Psychology," draws some interesting parallels between Freud and Hull. The title of McClelland's article is perhaps the most revealing.

the conditioned response. Under the influence of the atmosphere of dedication to the integration of the social and behavioral sciences at the Yale Institute of Human Relations, and of his own urge for synthesis (or, as May puts it in a personal communication, "sparked by his success in putting Pavlov and Thorndike together"), Hull (1936-1942) started a series of seminars.[44] The purpose of these

[44] In this atmosphere Hull's relation to psychoanalysis was quite complex. During his years at Wisconsin, Hull became preoccupied with hypnosis, an interest that he carried over to his early years at Yale. (Hull was actually markedly ambivalent about this preoccupation, as is evidenced by the frequent doubts and hesitations he expressed in his "Idea Books" [Hull, 1962, pp. 849-850, 852] about the loss of status which probably resulted from his involvement with it. One cannot in this matter avoid the comparison of Hull's timidity with James' forthrightness [James, 1920a, pp. 384-385].) His pursuit of this topic made some contact with psychoanalysis inevitable. He actually did refer to Freud in his volume on hypnosis (Hull, 1933). In his "Idea Books" (Hull, 1962), Hull mentioned psychoanalysis and Freudian psychology, in relation to a book on habit, in June, 1933 (pp. 853-854), and again in January, 1937, in relation to a number of "seminars to have in the immediate future." The projected seminars included one by Sears on "morals viewed from psychoanalysis" and another by Dollard on "morals viewed from anthropology" (p. 863).

Another factor in this psychoanalytic influence was Dollard, fundamentally interested in personality and culture, who had come from a year in Berlin where he had had an analysis with Sachs. During his earlier period at Yale he worked (1932-1933) with Sapir in his international seminar on culture and personality, and continued his concern with psychocultural problems (the latter is evidenced by *Caste and Class in a Southern Town* [Dollard, 1937]). At the same time he maintained his interest in psychoanalysis. Even before the Seminars started, Dollard (1935) had published *Criteria for the Life History*, a volume based on the case-history approach. One of the cases included was Freud's "Analysis of a Phobia in a Five-Year-Old Boy." Although he was not part of the Yale psychological group in this period, Dollard did have some informal contacts with two of Hull's associates—Neal Miller, who was a graduate student, and Mowrer, who was at Yale as a Sterling Fellow. Through these contacts some influence in a psychoanalytic direction might have been exerted on Hull, especially since Miller appears to have been one of his favorite students.

By 1935 Miller had apparently become sufficiently interested in psychoanalysis to use his Social Science Research fellowship at the Institute for Psychoanalysis at Vienna, where he had an analysis with Hartmann. Presumably an earlier kindled interest led him to Vienna. This interest, which must have been expressed during his graduate days at Yale, may actually be traced back to his Stanford period with Terman (see pp. 70-71).

At the same time Sears was probably playing a considerable role from a distance. Sears had been at Yale as a graduate student under Hull from 1929 until he received his Ph.D. in 1932. (He does not remember Hull's ever mentioning Freud in his hearing during his graduate period.) He then spent the years 1932-1936 at Illinois, where he taught courses in abnormal psychology and personality, and became interested in psychoanalytic theory. During this period Sears completed at least four studies relating to psychoanalytic themes: two studies of projection, one on attribution of traits (1936a), the other on ideas of reference (1937a), a study of functional abnormalities of memory with special reference to amnesia (1936b), and an experimental study of repression (1937b). He maintained a correspondence with Hull throughout his years at Illinois. During this

seminars was to achieve a synthesis of conditioning theory and psychoanalysis. They were attended by a number of psychoanalysts and analyzed psychologists. Although this attempt to apply conditioning principles to the mastery of psychoanalytic theories was certainly not the first one, it is the most important one for the history of Freud's influence on psychology.

In the January 20, 1936 announcement of the first meeting of the Hull Seminars on January 22, Hull stated the long-range objectives as well as the immediate program:

> This is the first of a proposed series of seminars which will be devoted to an attempt to integrate the major concepts and principles of the conditioned reaction with those of psychoanalysis. Stated in another way, it will be an attempt to derive phenomena and principles covered by psychoanalysis from those of ordinary habit, and to devise ways to submit these deductions to experimental or observational test. The seminar will proceed on the basic working hypothesis that all genuine behavior principles, once we properly grasp the conditions under which they operate, will be found active throughout

---

period, Hull was much stimulated by Sears' paper on projection at the 1934 Columbia meetings of the American Psychological Association. He was also sufficiently impressed by Sears' (1936b) repression paper in the *Psychological Bulletin* to order 100 reprints, and pass them around with "what appeared to be considerable pride and pleasure." (These comments on Sears are based on a personal communication, March 26, 1963.) In 1936 Sears was invited to return as a member of the Yale staff. It thus seems likely that Sears' work at Illinois, work which seems to have been undertaken on his own and which anticipated the Yale work on psychoanalytic themes, constituted a considerable psychoanalytic influence on Hull.

Another major influence was the coming, in the fall of 1935, of Earl Zinn to Yale, where he continued his Worcester psychoanalytic recording studies. Through Zinn, and Zinn's influence on Whiting and Murdock, psychoanalytic ideas became even more strongly represented at Yale.

Other psychoanalytic influences were Edward Sapir, the anthropologist, who was frequently visited by his friend Harry Stack Sullivan; and Erik Erikson, who was also there for part of the period in which the seminars were being held.

Thus the Hull Seminars grew out of at least this complex of factors in an atmosphere where there was considerable pressure and interest toward the integration of the social and behavioral sciences (see Dollard, 1964). When the Seminars actually started in January, 1936, they did so without the presence of Sears and Miller who had apparently played a considerable role in laying the ground for them. They did not take part in the Seminars until they returned to Yale in the fall of 1936. (Some of these data come from personal communications of Dollard, May, Miller, and Sears.)

The Seminars with which we are most concerned ran from January 1936 through the spring of 1937. Although some discussions in later seminars were devoted to the relationship of psychoanalysis and behavior theory, these are not so immediately relevant for our purposes.

the whole range of mammalian behavior. Excessively complex situations, such as those presented by the psycho-neuroses, will be fertile in presenting problems; situations presented by the conditioned reflex and other learning experiments, particularly with the lower mammals, because of their relative simplicity are more favorable for the isolation of basic principles or laws, the knowledge of which should aid in the solution of such problems. If principles of action in the latter situations are natural laws, they should be general and therefore should be found active in the former situations.

. . . The present meeting, in addition to considering such preliminary matters as may present themselves, will probably be devoted largely to the consideration of the libido as a reinforcing agent.

What does Freud mean by *psychic energy?*

What do the psychoanalysts mean by *cathexis?*

How are these concepts related to the striving of an organism to attain ends?

How can striving for ends be derived from the basic idea of conditioning or reinforcement? (See pp. 817-822 of Mr. Hull's [1935] review of Thorndike's *Fundamentals of Learning*. . .)

The replies of the participating psychoanalysts to these questions did not lend themselves to the formalization Hull and his associates were after. This soon became evident, as an excerpt from Hull's seminar announcement of February 14, 1936 shows: "If, however, the present development of psychoanalytic theory does not yield clean-cut postulates such as are necessary for the deductions of theorems by strict logical methods, a possible alternative will be to formulate for ourselves various sharply defined alternative hypotheses which are consistent with current psychoanalytic views and proceed to test these by the method previously indicated."

Shortly after this (March 4, 1936), Dollard questioned whether the goal sought was attainable; O. H. Mowrer, who acted as secretary, described Dollard's query: "Dr. Dollard ended by stating that although he feels that the rigor of psychoanalysis can be greatly increased, he is convinced that the 'analytic situation' offers at present the best method of studying the kind of problems presented by the neuroses and expressed doubt as to whether its findings can be at all adequately checked 'in laboratories designed for studying other animals or problems.' "

During the rest of the academic year, the seminar vacillated between unsuccessful attempts to get "usable formulations" from the psychoanalysts present and equally unsuccessful attempts to find, in the two or three writings of Freud agreed upon for study, systematic propositions which could be transformed into workable postulates.

When the seminar gathered for the next academic year, the futility of the learning theorists' attempts to get together on a systematic basis with psychoanalysts seems to have been accepted and the unsystematic character of the psychoanalytic literature recognized. Hull then returned to the vein in which he had written on February 14, 1936, as his November 14 announcement of the seminar of November 17, 1936, shows:

> On the assumption that psychoanalysis leaves much to be desired in the matter of theoretical structure, does it follow necessarily that this is a permanent defect? Is it not conceivable that, taking the present informal elaborations of postulates contained in the literature as a guide and point of departure, there may be formulated at a fairly early date a workable postulate system accompanied by operational definitions of critical terms, and that from these two there may be derived coherent theorem sequences covering extensive fields of phenomena in psychopathology, normal psychology, sociology, and anthropology?
>
> Assuming such a systematic theory of psychoanalysis to be possible of construction, what advantages, if any, could conceivably result from the necessarily considerable expenditure of energy? Is it probable that such a logical rectification of psychoanalytic theory would add materially to its scientific and integrative power?

But instead of this ambitious schedule, the participants in the seminar made piecemeal formulations of randomly selected Freudian propositions. Hull's November 28, 1936 notice for his first December seminar (December 2, 1936) indicates that Neal Miller led in this attempt: "In connection with Dr. Dollard's presentation there came up the question of whether the characteristic principles of Freudian psychology could conceivably be reduced to rigorous scientific theory analogous to that of Newton's *Principia*. As a bit of affirmative evidence in the controversy, Dr. Neal E. Miller presented a sequence of three formally derived theorems in which the subject matter of both the postulates and theorems was characteristically Freudian."

The preparatory notes of this seminar (written by Hull) and its minutes (drafted by Mowrer)[45] show that Hull persistently called for definitions of psychoanalytic concepts. None of those with a psychoanalytic point of view, however, with the exception of Erikson, even attempted to provide such definitions. Their answers to Hull's questions usually took the form of clinical or everyday examples. If they did venture into anything abstract, it was arbitrary and apparently bewildering to the listeners, as the present authors can testify from a reading of the record. Several interesting observations and investigations corroborating Freudian propositions and observations were, however, reported in this seminar. The psychologists, including Hull, did not tire of reiterating the idea that "there is something important in that theory," but no definitions or "cleancut postulates" of psychoanalysis were forthcoming. Failing in this, Hull, followed by Dollard, Miller, Mowrer, and Sears, turned to his own hypotheses. In their own formulations, they not only attempted to define concepts, but also tried to convey something about the psychological theory—the metapsychology—of psychoanalysis.

Whatever the intrinsic merits of these formulations, a question remains about their consistency with current psychoanalytic views. On this, opinions differ sharply. We believe (Rapaport, 1952, 1953a) that they are in essence inconsistent with Freudian theories. The drive concepts of Hull, Dollard, Miller, and Mowrer helped to obscure for the majority of psychologists the distinctive nature and often even the very existence of Freud's concept of the instinctual drive. The Yale studies had a similar effect on many other psychoanalytic concepts, for instance, frustration, identification, regression, repression, projection, and displacement (Rapaport, 1942a, 1942b). Nonetheless, the various formulations are part of Freud's influence, both as symptoms and vehicles of it. There can be no doubt that Hull, Dollard, and Mowrer—all of whose drive concepts differed from that of psychoanalysis—did more than any protagonists of the Freudian conception of drive to make it familiar-sounding and talked-about by psychologists.

May and Miller (personal communications) agree, in harmony

[45] The papers—notices, abstracts of meetings, etc.—of the Hull Seminars have never been published. The permission of several of the living major participants (Dollard, Miller, Mowrer) was obtained to use the seminar material in this volume.

with the transcript of the Hull seminars, that it was Dollard who triggered the investigations aimed at reproducing and studying psychoanalytic observations experimentally, bringing psychoanalysis into the center of the stage at the Yale Institute of Human Relations. As far as can be judged at present, the major share of the credit and responsibility for the acceptance of the conception of drive is Dollard's and Miller's. To Sears and Mowrer belong the rest. Without Hull, however, none of it would have been possible, though he seems to have gotten into it the way Pontius Pilate got into the Credo.

Thus Freudian terms and crudely analogous observations invaded the experimental literature on a scale never before attained, but the price paid was that Freud's concepts were turned into vague conceptions, barely related, and at times actually contradictory, to their original forms. This kind of "acceptance" is a further obstacle to coming to grips with the theory proper. In the history of ideas, however, it often seems that passage through such a stage is unavoidable.

THE INSTINCT CONTROVERSY

Even though our discussion of Piaget, Lewin, Thorndike, and Hull was touched off by the nature-nurture controversy, we have not as yet dealt in detail with its central issue, that of instinctual drive. We must now consider this, since it is an important vehicle of Freud's influence. Some of the psychologists who expounded various notions of instinct figured significantly in the spread of that influence.

Before sketching the highlights of the controversy that developed over instinct, we must first deal with two remarkable Englishmen, Rivers and McDougall.

Rivers. Though Rivers developed his own theories, he was strongly influenced by Freud and was closely conversant with his theory. One of the many examples of the care that Rivers exercised in distinguishing his concepts from Freud's is the following:

> Freud is accustomed to speak of this process as one of distortion and in many ways the term is appropriate. It has come to stand, however, in a close relation to a feature of Freud's scheme according to which it is the function of the transformation to disguise the

real nature of the dream, so that the sleeper shall not recognize the motives by which it has been prompted. Since for the present I do not wish to commit myself to this portion of Freud's scheme, I shall abstain from using a term with which it is so closely connected. I shall therefore speak of the process by which the latent content of the dream manifests itself as one of transformation. Those familiar with Freud's work will recognize that my "transformation" corresponds almost exactly to his "distortion" [1918, p. 389].

Rivers states his own theory, which crystallized from his experiences with war neuroses, in *Instinct and the Unconscious* (1920), a volume containing some reprinted articles and a series of lectures.[46] He accepts Freud's concepts of the unconscious, repression, and instinct, although he proposes a different explanation for each, and rejects the paramount role of the sexual instincts in neuroses in general and in war neuroses in particular. Yet his careful treatment of Freud's concepts, even though he dealt with only a few of them, remains an example of a real and far-reaching influence of Freud. Independent from psychoanalysis, Rivers accepted with acknowledgment and rejected without abuse or rancor (see particularly Rivers, 1923, p. 141 ff.). He came close to the ideal of the scientist absorbing influence precisely.

McDougall is something of an enigma. It is not easy to assess his role in the spread of Freud's influence despite its undoubted importance. The interests and erudition of this singular figure spanned a broad range of psychology—abnormal, physiological, general, social, and ethnopsychology. In each of these he pioneered and made substantial contributions. Among his catholic interests were three which ultimately condemned him in the eyes of many psychologists: instincts, parapsychology, and Lamarckian evolution theory. His *hormic psychology,* at the center of which stood a conative conception, was one of the more broadly conceived psychological systems.[47] It was just as broad as Freud's in its claims, if not in its execution; in fact, it was the only theory of a breadth comparable to Freud's. To what extent he was influenced by Freud in building this theory is unclear.

From his autobiography we learn that his planned analysis with

---

[46] These lectures were given at the Johns Hopkins Medical School in 1920 under the auspices of Adolf Meyer. They had previously been given in 1919 at the Psychological Laboratory at Cambridge.
[47] See particularly his *Outline of Psychology* (McDougall, 1923).

Jung was prevented by the outbreak of the First World War. After the war, he did undertake this analysis, ". . . so far as that process is possible for so hopelessly normal a personality as mine. I made an effort to be as open-minded as possible; and came away enlightened but not convinced" (1930, p. 211). A more important contact for McDougall was Rivers, with whom he collaborated early in his professional career. McDougall's initial contact with Rivers, however, came so early—1899—(1930, p. 201) that it is unlikely to have been an immediate channel of Freudian influence. Indeed, we have already noted McDougall's assertion that he did not become familiar with Freud's writings until after he had published his *Social Psychology* in 1908. Yet his admiration for Rivers may have been lasting and the basis for later Freudian influence.[48]

In subsequent editions of *An Introduction to Social Psychology* and in his discussion at the symposium on "Instinct and Intelligence" (1910), McDougall showed sufficient familiarity with the work of Freud and his collaborators to criticize them freely, objecting to their nondifferentiating treatment of motivation (1910, p. 266). In the context of criticizing academic psychology for a disregard of instincts in general, and sex in particular (1914a, p. 66) he reproved Freud for having fastened on a single conative tendency —sex. He claimed that his judgment of Freud's emphasis on sex did not arise from moralistic concerns (1914a, p. 78) but from Freud's indiscriminate lumping of too many varied motivations under one category.

In his 1918 survey of clinical psychology, however, he treats Freud as a comrade-in-arms in the struggle against "mechanistic psychology,"[49] although criticizing Freud's residual "mechanistic"

---

[48] But see McDougall's discussion of his relationship to generally accepted theories (1930, p. 204).

[49] "This method of approach and these consequences are best illustrated by the work of Professor S. Freud, who, whatever verdict may ultimately be passed on his psycho-therapeutic methods, will certainly rank as one who has given a great impulse to psychological inquiry. . . . In this way, in his reaction from the mechanistic psychology, he has brought to light two great allied facts: (1) The impulsive, demoniac, illogical nature of much of human thought and conduct; (2) the very partial and inadequate way in which consciousness or self-consciousness reflects or represents the workings of this impulsive force. Freud's insistence on these two facts is his fundamental contribution to psychology; and it is the recognition and emphasis of them, thanks largely to his labours, that is the keynote of clinical psychology at the present time" (McDougall, 1918, p. 5).

and "hedonistic" taint. In this criticism, the first two of his arguments are plainly based on misunderstandings, but the third clearly reflects a factual appraisal.

> Freud's development of these two truths has been marred by several errors: First, his attribution to the sexual impulse of much of conduct that is not properly so attributable, and his consequent exaggeration of the rôle of sex; secondly, he has not wholly freed himself from the errors of the mechanistic psychology, in spite of his detachment from tradition, so natural are these errors to the scientific mind; two especially he has retained—(a) instead of repudiating the mechanistic determination, he claims that he has for the first time established this principle in psychology; (b) instead of repudiating *Hedonism* he has made it his own and attempted to combine it with his recognition of the impulsive nature of conduct, as what he calls the *pleasure principle,* in a very confusing way that largely vitiates his thinking. A third great blemish is, that, having repudiated the traditional terminology of psychology and having neglected to define his own terms by careful analysis, his terminology is often obscure and misleading, and, as a further consequence, the large unanalysed conceptions with which he operates tend to become anthropomorphic agencies—the unconscious, the censor, the foreconscious, &c. [1918, pp. 5-6].

A similar mixture of interest and enthusiasm on the one hand and misunderstanding on the other permeates his publications during the earlier part of his American period (1925, 1926). Both reactions were based on McDougall's appreciation of the extent to which Freud approximated or deviated from his own hormic psychology.

Clearly McDougall read, and for the most part understood and appreciated, Freud. Thus it is particularly enlightening to see how his own system and interests limited a full understanding of Freud. For he did not seem to gain enough mastery of Freud's theory to appreciate fully its contribution to the topics at hand. Nevertheless, although Freud's work may not have influenced the foundations of McDougall's theory, it surely reinforced McDougall's persistence in advocating and expanding his own theory. Although it may be too much to claim that McDougall's work was a major vehicle for Freud's influence, it is certain that he served in his years at Harvard—1921-1927—as a force in this direction, as well as a link between James, and Prince and Murray and his group in the 1930's at the Harvard Psychological Clinic.[50] As Murray (1938, p. 37) said: "Outside the universities, the medical psychologists—and here we may, without serious omissions, start with Freud—have for five decades been constructing a quintessentially dynamic theory. For this theory the academic psychologists, with the exception of McDougall, found themselves entirely unprepared. . . . McDougall and the analysts have been kept apart by numerous differences, but in respect to their fundamental dynamical assumptions they belong together."

It may at first seem astonishing to find that Freud's concept of the instinctual drive was rarely brought specifically into discussions of instinct. Although the conception of instinct was vague, it could nevertheless be clearly differentiated from Freud's concept of instinctual drive. On further consideration, however, this general omission appears quite natural. As we have seen, the two major statements of his theory appeared in *Three Essays on the Theory of Sexuality* (1905b) and "Instincts and Their Vicissitudes" (1915a). The evidence seems to indicate that the 1915 paper, which was the more theoretical statement of the two, was rarely referred to by psychologists, while the 1905 book was read for what it said about sex. Even if there had been a clear-cut statement of Freud's instinctual drive concept which was commonly read, it might well have been found too unlike the general conception of instinct to be included in this controversy. But in spite of its marked differences, Freud's concept eventually became so strongly identified with the instinct conception that they were condemned or defended together.

In the case of instinct, we are again faced with the peculiarity of the process of influence. The conception of instinct is ancient

---

[50] In *Explorations in Personality* (1938) Murray wrote: "We were largely guided in the construction of our generalizations by the theories of Freud and McDougall, as well as those of Jung, Rank, Adler, Lewin and others" (p. 24; also see p. 38).

One of us (Shakow) was at Harvard both as undergraduate and graduate student during practically all of the period when McDougall was there and took most of the courses and seminars he offered. What surprised a student without any biases except a "motivation to understand human nature" was McDougall's lack of following, particularly among the "experimental" students, despite his world prominence. This was particularly striking during graduate days, when McDougall had few students doing their dissertations with him. It was hard to get away from a feeling that the more immediate *Zeitgeist* was just not with him. His influence on the "dynamic" students Murray speaks of occurred after he had left Harvard.

(see Wilm, 1925; Drever, 1917), but its importance for psychology came at the turn of the century in the wake of Darwin's influence, the general aspects of which we considered earlier. Apparently, even as early as the 1910's the general notion of instinct aided the spread of Freud's influence. The 1910 British symposium, "Instinct and Intelligence" (Myers et al., 1910) and the 1919 British symposium discussed above, "Instinct and the Unconscious" (Rivers et al., 1919), clearly indicate the status of this conception. These symposia also indicate that it had more vigor in England than in the United States. In the second decade of the century, however, many of its supporters turned against the concept, and it became the target of the "objectivist," "behaviorist" revolt. Although it managed to survive the assault, the net historical effect of this was, for a period in American psychology, a virtual taboo on the nature conception in general and the instinct conception in particular. Although in the United States the process was slow, the negators of the instinct concept did win a temporary victory.[51]

[51] The "victory" was portrayed by L. L. Bernard in his book (1924) and articles (1921, 1923) on instincts. In "Instincts and the Psychoanalysts" (Bernard, 1923, pp. 365-366) he wrote: "... it is now time for the psychoanalysts to advance from the naïve biological and inheritance interpretation of conflict and psychoneuroses to a more sophisticated and analytical environmental analysis. It can scarcely be questioned that the psychoanalysts have brought to the attention of the psychologists and especially the psychiatrists some extremely valuable data. They have emphasized a phase of consciousness of the utmost importance individually and socially which, because of the strong predilection for an intellectualistic interpretation of social and individual action regnant in the nineteenth century, had been neglected or overlooked. Whether their contribution is to rank as one of the three great discoveries of method in science, comparable, as Freud seems to think, to the work of Darwin, remains yet to be determined. Nor can it be determined until the theory becomes dominantly scientific and drops its metaphysical preconceptions.... It must be admitted that the instinct interpretation has been forced upon psychoanalytic theory largely as a short cut method of making it square with the approved biological and psychological interpretations of action and attitude, of conduct. But the psychologists and biologists are coming to see that the individually and socially significant phases of conduct, in members of the human type at least, are not inherited, but are determined by environmental pressures....

"While it is important to analyze the so-called instincts of the psychoanalysts and the social and educational psychologists into true inherited action patterns (where these can be isolated) as a method of arriving at the actual original nature of man, it is of even more importance to account for the large residue remaining from these so-called instincts which must be attributed to an environmental origin. The acquired element in most human action patterns is much larger than the instinctive.... While a further analysis and better understanding of the inherited nature of man—especially if it results in getting down to the fundamental and inherited activity units—will help in solving this problem, the chief aid must

J. B. Watson, who spearheaded the drive against the "nature" conception, and especially against instincts, began, as we have mentioned, in the opposite camp. In contrast to his later famed slogan which may be paraphrased as "Give me any child and I will make of him what you want," in 1913 he wrote: "The psychology which I should attempt to build up would take as a starting point . . . the observable fact that organisms, man and animal alike, do adjust themselves to their environment by means of hereditary and habit equipments" (1913, p. 167). Harrell and Harrison (1938), studying the course of the development of Watson's theories, summarize this aspect of it as follows: "True to his Darwinian and his functional heritage, Watson initially published elaborate lists of instincts and only performed a *volte face* after the attacks of Dunlap [1919, 1920] and Kuo [1921, 1922]. His works present chronologically an ever decreasing enthusiasm for instinct which was reinforced by the introduction into psychology of the conditioned response" (p. 381). When Watson, under Dunlap's and Kuo's influence, turned against the concept of instinct, his (as well as the other behaviorists' and functionalists') previous marriage to it was forgotten. Nothing remained of Watson's inclination to psychoanalysis except his interest in sex and his misunderstanding of Freud's theory of the Oedipus complex, a misunderstanding which led him to advise (Watson and Watson, 1928, pp. 69-87) a mechanical handling of infants to avoid oedipal involvement. Bernard's (1924) volume on instincts is a monument to this rejection of instinct. Yet like all victories—particularly in a struggle of ideas—this one was not complete.

It would seem that Freudian influence, although impeded by the victory of the anti-instinct trend in American psychology, had an important share in maintaining the instinct concept in the texture of psychology. For example, Floyd Allport, in spite of his behavioristic leanings, did not jettison the idea of instinct. His *Social Psychology* (1924) was the first text on social psychology to give a careful if brief discussion of Freudian theory, based though it was

---

come from an understanding and control of the environmental pressures which are overtaxing man's native equipment. Such an analysis of environment and its influence in producing conflicts will constitute a more scientific approach to an explanatory psychoanalytic theory."

on secondary sources. Chapter XIV, on social adjustment, seems to be strongly influenced by Freud's conceptions.

E. C. Tolman. Freudian theories affected Tolman much as they affected Floyd Allport. Tolman's disappointment with psychology at Harvard has already been mentioned. It is no surprise, therefore, that he held out against the behaviorist attack on instincts (1920, 1922, 1923). It is, however, a surprising comment on the nature of influence that Tolman's first encounter with psychoanalysis actually served to quiet some of his doubts about behaviorism. In a personal communication (December 22, 1955), Tolman wrote:

> When I was starting out to be a behaviorist, I remember that it seemed to me then (perhaps in a rather illogical fashion) that Freud's demonstration of so much going on in the unconscious helped to support the behavioristic position. If introspection could not tell you anything about the whys and wherefores of unconsciously determined behavior it probably was equally useless as regards much of so-called consciously determined behavior. I don't think that I ever made this point in writing. And it certainly is a distortion of the Freudian doctrine. But nonetheless it did at the time give me emotional support.

It seems clear, however, that the full impact of Freud's influence on Tolman did not come until later. In his autobiography (1952, p. 339), he wrote: "... most of the credit ... should go to my year's stay in Vienna and especially to Egon Brunswik, who opened my eyes to the meaning and the viability of the European psychological tradition, both academic and psychoanalytical, and who gave me new insight into the essentially 'achievement' character of behavior." But, perhaps above all, Tolman's receptiveness to psychoanalysis was an outgrowth of his personality—his lack of arrogance and his tolerance for other points of view.

Psychoanalytic influence[52] is evidenced by a subtle and unobtru-

---

[52] A student of Tolman's told one of us (Shakow) that at California in the post-World War II years his lectures were studded with references to Freud, and he once stated that if he were coming into psychology now—1952—he would be a clinical psychologist. In 1949 or 1950 he sat in on the fourth-year psychotherapy case conference seminar at Berkeley, saying in his typically generous and self-effacing way, "to find out about psychotherapy from the people who are doing it."

Freud's influence did not affect Tolman as it affected some academic psychologists. We refer to those who, once let loose in the clinical pastures, throw off the discipline of their academic thinking, and not having as yet acquired the discipline of clinical responsibility, engage in crude, unbridled speculation.

sive self-appraisal in Tolman's autobiography and is partly woven into the very fabric of his theory. About the latter, he wrote:

> ... I have taken over from Freud: (1) the notion that the determiners of much behavior are not to be found in introspective consciousness; (2) a sort of hydraulic notion of drives and of a general libido—though not specifically an erotic one; (3) notion of cathexes or channels by which objects get values or valences; (4) the validity of most of the defense mechanisms and a feeling that they must somehow be fitted into a general theory of learning, lack of learning, distortion of learning or what not; and (5) a conviction that there *is* some important difference about how perceptions, expectancies, beliefs and motives which get into consciousness and those which do not get into consciousness. But I haven't been able to do much about this latter.[53]

Tolman's influence was probably far less widespread than that of the Yale group—Hull, Dollard, Miller, and Mowrer. Yet his theory, methods of thinking, and experiments seem to have been the main, if not the sole, check on the hegemony Hull's theories enjoyed in the late 1930's and 1940's. Tolman kept open such issues as latent learning, expectancy, and discontinuity, areas which in the long run should prove crucial for the development of a psychology of learning both relevant to and compatible with psychoanalysis.

Woodworth. Our discussion of the instinct controversy would be incomplete without a consideration of Woodworth. Woodworth indicates in his autobiography (1932) that he was influenced by Stanley Hall and particularly by James. In 1891 James set Woodworth to work on a study of dreams. Although the findings of this study were never published, some of them antedated Freud's.[54] He reports

---

[53] Personal communication, December 22, 1955. This retrospective view of his relation to psychoanalytic theory is amply substantiated and documented in Tolman's writings (particularly 1942, 1943, 1945, 1949a, 1949b).

[54] "James, in his abnormal psychology—a course in which he was at his best, and in which he became well known to his students through the visits to institutions on which he piloted us—James set me to work on dreams. Besides consulting the literature, I recorded many of my own dreams and made certain experiments on the speed of continued association and revery in waking conditions, as a check on the often asserted extraordinary speed of dreams. I found the speed sufficient in waking revery to account for all the instances of rapid dreaming that had seemed so remarkable. I also was led by my readings and records to a hypothesis on the cause of dreams that I have often wished I had published, as it has a certain resemblance, along with a difference, to Freud's conceptions which were published a few years later. Ives Delage had pointed out that we do not dream

THE UNCONSCIOUS AND MOTIVATION 151

that around the same time he said to Thorndike that he wanted to work in "motivology." His persistence in this intention throughout his long and productive career is amply attested to by his publications (for example, 1918, 1927, 1958). Despite this focus, his adherence to the exact science program has never been questioned.

Woodworth's (1918) volume of his Jessup lectures, given in 1916-1917, entitled *Dynamic Psychology*,[55] appears to have been a beacon light during the period of rigid behaviorism for those who, in spite of the lack of exact methods for the study of motives and personality, did not abandon interest in them. On the subject of instinct Woodworth wrote in *Dynamic Psychology* and later in "A Justification of the Concept of Instinct" (1927) with an unparalleled incisiveness. His argument could well have been that of a most far-sighted psychoanalyst who was ready to meet psychologists on their own terms and grounds:

> One link in the chain, indeed, the getting of food to the lips, depends on accidents of the environment, and is a loose link and subject to modification through learning. Yet it would be absurd, after some modification of this link, to speak of the whole chain as a habit complex. Even after the adult has regularized his hours and places of eating, his choice of foods, and his table manners, it would be absurd to speak of nutritive behavior as the "habit of nutrition", since the sequence of processes, taken as a whole, remains as instinctive as ever.
>
> What is so clear in the case of hungry behavior is probably true also of thirsty behavior, of sleepy behavior, of sex behavior, and in other instances—perhaps even of fighting, though here, as often, it

---

of matters that fully occupy us during the day, but of something else. I thought I could see that we dreamed about matters that had been opened up but interrupted or checked during the day. Any desire or interest aroused during the day, but prevented from reaching its goal, was likely to recur in dreams and be brought to some sort of conclusion that was satisfactory in the dream, while activities that had probably taken much more time and energy during the day, but had been carried through to completion, were conspicuous by their absence from the dream. But the wishes 'fulfilled' in the dream, according to my idea, were of any sort—sometimes mere curiosity—and the suppression of them which had occurred during the day might be the result of external interruption as well as of moral censorship" (Woodworth, 1932, pp. 365-366).

[55] We have not succeeded in tracing the origins of the term "dynamic psychology" in this modern sense. It is worth noting, however, that F. L. Wells' reviews and summaries of psychoanalytic, functionalist, and related literature appeared in the *Psychological Bulletin* from 1913 to 1916 under the title "Dynamic Psychology." Wells, in a communication (December 31, 1962), said: "Sorry, I cannot now recall what was the 'precipitating cause' of my using the term Dynamic Psychology in this connection."

is unfortunate that the name given to the instinct applies primarily to the adult and greatly modified condition of the behavior complex. When we can trace out a genetic continuity from the early and native to the adult form of a given type of performance, and when the real core of the performance remains the same through all modifications, then we can properly speak of an instinct. Unmodified instincts of any great complexity will probably not be found in the human adult; and only careful ontogenetic study will show how wide the scope of instinct, unmodified or modified, may be. So far from being a sedative to research—and this is another of the objections that has been raised against instinct—the concept of instinct is sure to be in the future, as it has been in the past, the incentive to painstaking study of the developing individual.

In the last analysis, the difficulty with scrapping instinct is that instinct does not stand alone. It is one of a system of interrelated and contrasting concepts, among which reflex, emotion and habit are the most important. If we eliminate instinct but keep the alternative concepts, we force our descriptions of behavior into an incomplete and insufficient set of molds. We take the edge off of the concept of a reflex. We introduce the false connotation of "mere habit" into our account of modified instinctive behavior. We lose sight of the continuity of individual development. We make a breach between human and animal psychology. We may be driven to the absurd extreme of denying to biological heredity any important part in the life of the human adult. Either keep instinct, I should say, or else let the whole outfit go. Clear the decks of all these old concepts, and take a fresh start with the concrete actualities of behavior. Until we are ready to try this radical experiment—which, after all, might prove worth trying—we had better keep instinct, if only as a foil to habit. Without the concept of instinct to hold it in check, the concept of habit is bound to lead us very far astray [1927, pp. 6-7].

Thus Woodworth apparently anticipated some of Freud's findings in his dream studies and, through his interest in motives, contributed to a general receptiveness to Freud's influence. In addition, he anticipated and prepared the ground for present-day ego psychology. In *Dynamic Psychology* he wrote:

In short, the power of acquiring new mechanisms possessed by the human mind is at the same time a power of acquiring new drives; for every mechanism, when at that stage of its development when it has reached a degree of effectiveness without having yet become entirely automatic, is itself a drive and capable of motivating activities that lie beyond its immediate scope. The primal forces of hunger, fear, sex, and the rest, continue in force, but do not by any means, even with their combinations, account for the sum total of drives actuating the experienced individual [Woodworth, 1918, p. 104].[56]

Woodworth became the acknowledged dean and elder statesman of scientific psychology. His union of the aspirations of the exact science program with an unflagging interest in motivation makes him a unique figure for the study of Freud's influence. We have already noted[57] his shift from the position of a sharp and sometimes irritated critic who saw merit in Freud's factual discoveries but rejected his theories, to that of an appreciator of the role Freud's discoveries and theories played in enriching psychology, who regretted that these discoveries and theories had not been subjected to the accepted tests of scientific validity.

We might raise the questions, why did not Woodworth's profound and lifelong interest in "motivology" and his critical interest in psychoanalysis lead him, or any of his many students, to an experimental exploration of motivation or to an experimental test of psychoanalytic theories? Indeed, why did not Woodworth publish, or return to, his early studies of dreams? Surely Woodworth, in contrast to the psychoanalysts and many clinical psychologists, did have command of the methods of psychological experimentation available at the time. One possible answer that presents itself is the one Thurstone considered in his autobiography (1952, p. 318): despite his interest in and acknowledgment of the perhaps central importance of personality study, he turned to other problems in which he could "invent experimental leverage." Whatever variety

---

[56] Woodworth's range is impressive. In addition to having anticipated in part Lewin's conception of "interrupted tasks" (see Birenbaum, 1930; Rickers-Ovsiankina, 1928; Zeigarnik, 1927; also see footnote 54, pp. 150-151), he also anticipated Gordon Allport's functional autonomy (1937a), Hartmann's (1950a) automatization and autonomy conceptions, and even the present-day curiosity, novelty, manipulative, and competence (see R. W. White, 1959, and particularly, 1963) drive conceptions. Woodworth elaborated his conception in *Dynamic Psychology*, during the running argument with McDougall's *Social Psychology* (1914b). (Woodworth used the 1914 eighth edition of McDougall's *An Introduction to Social Psychology*, originally published in 1908.) It is worth noting that McDougall, in his response to Woodworth, said that he had already propounded such a conception in his *Social Psychology:* " 'In the developed human mind there are springs of action of another class, namely, acquired habits of thought and action' " (1920, p. 282). A critical scrutiny of McDougall's conception indicates, however, that it lacked a concept of autonomy. In any case, it appears to have gone unnoticed.

[57] See p. 69 and footnote 32, Chapter 4.

of reasons lay behind the mutual misunderstandings between psychology and psychoanalysis, we see raised once again the point we have already mentioned: the exact methods which were necessary to test psychoanalytic propositions and to explore motivation and personality experimentally were just not available.

DYNAMIC PSYCHOLOGISTS

Finally, in our survey of the complexities of Freud's relationship to ideas of motivation in psychology, we shall look at several outstanding dynamic psychologists who were influenced by Freud.

F. L. Wells. We have already encountered F. L. Wells, since Jung's death the only person living from the famous picture taken at the 1909 meeting at Clark University. Wells was much concerned with dynamic psychology, and was constantly expanding his range beyond the Freudian. It seems that his extreme nonpartisanship, his general erudition, and his wide-ranging interest in folkways[58] would not let him remain within ordinary bounds. Wells gave considerable space to Freudian themes in his books, although he had relatively few firsthand references to Freud;[59] for example, his extensive discussions of defense rarely referred to Freud or to psychoanalysis. He helped spread Freudian influence by his independent articles on psychoanalytic themes. His reviews in the *Psychological Bulletin*, beginning in 1912, were among the main sources through which psychologists became acquainted with psychoanalytic literature during this period.[60]

These reviews and articles are accurate and fair-minded as well as critical and speculative. For instance, in his review of *The Inter-*

---

[58] It is noteworthy that in the Preface to *Mental Adjustments* (Wells, 1917a, p. viii) he acknowledged particularly his debt to Frazer and Sumner.

[59] In *Mental Adjustments* (Wells, 1917a) his main reference books were Pfister, Jung, and Prince, and he made no bibliographic reference to Freud. His discussions of Freud and psychoanalysis were limited to sketches of mental images, the unconscious, dreams, transference, regression, sublimation, repression, and the importance of early experience (see pp. 41, 105-106, 108, 109-110, 126, 136, 150, 288, 307). In *Pleasure and Behavior* (1924) the psychoanalytic notions he covered were sublimation, Oedipus complex, conflict and introversion, and dreams and daydreams (see pp. 24-25, 135-136, 223-224, 229-230, 253, 258).

[60] Wells' reviews succeeded those of Adolf Meyer, August Hoch, and other psychiatrists in the same journal. Although Meyer and Hoch published reviews in a psychological journal, and although they had considerable influence on psychology, we are not discussing them in this volume since Burnham (unpublished manuscript) will be considering them at length. For a summary of some of the reviews of Meyer and Hoch see Burnham (1958, pp. 55-60).

pretation of Dreams in *The Journal of Philosophy, Psychology, and Scientific Methods* (1913c), Wells summarized the major concepts and the organization of the book in a balanced and concise fashion. He praised Freud's style highly, as was to be expected of an expert in German and a connoisseur of fine literature, but considered that the volume was "not very systematically put together . . . abounds in repetition . . . rambles interestingly along, more or less free association fashion" (1913c, p. 554), and briefly but sharply criticized the concept of "wish."

He gave a sarcastic and devastating criticism of the translation, and was even more sharply critical of Brill's introduction:

> "No one is really qualified to use or judge Freud's psychoanalytic method," runs part of the translator's preface, "who has not thoroughly mastered his theory of the neuroses—"The Interpretation of Dreams," "Three Contributions to the Sexual Theory," "The Psychopathology of Everyday Life," and "Wit and its Relation to the Unconscious," and who has not had considerable experience in analyzing the dreams and psychopathological actions of himself and others. That there is required also a thorough training in normal and abnormal psychology goes without saying." This is at best an ungallant flight from criticism, since no one lives who has these qualifications; hyperbole that may be justified in proselytizing for a faith, but in scientific matters one is better concerned with the justice of the criticism than with the competence of the critic [pp. 554-555].

Wells also added, at some length, a clinical vignette and a selection of a *Bestiary* from a medieval text as illustrations of symbolic relationships independent from the psychoanalytic method. The end of the review may perhaps be taken as Wells' motto: "He is the most fortunate who is not prevented by factors of personal affect from seeing and using what is advantageous in all" (p. 555).[61]

In his articles Wells was perhaps less friendly to psychoanalysis. He was more inclined to criticize sharply what he considered arbitrary in the methods and claims of psychoanalysis, while simultaneously engaging in speculations not backed by either the psychoanalytic or the experimental method. In his "Critique of Impure Reason" (1912) he endeavored "to point out some special reasons

---

[61] In a personal note dated December 31, 1962, Wells said: ". . . I owed understanding of this sentiment largely to psychoanalytic influence, though at a verbal level it goes back at least to Julius Caesar."

why these doctrines have not had, and in their present form ought scarcely to expect, sympathetic recognition at the hands of a discriminating psychology" (p. 89). Although he did not deny either the role of symbolism in dreams or that of "the hidden tendency" in parapraxes, he concluded: "Whatever of these theories be true or false, there seem to have been but scattered attempts to submit them to the test of experiential [experimental?] conditions" (p. 92). He also took exception to the "resistances" argument, using the reverse of it on psychoanalysts to ask whether or not their theory attracted a certain kind of person: ". . . a type of personality that would be attracted to psychoanalysis by the very prominence it gives to sexual factors, . . . perhaps affording to the sexual feelings a not disagreeable stimulation of the safer and cheaper sort" (p. 93). But his vision was much keener than is implied by the above. In "On Formulation in Psychoanalysis" (1913a) he wrote: ". . . upon the basis of a body of observational data, probably the most intimate ever focussed upon psychological questions, are constructed many theories of mental function, scarcely one of which has been assimilated to the psychology of scientific method" (p. 217). On the other hand, he asked: "Has due care been exercised to keep the interpretation of your splendid body of observational data within the limits of what they really showed, or is it often subordinated to impressiveness of statement, with just a tinge of what we clinically know as the 'desire to astonish'? Have you never said 'Freud has discovered,' where he only surmised? The same looseness of formulation that, perhaps, facilitated their applicability to data of clinical observation, has unquestionably retarded their assimilation with the more rigid standards of experimental proof" (p. 227). He felt "strongly that an ameliorated formulation will not only make it easier for every one to appreciate adequately what is already known, but will obviate many natural barriers of resistance to the correct interpreting of future observations" (p. 218). Nevertheless, if we look at Wells' papers (1916, 1917b), and even a late paper (1935a) which anticipates some of the concepts of psychoanalytic ego psychology, we find that his massing of literary allusions and anthropological references left him open to the same kind of criticism which he directed at psychoanalysis. Thus we see this perhaps most sympathetic critic of psychoanalysis—scholarly, erudite, insightful[62]—caught up in difficulties similar to those of Freud and his followers.

H. A. Murray might be labeled as an eclectic Freudian-Jungian-Adlerian psychoanalyst, but is primarily a Henry Murrayan. His *Explorations in Personality* (1938) and his leadership in the Harvard Psychological Clinic[63] and the O.S.S. Assessment program played as significant a role as the Yale group in spreading concern and interest in the exploration of motivation. The Harvard group actually did more than any other to spread Freudian interest in the human personality as a whole. Murray brought a great deal to the study of personality. He not only triggered a good part of the projective testing "movement" through his Thematic Apperception Test, and encouraged an interest in healthy human assets, but also contributed his pluralistic theory of motivation. In Murray's pluralistic theory, we find a presentation of Freud's conception, but not his concept, of motivation. It seems related to Shand's, and to McDougall's, which we have already discussed.[64] His concept of needs is supplemented by his concept of presses and by a concept of sentiments compounded of Shand's and McDougall's concept of sentiment.

Murray also stimulated systematic study of the role of reality factors through his concept of presses. Since 1911,[65] psychoanalytic theory has increasingly taken cognizance of reality factors, but when Murray began to write about presses in the mid-1930's, psychoanalysis had not translated its own interest into detailed study. In this respect, present-day psychoanalytic ego psychology still lags behind.[66] Murray's needs, sentiments, and presses have

[62] And an old student of his (Shakow) must add "with a wonderful sense of humor." Who else would organize a whole year's course on "Mental Adjustments" around slides made up from cartoons taken mostly from *The New Yorker?*

[63] In our previous discussion of Prince (p. 104 ff.) we did not say anything about his part in the foundation of what he decided to call the Harvard Psychological Clinic. In 1926 he brought some money to Harvard from an anonymous donor with a wish to establish a Department of Abnormal Psychology. Instead, he was appointed Associate Professor of Abnormal and Dynamic Psychology within the Department of Psychology. When the Harvard Psychological Clinic was established within the next few years, Prince became its Director. He remained in this post until his death in 1929, when Henry Murray took over.

[64] See McDougall's "Motives in the Light of Recent Discussion" (1920).

[65] The date of Freud's "Formulations on the Two Principles of Mental Functioning."

[66] An independent and incisive attempt toward the study of reality factors was made by Heider (1958).

prompted many investigations which are likely to be recognized in the long run as studies of ego and "interests."

Other Dynamic Psychologists. MacCurdy was another outstanding dynamic psychologist. His approach is critical, as shown by his extensive and detailed criticism of Freud's general theories in *Problems in Dynamic Psychology* (1922). His *Psychology of Emotion* (1925), however, stands as witness to Freud's impact on him, an impact mediated by Adolf Meyer and August Hoch. But his work was hardly read and rarely referred to, even though it is one of the most careful phenomenological studies in the psychological literature in the English language.

There was also Dom T. V. Moore, whose textbook (1924) gave perhaps the most extensive place to Freud's ideas of all the textbooks of the period. He is also the only one who, up to 1919, had carried out studies (1919) similar to the hypnagogic "experiments" of the psychoanalyst Silberer. His findings were along similar lines. He apparently originated the concepts "psychotaxes" and "parataxes" (1921), the latter of which came to play a central role in the psychoanalyst Harry Stack Sullivan's thinking.[67]

Summary

In this chapter we have attempted to trace the fate of Freud's concepts of the unconscious and of motivation. We have already seen both the favorable and unfavorable effects of the long history of the conception of the unconscious upon psychology's reception and understanding of Freud's theory.

In the case of motivation, we have seen how Freud's theory was caught up in the controversies related to the polarities of determinism-teleology, mechanism-vitalism, pro- and antihedonism, and nature-nurture. These controversies served as obstacles to the penetration of Freud's concepts, but nevertheless helped to spread his general conception of motivation. The very involvement of his theory on both sides of the controversies clearly demonstrates the misunderstandings of it which were prevalent.

---

[67] In passing, we might remark that since these concepts add nothing to Freud's concepts of primary and secondary processes, one wonders how Sullivan read Freud.

When we examine the specific course of Freud's theory of motivation, we see its relationships to certain aspects of the association and act psychology of his predecessors Herbart and Brentano ("active ideas" and "intentionalism"), and its similarities to such sibling theories as those of Thorndike, Claparède, and Ach. Definite likenesses can also be seen between Freud and the theories which derived from these latter three psychologists—those of Piaget, Lewin, and the adopters of Thorndike's "law of effect," most particularly in Hull and the Yale group.

Piaget's theories show parallels to Freud's theories in their union of nature and nurture, in the pervasive role they give to motivation, and in their hierarchic conception of motivation. Lewin's theories of tension systems and his concern with emotions can also be seen as parallels to Freud. The attempt made by Hull and the Yale group to reconcile psychoanalysis with conditioned-reflex theory generally resulted in an invasion of the literature by Freudian terms, but at the price of turning Freud's concepts into conceptions only barely related and sometimes contradictory to the original concepts. There can be no doubt, however, that Hull's drive concept and those of Dollard and Miller and Mowrer, all of which differed from the psychoanalytic one, did a great deal to make Freudian ideas familiar and of great interest to psychologists.

If we follow Freud's concepts along another line of development, along the line of instinct, we see a somewhat similar result. The comparison of the "instinct" conception with Freud's concept of "instinctual drive" reveals developments which were both an aid in a general way to keeping the "instinct" idea alive and a hindrance in a specific way to Freudian influence. We see this both in those who rebelled against the instinct idea—Bernard, Watson, Kuo—and in those who, like Tolman and Woodworth, needed some kind of nativist conception for the completion of their psychological systems. In the case of McDougall, who was particularly concerned with a nativist basis for his psychology, Freud's emphasis on the drive concept appears to have had the effect of reinforcing his persistence in his own hormic psychology.

It is difficult to epitomize the meandering course of Freud's influence on the birth and development of motivation theories in psychology. One can only be amazed by the intricate intertwining of influence and by the unpredictable channels through which influences are effected. What appears highly probable, however, is that the passage through a stage of "acceptance," which amounts mainly to taking the specificity out of concepts and turning them into vague conceptions, is unavoidable in the historical process.

6

APPRAISALS, SURVEYS, AND REFERENCE WORKS BY PSYCHOLOGISTS DEALING WITH PSYCHOANALYSIS

Many other substantive areas in psychology that are close to and affected by psychoanalysis have come to the fore in recent years. Among these are cognition without awareness, dream studies related to psychophysiology, personality and affective processes in perception, studies in attention cathexis and other developments in relation to ego psychology, and ethology. There are, besides, many psychoanalytic concepts whose course of influence we have either not dealt with at all or have merely touched upon. But since we must set certain limits upon our work, we will close our attempt to trace Freud's influence with an examination of general survey material in the psychological literature. This material includes, on the one hand, studies directed primarily at psychoanalysis, such as general appraisals of psychoanalysis, surveys of experiments testing psychoanalytic theories, and consideration of special psychoanalytic themes in the *Psychological Bulletin;* and on the other hand, studies directed primarily at psychology, such as histories, readings, and dictionaries of psychology.

Appraisals of Psychoanalysis

The four general appraisals we shall consider were made by Dunlap (1920), Jastrow (1932), Albert Ellis (1950), and Rapaport (1959).

Knight Dunlap, one of the most vociferous and often irresponsible critics of psychoanalysis, wrote frequently, though informally,[1] about sex, childhood, marital relations, and other "Freudian" themes. Dunlap's *Mysticism, Freudianism and Scientific Psychology* (1920) endeavored to demonstrate that psychoanalysis was a new brand of mysticism which violated logic and the scientific canon, and that its findings should be rejected outright. He simultaneously characterized the undeniable core of Freudian propositions as "old hat":

> In an equally naive way the Freudians deduce from time to time other important "discoveries" from the Freudian principles. The great importance of sex in human life is something which is supposed to have been entirely unknown until pointed out by Freud. It is a constant surprise to disciples of the Vienna physician that a psychologist may recognize, and even emphasize, the fundamental role which sex ideas and sex activities play in mind and conduct and yet not be a Freudian. Even the principles of the association of ideas, are, by frequent implication, products of psychoanalysis. The fact that all the details of conscious conduct are causally directed by the results of previous experience was, according to psychoanalysis, never surmised until Freud's *Psychopathology of Everyday Life* appeared. Students unacquainted with psychology, who get their first knowledge of commonplace psychological facts from Freudian sources, necessarily look upon Freud as the founder of modern mental science [p. 94, note].

In the same volume, he says:

> Concerning "repression" there are certain important observations which should be made, although these observations do not strictly pertain to our general critique of the Freudian system. There is a psychological fact which corresponds in a rudimentary way to the

---

[1] One of Dunlap's most "informal" writings is "A Scientific Psycho-Analysis of Some Classic Verses," a parodic reinterpretation of classic nursery rhymes. (Evidence that this production is Dunlap's will be found in Dunlap, 1914, p. 151.)

In this connection we might mention Titchener's "An Attempt at Freudian Analysis," a symbolic interpretation of the motives of a "favorable reviewer of recent Freudian literature," a certain "Mr. X." (The evidence that this is Titchener's is based on Boring's memory and on both internal and external evidence. See the memorandum from Boring for the Titchener Papers at Cornell, dated August 3, 1961. The author parodied is Rudolph Acher.)

The fact that Freudian symbolic theory lent itself so readily to such off-color manipulations probably played a role in strengthening negative attitudes—here was a frivolous occupation for lighter moments, one which could be easily rationalized into skepticism in more serious moments.

mystical "repression." In the first place things which are now "in consciousness" may be in a few moments forgotten. We are constantly forgetting things and in many cases this forgetting is aided and accelerated by voluntary processes. In common language: we try to forget and this trying is sometimes efficacious.

We do not, of course, suppose that what is forgotten still exists, in the same form as before, but stored in an "unconscious warehouse" of the mind. An idea is not a thing like a written document which, after being in the active files is taken out and stored in the transfer case. It is more like an *act* such as snapping the fingers or striking a blow [p. 105].

Proportionate to what might be expected, Dunlap's chapter on psychoanalysis has relatively few direct quotations from or bibliographic references to Freud; the references are mainly to Freudian psychoanalysts, and a number are also to Jung. Yet Dunlap's preoccupation with arguments against psychoanalysis made him think about Freudian themes. In the process he rediscovered that some of them had a place in psychology, and he marshaled—for better or for worse—his observations of neurotic acts and sex abnormalities. There is no doubt that Dunlap was much read at the time, although his general iconoclasm probably restricted his influence.[2]

In 1932 Jastrow produced *The House that Freud Built,* the most extensive "treatment" of psychoanalysis put forth by a psychologist up to that time. (He had published a volume entitled *The Subconscious* in 1906 without apparent awareness of Freud's concept of the unconscious.) It should be pointed out that by this time he had left Academe for more popular psychological activities. The tone of this volume (1932), mentioned earlier in a different context, is in a way different from Dunlap's. Instead of Dunlap's cold, contemptuous criticism and rejection, we find Jastrow combining an appreciative acceptance of some of the "valid core" with his scorn and derogation.[3]

> There is something enduring in the Freudian quest and in the Freudian solution. Despite manifold errors and gross extravagances, despite glaring fallacies and flagrant violations of sense and sanity,

[2] His iconoclastic view of life is perhaps best reflected in what Wells (1935b) has called the "Dunlap Dilemma" (Dunlap, 1934, pp. 207-208).
[3] For Jastrow's warm attitude toward psychoanalysis, see Jastrow's autobiography (1930, pp. 144, 154-155).

there remains a valid core of insight in the germ idea of psychoanalysis. A tolerant mind can hardly dismiss the project as another instance of medical or psychological folly or futility, though by and large there is as much madness in its method as method in its madness [p. 5].

Before Freud we were studying "the subconscious" too much on a descriptive level. . . . By the single stroke of an illuminating idea, Freud wrote the word "suppression" on the psychological map; and it has come to stay. . . . Here was unearthed a novel phase of the subconscious, not an automatism, but a strangely motivated disability [pp. 162-163].

But Jastrow also says:

In this chapter I have had to present . . . the reasons why the Freudian "Ucs" is completely unacceptable. . . . I can state the conclusions . . . simply. There is no evidence that any such region or process exists; the functions attributed by Freud to the "Ucs" are unnatural. That subconscious processes appear in the neuroses, in dreams and in lapses is abundantly clear. Their legitimate explanation forms a large problem in psychology [p. 175].

To bring sex into the focus of psychic motivation was an essential step in depth psychology . . . The credit for its establishment may in part be assigned to Freud; the discredit of the untenable execution of the project is responsibly his, and flagrantly that of his followers [p. 196].

Jastrow's volume lacks bibliographic and page references, and direct quotes, and what psychoanalysis has to say is drowned out by what Jastrow has to say about psychoanalysis. The evidence does not indicate that Jastrow had read more than Freud's Clark Lectures and a smattering of *The Interpretation of Dreams, Introductory Lectures, The Ego and the Id, The Psychopathology of Everyday Life,* and perhaps a few others.[4] Although Jastrow was much read among the general public, he does not seem to have had much impact on academic psychology.

Albert Ellis, an outsider to academic psychology, wrote "An Introduction to the Principles of Scientific Psychoanalysis" (1950). Of the thirteen sections in his article, nine are devoted to the "dangers" of psychoanalysis, which according to him are its "theoretical biases," its "personal biases," its "compartmentalization of

---

[4] See footnote 52, Chapter 4.

personality," its "typologies," its "cultural biases," its "instinct theories," its "developmental theories," its "concepts of intuition," and its "concepts of research." His sources are secondary (as evidenced in the single secondary source on concepts of intuition) or on the borderline of what we have termed "tertiary" (as some of his references are on "theoretical biases"), or a mixture of the two. The monograph does have a bibliography of some 180 items, of which by rough count five refer to Freud, five to Ellis himself, six to Jung, forty-odd to Freudians, and approximately thirty to dissidents of one sort or another. But whoever might conclude from this part of the discussion that Ellis will reject psychoanalysis outright, as did Dunlap, would be absolutely incorrect. He is a self-invited St. George who does not want to slay the dragon; rather, he singlehandedly attempts to transform each of its nine destruction-spewing heads into as many teats flowing with nourishment. Although Ellis is not in the tradition of academic psychology and his views are probably not representative of psychology in general, the very fact that this kind of "study" could have appeared in 1950 sheds light on the vagaries of "influence."

The last appraisal is Rapaport's "The Structure of Psychoanalytic Theory: A Systematizing Attempt" (1959).[5] It tries to do what the title promises, documenting discussion of psychoanalytic theory with bibliographic source and page references. It was organized according to an outline suggested by Koch for the "project" of the American Psychological Association, *Psychology: A Study of a Science*. It therefore presents psychoanalysis mainly as part of the theoretical resources of psychology.

Rapaport described his work as "an early attempt at systematization." An outline of his twelve major headings may serve to give an indication of the nature of his tightly knit presentation.

A few introductory remarks are followed by a general chapter in which background factors and orienting attitudes are considered. The background factors include some probable early influences on Freud. The subjects included in the orienting attitudes are: predic-

[5] The evaluation of Rapaport's work here is mine (D. S.). The original statement about his contribution, written approximately a year before his death, was characteristically Rapaportian (when writing about himself): short and factual, without any qualitative comment. I have added the abstract of the contents and the few comments.

tion in psychology, levels of analysis, the comprehensiveness of empirical reference, quantification and mensuration, and formal organization. Also presented here is a "combined model" which Rapaport developed from the four separate models implied in Freud's theory. With this model Rapaport made explicit the corresponding psychological models: reflex-arc (topographic), entropy (economic), Darwinian (genetic), Jacksonian (neural integration hierarchy).

In the next major section Rapaport "sketches" the "Structure of the System," as a prelude to examining the variables of psychoanalytic theory. He points out that the subject matter of psychoanalysis is behavior (the empirical point of view). He then describes the various characteristics and determinants of behavior as seen psychoanalytically, again correlated explicitly with the related psychological points of view: behavior in psychoanalytic theory is integrated and indivisible (the Gestalt view); it does not stand in isolation (organismic); it is part of a genetic series and of temporal antecedent sequences (genetic); its crucial determinants are unconscious (topographic); it is drive determined (dynamic); it disposes of and is regulated by psychological energy (economic); it has structural determiners (structural); it is determined by reality (adaptive); it is socially determined (psychosocial).

The next part considers "the evidential grounds for the early assumptions of the system": psychological determinism, unconscious psychological processes, forces, and conflicts, and psychological energies and their origin in drives. The strategic character of these initial evidential grounds, and the relation of the observations to the theory, are then dealt with.

The five sections which follow deal with the problem of the construction of "function forms" in psychoanalysis as compared with those of the Lewinian and the S-R systems, the problem of quantification, the formal organization of the system, the range of the system's applications, and the history of the system's research mediation.

The evidence for the system is then discussed by a presentation of both the positive evidence and the major sources of incompatible data, and is followed by a consideration of "critical" tests of the principal assumptions.

The next section deals with the methods, concepts, and principles of broad application and of long-term significance, particularly the concepts related to the dynamic, economic, structural, genetic, and adaptive points of view.

The rest of the presentation is a kind of stock-taking. It considers the theory's achievements and its convergence with other theories, the tasks for the future development of the theory, including the empirical evidence needed, the obstacles to the development of the theory, and finally the practical obstacles to theoretical advance for psychology in general.

Perhaps the greatest contribution of Rapaport's masterly appraisal, in addition to its being the most systematic presentation of psychoanalysis ever attempted, is its achievement in relating psychoanalysis to psychology at large. Rapaport succeeded in explicating those relationships of psychoanalytic theories to psychology which had previously been merely implicit. The work's highly condensed nature demands scholarly concentration and repeated reading. Whatever its merits or shortcomings, the fact that it was written under such auspices is in itself a basis for gauging how far Freud's influence has come.

Surveys of Experiments Testing Psychoanalytic Theory

The three major surveys of experiments testing psychoanalytic theories are Rapaport's *Emotions and Memory* (1942a), Sears' *Survey of Objective Studies of Psychoanalytic Concepts* (1943), and Hilgard's "Experimental Approaches to Psychoanalysis" (1952).

Rapaport's book[6] surveys experiments on memory and a few on perception. The experiments considered by and large have to do with the concept of repression. In addition to these experimental studies, it includes a discussion of some using diagnostic tests. A positive feature of this study is its inclusion of an analysis of the psychoanalytic concept of emotions and of repression. Since it is written from the psychoanalytic point of view, its failure to take into account the earlier presentations of psychoanalytic ego psychology (Freud, 1923, 1926a; Anna Freud, 1936; Hartmann,

[6] The evaluation here is largely mine (D. S.). See footnote 5, p. 165.

1939) must be considered a deficiency. It is a deficiency, however, that is quite understandable considering the time of its writing.[7] It is also somewhat mitigated by Rapaport's conclusion that some of the experimental results represented ego-level equivalents of repression and his independent formulation of a hierarchic conception similar to that of psychoanalytic ego psychology.[8]

Again on the positive side, Rapaport subjected to critical scrutiny the experimental methods employed to induce "repression." He evaluated the relevance of these methods to psychoanalytic theory and devoted a chapter, "Direct Experimental Evidence," to those methods which seemed relevant. (This chapter includes a review of the Pötzl and Allers-Teler experiments, which have become significant for some recent experiments bearing the stamp of Freud's influence.) Although the study does fall down in not giving a *systematic* analysis of the criteria for distinguishing between relevant and irrelevant experimental methods, perhaps this was too much to expect.

The shortcomings of this survey illustrate that the difficulties which faced psychoanalysis were not only resistance to the theory and lack of sufficient interest and conversance with it. In spite of considerable interest in and familiarity with the theory, Rapaport did not explore the relevance of ego psychology to the problem of repression.[9] Even more strikingly, in spite of his conversance with the theory and interest in the problem of method he did not provide the insight into methods which might have led to a systematic treatment of the criteria of relevance.

Sears' (1943) *Survey of Objective Studies of Psychoanalytic Concepts* is far broader in scope.[10] It covers not only experimental

[7] It was written at the time when Hartmann's systematic statement of ego psychology (Hartmann, 1939) was first published in German.

[8] See "Preface to the Second Unaltered Edition" of *Emotions and Memory* (Rapaport, 1950b).

[9] MacKinnon and Dukes (1962) provide a discussion of the repression concept in the context of ego psychology. Madison (1956) has conscientiously attempted to trace the changes in the meaning of "repression" in Freud's writing.

[10] At approximately the same time Sears (1944) wrote a chapter for Hunt's handbook, which states that in the preparation of the chapter "the writer has drawn heavily from a more extensive appraisal of the problems and experimental literature relating to psychoanalytic theory prepared for the Social Science Research Council" (p. 307). There were, however, some deliberate differences in emphasis and content according to Sears (personal communication, March 26, 1963).

material, but questionnaire and observational studies as well. On the other hand, it does not include studies using diagnostic testing methods, is limited in its coverage of studies on "repression,"[11] and in spite of its wide scope, is far from exhaustive. Even so, it surveys approximately one hundred studies stimulated directly by Freudian concepts or propositions.

It was, of course, necessary for Sears to place some limitations upon himself, both in relation to his own goals and those of the Subcommittee on Motivation of the Social Science Research Council which sponsored the project. But perhaps the major limitation of Sears' study involves its basic philosophical orientation. His strongly behaviorist-environmentalist point of view seems to have prevented him from recognizing the nativistic-genetic quality of psychoanalytic theory. In keeping with the then prevailing behaviorist frame of reference, his discussions appeared to be directed at translating psychoanalysis into learning-theory terms. Thus a proposition of Freud's on oral eroticism becomes ". . . pleasure-sucking is a function of practice at sucking in association with eating" (p. 7). It is, of course, too much to expect Sears to have transcended the limitations of the *Zeitgeist* of his particular environment. Nevertheless, if he had been able to do so, as an experimental psychologist who *was* interested in psychoanalytic theory, he might have been more creative about experimental approaches *combining* the nativistic with the learning-theory orientation.

In general Sears found that the studies he surveyed in the first part of the volume, those which dealt with propositions less abstract and closer to observation ("Erotogenesis," "Erotic Behavior of Children," "Object Choice," and "Distortions of Sexuality"), tended to confirm Freud more than did those which dealt with more abstract concepts ("Fixation and Regression," "Repression," and "Projection and Dreams"). "The truly theoretical aspects of psychoanalysis involve such concepts as inhibition, sublimation, reaction formation and projection. These connecting links between the facts of clinical observation are what make Freud's writings distinctive

---

[11] It should not be overlooked, however, that Sears had already published a long article on amnesia which included an extensive discussion of repression (Sears, 1936b). He referred to this paper several times in his monograph with the apparent intention of having its content considered as closely related to his discussion there. It was perhaps the most extensive discussion of Freud's theory of repression published up to that time in a psychological journal.

from those of other students of psychopathology. And yet it is these very concepts that remain hidden in the objective data. Nothing supports them; nothing refutes them" (Sears, 1943, p. 75).

At times he seems to have been unconcerned about the relevance of the method to the proposition being tested. When doubt on an issue of this kind arose, he was likely to handle the discrepancy in this way: "The success with which animal psychologists have attacked fixation and regression is dimmed somewhat by the fact that experimental regression is not entirely representative of the Freudian clinical phenomenon. There is sufficient systematic relation between them, however, to suggest that most of the experimental findings can be applied safely to the latter" (p. 102). In another section, Sears concluded that "There is no aid to the interpretation of any particular dream in knowing that dreams are efforts at 'wish-fulfilment'. . ." (p. 132). One wishes that Sears had taken more seriously both these discrepancies and the respective theoretical positions involved.

Sears appears to have been so convinced of the inadequacy of psychoanalytic method that he did not pay sufficient attention to the relevance and limitations of alternative experimental methods. For instance, he said: "The experiments and observations examined in this report stand testimony that few investigators feel free to accept Freud's statements at face value. The reason lies in the same factor that makes psychoanalysis a bad science—its method. Psychoanalysis relies upon techniques that do not admit of the repetition of observation, that have no self-evident or denotative validity, and that are tinctured to an unknown degree with the observer's own suggestions" (p. 133). We shall have more to say about "bad science" shortly.

In spite of occasionally seeing the limitations of experimental method (for example, p. 120), in general he failed to do so. This failure is perhaps typified in his consideration of the promise in further studies of object fixation. He wrote: "With little expense, and with virtually no waste motion on the development of new experimental techniques, a vastly significant contribution to the problem of secondary motivation could be made by animal psychologists" (p. 142). He apparently did not entertain the possibility that "new" techniques might be the key to the experimental study of psychoanalysis. He did, however, recommend longitudinal and cross-cultural studies of child development.

Sears considered "object fixation," "instrumental act fixation," and regression to be the best established and the most promising areas for future experimental investigation. His final conclusion was that "social and psychological sciences must gain as many hypotheses and intuitions as possible from psychoanalysis but . . . the further analysis of psychoanalytic concepts by nonpsychoanalytic techniques may be relatively fruitless so long as those concepts rest in the theoretical framework of psychoanalysis" (p. 143). In this respect Sears had a worry shared by many others and stated by Hilgard (1952, p. 43): "If experiments supporting psychoanalytic interpretations are any good, they ought to *advance* our understanding, not merely *confirm* or *deny* the theories that someone has stated."

But whatever the characteristics of this survey written in the early 1940's, they are significant in an evaluation of Freud's influence. In part they show that Heidbreder's appraisal, written at approximately the same time (1940), represents only one side of psychology's attitudes toward psychoanalysis. They also highlight again the peculiarity of influence. It is not usually an active process in which the idea in its "true" form penetrates those influenced. It is very largely a passive process in which aspects of the idea are assimilated, but much is discarded or perhaps not perceived at all. The aspect of it which is "selected" undergoes a marked change, often becoming unrecognizable, as it becomes an organic part of what is being influenced.

Even if in the evaluation of Sears' survey it is at times difficult not to agree with Hilgard's (1952, p. 42) observation that it is "a fairly unfriendly statement of the case," there is no question about its being a very considerable contribution. In seriously undertaking this difficult task, Sears provided a focal point for the consideration of the experimental approach to psychoanalysis. It would be a mistake to underestimate the importance of his survey at the time. In fact, Sears' importance in the history of the relationship of academic psychology to psychoanalysis has perhaps not been sufficiently recognized. He was one of the earlier and more prominent contributors to both the theoretical and experimental aspects of the attempt to bridge the gap beween the two fields.

Hilgard's (1952) survey (like his two articles, 1956b, 1957) is less systematic and complete in intent than Sears'. Although it is in some aspects similar to Sears', it reflects the achievements and the change of climate which had occurred over the decade. This survey is pervaded by a critical but positive interest in and attitude toward psychoanalysis.[12] Hilgard does not insist on a single method of experimentation; he includes both observational studies and some based on hypnotic and projective techniques. He holds generally to the view that the amenability of psychoanalytic propositions to investigation should not be a criterion of their validity. Unlike Sears, he does not attempt to translate psychoanalytic propositions into the terms of a single theory. The total lack of theoretical analysis might be seen as a shortcoming, but, considering the limited range and brevity of the survey, this would be unfair.

Like Sears, however, Hilgard takes for granted that experimental approaches to psychoanalysis are both possible and already available. Thus he deals only with experiments which he finds promising, or indeed already successful approaches. Some of these choices of promising experimental techniques (Blacky Test, Rogers' methods of therapy research) might be considered unfortunate. Again like Sears, Hilgard advocates that psychoanalysis should be judged by criteria of validity common to all laboratory sciences.

> Anyone who tries to give an honest appraisal of psychoanalysis as a science must be ready to admit that as it is stated it is mostly very bad science, that the bulk of the articles in its journals cannot be defended as research publications at all. Having said this, I am prepared to reassert that there is much to be learned from these writings. The task of making a science of the observations and relationships may, however, fall to others than the psychoanalysts themselves.
>
> If psychoanalysts are themselves to make a science of their knowledge, they must be prepared to follow some of the standard rules of science [p. 44].

---

[12] "Whatever the psychoanalysts do about research, the obligation is clearly upon experimental, physiological, and clinical psychologists to take seriously the field of psychodynamics, and to conduct investigations either independently or in collaboration with psychoanalysts. It is a tribute to Freud and his psychoanalytic followers that the problems faced by psychologists in their laboratories have been enormously enriched by the questions the analysts have taught us to ask" (Hilgard, 1952, pp. 44-45).

The significance of this tone is not that it may hurt psychoanalysts' sensitivities, but that it points up the conditions under which Freud's theories exert their effect. Psychology too often persists in judging relatively unexplored areas in terms of "good" or "bad" science, and encourages the assumption that we already know "the standard rules of science" which are applicable.[13] Thus while Hilgard's survey is a landmark in the spread of Freud's influence on experimental psychology, it also shows the continuance of the impediments to influence which appeared in Sears' survey. It stands to reason that, even if it were proper to borrow an ideal of science from an advanced stage of the physical sciences, such an ideal can hardly be realized in a science which is in an early phase of development (Shakow, 1953).

Dingle (1952), the British science historian, raises even more sweeping objections to the implications of philosophy of science in the development of a science.

> This is a discipline conducted for the most part by logicians unacquainted with the practice of science, and it consists mainly of a set of principles by which accepted conclusions can best be reached by those who already know them. When we compare these principles with the steps by which the discoveries were actually made we find scarcely a single instance in which there is the slightest resemblance. If experience is to be any guide to us at all—and what scientist can think otherwise?—we must conclude that there is only one scientific method: produce a genius and let him do what he likes. . . . the best we can do is to learn how to spot natural genius . . . and protect it, by fiery dragons if need be, from the god of planning [pp. 38-39].

We find, then, that these surveys indicate great strides in Freud's influence through the 1940's. They also seem to show, however, that most of the time this advance was not accompanied by increasing understanding or explication of the theory itself. This might have been due to the theory's lack of systematic sources or to special attitudes of those to whom it was addressed. Or it may be an illustration of a thesis we have already proposed: that the understanding of a theory may to a considerable extent be dependent upon the development and availability of experimental methods for testing it.

---

[13] What part the auspices under which Hilgard's lectures were delivered—the Hixon Lectures at the California Institute of Technology—played in this emphasis is one of the never-answered questions of the sub-*Zeitgeists*.

Articles on Psychoanalytic Themes in the *Psychological Bulletin*

With the exception of Hilgard's survey, we have no over-all evaluation of experimental or other evidence about the validity of psychoanalytic theories after 1943. The next best source of information about the period 1943-1958 appears to be the *Psychological Bulletin*. This journal, devoted to survey articles and special reviews, can be expected to reflect the views of psychology about the experimental evidence for and against psychoanalytic theories, and should also give some inkling of the status of Freud's influence on psychology. We cannot expect, however, that it will provide a completely reliable measure of this influence. The *Psychological Bulletin* is not intended to be encyclopedic. By and large it receives rather than solicits its survey articles, so that its contents represent the interests and predilections of single individuals. Nevertheless, the articles do indicate what subject matters have come to command the interest of psychologists and have found someone capable of, and interested in, giving a survey of them.

Gardner Murphy's 1944 presidential address to the American Psychological Association was printed in the *Bulletin* (1945) under the title "The Freeing of Intelligence." Murphy surveyed the guiding ideas of his own and of his associates' research on cognitive responses in relation to needs. The central idea for the relation of cognition to impulse may be characterized by the term autism.[14] Upon inspection, however, Murphy's autism proves to be a portmanteau expression for a wide variety of the effects of the pleasure principle, all of which it subsumes indiscriminately, instead of further differentiating them. He agreed that cognitive processes are also guided by habit and admitted the importance of primitive habit, "especially thinking by analogy," as demonstrated by Piaget and others. But he was "unwilling to admit that habit can be distinguished from motivated behavior; I would emphasize that habits become ingrained by *serving needs* . . ." (1945, p. 5). His concept of autism indeed represents a Freudian influence, but one under-

[14] A word introduced into the literature by Bleuler (1912) during his psychoanalytic period and given currency by Piaget (1923, 1924) as well as by Murphy (1945, 1947, 1950).

stood in Thorndikean (and perhaps Hullian) reward and punishment terms:

> If we now set out to order the specific relations of cognition to the life of impulse, we might schematize the steps as follows:
> First, ... perception, recall, and thought tend to take a direction such as to bring to the individual a cognitive situation satisfying to his needs.
> Second, this movement of cognitive processes in the direction of need-satisfaction is often unconsciously directed, the individual achieving a wish-fulfilling end by steps which do not betray to him the origin of the impulse which he follows. This appears to be simply because one of the needs is to keep himself happy regarding his own motivation. In the cases reported by psychoanalysis, the individual reaches his goal, remaining unaware that the pseudo-logical steps taken serve an unconscious need.
> Third, that cognitive processes move towards need-satisfaction appears to be a special case of the law that *behavior in general* moves in the direction of need satisfaction. I refer here to the whole mass of data on the psychology of learning which, however phrased, define the customary elimination of the frustrating aspects and the fixation of the satisfying aspects of behavior processes.
> Fourth, as to perceptual dynamics, it would appear that relatively unstructured perceptual situations are given structure in terms of *figure and ground,* by virtue of the fact that those elements stand out as figure which have previously been present as aspects of satisfying situations [pp. 5-6].

Murphy also presented some interesting ideas about the place of dreams and of casual mental states, and mentioned an early experiment on the "new look" in perception—all areas of central importance to psychoanalysis.

Almost ten years later, Ramsey (1953) also turned to the subject of dreams in his article, "Studies of Dreaming." In spite of his topic, Ramsey made no attempt to deal with psychoanalytic studies. He did recognize, however, some of the implications of his self-imposed limitations. "The restriction of the review to the more quantitative studies does not imply that less systematically controlled and reported observations are without value. . . . The reviewer appreciates the clinical validity of the dynamic nature of dreaming and its relationship to the total functioning of the personality. The complex role and meaning of dreams in the life of the individual are not easily attacked at the present time by quantitative research methods" (p. 432). Those familiar with the literature on dreams will, nevertheless, notice signs of Freud's influence in Ramsey's references to Pötzl, Schrötter, Nachmansohn, Roffenstein, Farber and Fisher, who are central to the survey.

R. H. Fortier (1953), in his survey of the same year, "The Response to Color and Ego Functions," centers on Schachtel's theory but fails to see its link with psychoanalytic theory. Of course, Schachtel's own presentation, and Fortier's failure to analyze Rorschach's conception, did not make this oversight difficult.

Going back a few years, we find Orlansky's (1949) "Infant Care and Personality," an ambitious undertaking which certainly reflects Freudian influence in the 149 references it musters. Although this survey has a rather different quality from those which we have examined thus far, it contains some of the faults we have noted in connection with them. It begins with "no illusion as to the adequacy of much of the data which will be presented," (p. 2), but it also expresses "the opinion that the evidence permits definite, if negative, conclusions in regard to the effect of certain features of infant care upon personality . . ." (p. 2). Although Orlansky finds the studies of Hunt, A. Wolf, Huschka, some of D. Levy's, and a few others to be positive evidence for the psychoanalytic view, he concludes that the findings have "been largely negative, and we have been led to substitute a theory which emphasizes, instead, the importance of constitutional factors and of the total cultural situation in personality formation; the importance of post-infantile experience is also indicated" (p. 42). In the matter of theory, Orlansky rejected Gorer, Erikson, La Barre, and Róheim, but accepted Kardiner and Du Bois.[15] Here, then, in the favoring of Kardiner's psychosocial "psychoanalytic" theory and the rejecting of the others, we see the Freudian influence coming in the side door. Despite Orlansky's attempt to reason theoretically, the survey is poorly oriented in the field of psychoanalysis, as indicated by the lumping together of the theorists mentioned above. It proposes a

---

[15] Moreover, like Dollard et al. (1939), he attributes the frustration-aggression hypothesis to Freud and psychoanalysis as well as to Dollard et al. He rejects the hypothesis, just as many psychoanalysts would, but on logical and empirical grounds different from what theirs would be.

"new" theory without having analyzed the old theory for its ingredients. The crucial shortcoming, however, is Orlansky's lack of awareness that the inadequacy of data stems from the inadequacy of the available methods for studying the kind of complex relationships he is surveying.

Beach and Jaynes' (1954) survey, "Effects of Early Experience upon the Behavior of Animals,"[16] is perhaps a good antidote to Orlansky's. In some respects it is the most important of the reviews of this period. The authors freely acknowledged Freud's influence and put it into perspective with the other influences operative in this field of study:

> In recent years the amount of attention paid to this subject has increased significantly, and the change is attributable to several different sources of stimulation. Some of the first systematic experiments dealing with behavioral development were generated by the problem of the relative importance of 'maturation' and 'practice' in the perfection of simple response patterns, such as the pecking behavior of young chicks or the swimming behavior of larval amphibians. Additional impetus was given to investigations in this field by the impact of Freudian theory [Freud, 1905b], which led to various studies, such as those which limited food supply or feeding responses in young animals and then measured the effects upon certain types of behavior in adulthood. A third influence, slower to gain recognition in America, has derived from the observations and theories of Konrad Lorenz and other European biologists who examined the effects of early social stimulation upon the adult behavior of various species of birds.
> The most recent increase of interest in the effects of early life experiences upon the behavior of adult animals is traceable to theories that stress the importance of perceptual learning in infancy upon subsequent performance in tests of learning [pp. 239-240].

The authors then go on to mention Hebb's *The Organization of Behavior* as a stimulus to experimentation in this theoretical field.

---

[16] Papers on early developmental effects in animals had begun to appear regularly two years after Hunt's article on hoarding (1941), an obvious attempt to test a Freudian proposition. In the first five years after Hunt's paper there were ten such papers published in the *Journal of Comparative and Physiological Psychology,* and in the second five years twelve. In the third five-year period the number increased to twenty-four, and in the fourth five years, at least twenty-one such articles were published in this journal alone. Whether or not the Beach and Jaynes article directly instigated any of these, it is strong evidence of the rising interest in the experimental study of early development.

Perhaps more important than the perspective they offer, however, is Beach and Jaynes' awareness of the methodological problem, for they recognize the objective difficulties impeding decisive experiments in this area.

> Reviewing the studies in the foregoing pages [130-odd references] has left the authors with two basic convictions. The first is that a fuller understanding of the effects of early experience upon subsequent behavior is fundamentally important for a science of psychology and for the broader field of animal biology. A second and equally strong impression is that much if not most of the presently available evidence bearing upon this problem is equivocal and of undetermined reliability.
> ... It must be admitted that there are instances in this area where independent control of all the relevant variables is difficult, if not actually impossible [pp. 256-257].

To turn to another category of article, we might briefly mention Terman's review (1948) of the first volume of the Kinsey Report. Terman's article is of interest expressly because it makes no reference to Freud. The "anonymous acceptance" which Herma, Kris, and Shor (see Chapter 1, footnote 5) spoke of seems to have been at work here.

Another *Bulletin* item of interest to us in the same year is a special review in which Boring (1948) discussed the first volume of the *Current Trends in Psychology* series. As is clear from the review, the book provides some idea of a particular obstacle to recognition of Freud's contribution to psychology. E. L. Kelly's discussion of clinical psychology gives no inkling of Freudian influence. Rogers' discussion of psychotherapy suggests that psychoanalysis is becoming more like client-centered counseling. Sears' discussion of child psychology lists three current developments, each of which reflects Freud's influence: (1) the human observer as an instrument replacing the brass instrument; (2) the increasing use of projective techniques (doll play and finger painting in particular); (3) the comparative intercultural method (Mead, Hallowell, Kluckhohn, Dollard, Whiting). Freud's role in those developments, however, is barely perceptible from his presentation.

Boring's comment, though written with a different intent, is revealing of this particular obstacle: "One last remark, a fitting one from him who has for twenty years been puzzling over the manner in which ego-involvement affects research and scientific judgment. In these papers every man found what he was doing important and psychology trending in his direction" (p. 84).

Let us now turn to Boring's own "A History of Introspection" (1953). He devoted one section of this paper to "Patients' Protocols" and one to "Unconsciousness." In his conclusion, he said:

> There have been in the history of science two important dichotomies that have been made with respect to introspection. (*a*) The first is animal psychology *vs.* human psychology: human beings are supposed to be able to introspect, and animals are not. (*b*) The second is the unconscious mind *vs.* the conscious mind, with introspection the means of observing consciousness. These two dichotomies reduce, however, to one: inference *vs.* direct experience.
> . . . Introspection's product, consciousness, appears now in the bodies of its progeny: the sensory experience of psychophysics, the phenomenal data of Gestalt psychology, the symbolic processes and intervening variables employed by various behaviorists, the ideas, the manifest wishes, the hallucinations, delusions, and emotions of patients and neurotic subjects, and the many mentalistic concepts which social psychology uses. . . . In general, however, it seems to the writer that there is no longer to be found any sharp dichotomy setting off the introspectable from the unconscious. That once fundamental distinction disappeared with the dissolution of dualism. Consciousness nowadays is simply one of many concepts which psychology employs, usually under some other name, whenever it finds the category useful for the generalization of observations [pp. 186-187].

Boring did show his awareness of the contributions of psychoanalysis to the problem of introspection and consciousness. On the other hand, he omitted mention of Freud's method of handling inferences concerning conscious and unconscious materials, as well as his theory of "consciousness as a sense organ,"[17] so that here again we can perhaps see the limitations of "influence."

In the same volume of the *Bulletin* as Boring's article we find R. I. Watson's "A Brief History of Clinical Psychology" (1953). Early in his article, Watson says that the "Boston group"—William

[17] This is a concept Freud derived from or developed concurrently with Theodor Lipps (see Freud, 1887-1902, p. 262). Also see Chapter 3 of *The Question of Lay Analysis* (Freud, 1926b).

James and G. Stanley Hall and their associates—had a closer relationship to dynamic psychiatry and clinical psychology than did the structuralists. "Heresy though it may be, it cannot be denied that at that time academic psychology had relatively little to contribute to clinical psychology" (p. 324). With this in mind Watson sketches the dynamic tradition in psychology and discusses psychoanalysis as part of psychology and as one of the significant roots (if not *the* significant one) of clinical psychology. "Many of the present developments in clinical psychology . . . stem in large measure from the dynamic tradition. In terms of the sources of these influences, Sigmund Freud, of course, looms largest" (p. 334). He then lists what he considers to be the three "specific manifestations of the dynamic tradition" which the psychoanalytic influence most directly affected: projective techniques, the American Orthopsychiatric Association, and the Harvard Psychological Clinic. Even if our own ego involvements would have included the Worcester State Hospital and the Menninger Clinic, Watson's appraisal includes many of the essential elements.

As might be expected, historical appraisals seem more sensitive to the influence of Freud than factual theoretical discussions or empirical surveys. Perhaps in Boring's vein we might say that writers of historical surveys have less "ego involvement" (or fewer blind spots?) than writers of theoretical discussions or surveyors of experiments. Inevitably these latter are likely to be specialists in the fields they survey, with considerable investments and commitments in those fields.

While we have thus far seen concrete examples which fit our initial description of the course of Freud's influence on psychology, the dawning recognition of the methodological problem has somewhat softened psychology's judgment of psychoanalysis.

Histories of Psychology

Before closing this chapter of surveys and reviews it seems appropriate to consider several comprehensive treatments of psychology—histories, readings, and dictionaries—because of the widespread effect they have on students in the field. We will concentrate our discussion on those volumes which are likely to have had the greatest influence on psychologists. Since we have already examined the relatively early inclusion of psychoanalysis in Woodworth's *Contemporary Schools* (1931, 1948) and in Heidbreder's *Seven Psychologies* (1933), we shall not consider them again here. We shall, however, extend our previous discussions of Boring's *History*.

The two major histories of psychology to date are Boring's and Murphy's. Both of these have gone through two editions, 1929 and 1949 in the case of Murphy, and 1929 and 1950 in the case of Boring.[18] These volumes have been important vehicles of influence in psychology from the time of their initial publication.

In our earlier discussion, we noted Boring's rather dramatic change of opinion about Freud between 1929 and 1950. In the 1929 edition of *A History of Experimental Psychology,* Boring made only four passing references to Freud. In his final "Assessment" he concluded: "There have been no great psychologists. Psychology has never had a great man to itself. Wundt was not a great man of the order of Helmholtz or Darwin. . . . The influence of Helmholtz was considerable, and the influence of Darwin in America and England was profound, but both of these men affected psychology only from the outside, as it were" (1929, p. 660). Nevertheless, with his characteristic honesty and the true historian's readiness to re-examine even his own dicta, Boring subsequently decided that his judgment with regard to great men in psychology needed "considerable revision" (1950b, p. 743). This time he devoted some twelve pages to Freud directly and had significant references to him on some thirty other pages. His "revised judgment":

> In the first place, let it be said that the history of psychology is its past. The great men who were in it stand by whatever their influence was eventually to be. Helmholtz may never have belonged to a *deutsche psychologische Gesellschaft* or Darwin to a British psychological society, yet they stand great figures in psychology's past— Darwin as the greater. So Freud. Psychologists long refused him admission to their numbers, yet now he is seen as the greatest originator of all, the agent of the *Zeitgeist* who accomplished the invasion of psychology by the principle of the unconscious process. If the author were to pick out psychology's great, in order to satisfy the reader's curiosity, then he would say that, judged by the criterion

[18] Is this almost simultaneous appearance another evidence for the *Zeitgeist?* The times needed a history and—twice—two excellent persons responded.

of their persistent posthumous importance, there are at least four very great men in psychology's history: Darwin, Helmholtz, James and Freud. Measured by the same criterion, Darwin and Freud have produced a greater revolution in thinking than have Helmholtz and James. Freud's effect is, however, still too recent to compare with Darwin's. For that we must wait fifty years [1950b, p. 743].

Boring's change in opinion of Freud is perhaps the best possible reflection of the change in attitude of psychology as a whole.

In contrast to Boring, Murphy, in his excellent history entitled *An Historical Introduction to Modern Psychology,* gave considerable space to Freud from the first. His discussions are generally favorable to psychoanalysis. The earlier edition (1929a) has a chapter on psychoanalysis of about twenty-five pages, of which about twenty-one are devoted to Freud and four to dissident schools. The second edition (1949) has two successive chapters on psychoanalysis. The first of these chapters, entitled "Sigmund Freud," is essentially the same as the chapter on psychoanalysis in the 1929 edition, with additional material on ego psychology and some remarks about the accumulating experimental evidence. Murphy concluded with the observation: "The psychoanalytic method has not only become a general way of looking at human beings, but has within the same years become a system of explicit hypotheses inviting critical examination by the methods developed in experimental biology" (1949, p. 330). The second of these chapters, "The Response to Freud," devotes a few additional pages to Freud, but focuses primarily on the dissident groups (some seventeen pages). We should note, however, that there is also a brief discussion of Erikson in this section. In various other places in the later edition Murphy pointed to the influence of psychoanalysis on child psychology and its increasing use in clinical psychology. He also saw the integration of its conceptions with those of biology, social psychology, and the general psychology of personality.

Two other volumes are major historical writings of the period, although they are not the qualitative equals of the two we have just considered. The first of these is Flugel's *A Hundred Years of Psychology,* which was issued as a volume in Duckworth's "Hundred Years Series." It first appeared in 1933, and after several reprintings, a second edition was published in 1951. The later edition is apparently essentially the first with a rather limited "additional part on developments 1933-1947." Flugel gave greatest emphasis to three major topics: Wundt and Fechner; British psychology, particularly Spearman and McDougall, with considerable space allotted to Galton, Spencer, and Darwin; and psychoanalysis. That he gave such prominence to psychoanalysis is not surprising, since Flugel was one of the really rare psychologists who early identified himself with psychoanalysis and continued to maintain his relationships to both groups. Flugel referred quite frequently to Freud and psychoanalysis throughout the volume. This was in addition to a chapter devoted to "Freud and Psychoanalysis," which provides a succinct review of some of the most important psychoanalytic concepts. In his supplementary chapter in the second edition he commented on the progress and contributions of psychoanalysis and expressed his evaluation of Freud. "Psycho-analysis . . . has directly or indirectly affected so many aspects of psychology. . . It suffered a great loss in the death of its founder . . . one who, perhaps more than any other, was responsible by his own individual effort for creating an outlook and a way of thought that have profoundly affected the whole course of the 20th century approach to problems of the mind" (1951, pp. 389-390).

Brett's *A History of Psychology* is also a major history of this period. Brett, however, devoted only about two pages to psychoanalysis (1921, pp. 305-308). The one-volume version of the three-volume Brett, which was edited and abridged by R. S. Peters (1953), is another matter. Peters has added a chapter on twentieth century trends. Although his discussion of the more current material is quite meager when compared with the Boring and Murphy volumes, he devotes some fifteen pages of this sixty-seven page chapter to Freud directly, and three or four pages to Freud's followers. Considering the size of the chapter, this represents a surprising amount of space given to psychoanalysis. Peters himself justified the length of his account of Freudian theory (which was apparently based on J. F. Brown's *Psycho-Dynamics of Abnormal Behavior*) by Freud's "overwhelming importance and influence in twentieth-century psychology" (p. 693). Although his section on Freud is somewhat imperceptive, the general atmosphere of the discussion is favorable, for he recognizes the importance of imaginative approaches to problems as opposed to "premature attempts to measure" (p. 509).

A more specialized history of psychology is Zilboorg and Henry's *A History of Medical Psychology* (1941). As we would expect from its concern with the medical aspect of the history of psychology, it devotes more space to Freud than do the general histories. Freud is one of the three most quoted authors, along with Weyer and Pinel. For Zilboorg, who actually wrote the sections with which we are concerned, these three were the great men of medical psychology. They all represented the spirit of humanism, the need for tolerance and understanding of the patient.

Among the less important histories of general psychology are those of Müller-Freienfels (1935) and Spearman (1937). Müller-Freienfels' *The Evolution of Modern Psychology,* translated from the German by W. Béran Wolfe in 1935, treats the evolution of psychology mainly from a European point of view. The volume never became popular on the American academic scene, perhaps in part because of Müller-Freienfels' own lack of prominence. The considerable emphasis, however, on "superindividual superconsciousness" and the use of such section headings as "Is There a 'Soul'?" did not enhance its popularity. The history does include sections on Freud and psychoanalysis, and on Adler and Jung, with a tendency to be more sympathetic to Jung than to Freud.

Psychology Down the Ages, Spearman's (1937) two-volume history, was also not particularly well-received in this country, probably owing to its unsystematic nature. Its greater popularity in Britain may have been because of Spearman's outstanding position in psychology there. Spearman mentioned Freud in scattered references and in a chapter on "complexes of behavior," but mainly talked of Freud in relation to the unconscious. Although he was on the whole skeptical of Freudian ideas, he did recognize the tremendous impact of Freud's contributions. He said: "Much perhaps of the current doctrines of the unconscious is confused, inaccurate, and even extravagant. But at any rate enough seems to have been achieved already to effect a revolution. Here, at last, that which in other sciences is the general rule, occurs for once in psychology also: to wit, all the older literature has become more or less obsolete" (Vol. 1, p. 385). In his statement about a "revolution," Spearman was apparently referring to what Kuhn (1962) has called the breaking of a "paradigm"—the basis for scientific revolutions.

J. M. Baldwin's *The Story of the Mind* (1904), and his early *History of Psychology* (1913), and Dessoir's *Outlines of the History of Psychology* (1912) contain nothing on Freud. Hulin's (1934) *A Short History of Psychology* has a short section which is reasonably favorable.

Another work, while more a systematic account of a particular topic than a history, has enough similarity especially to the Boring and Murphy histories to be considered at this point. We refer to Hilgard's *Theories of Learning* (1948, 1956a). The first edition of this work was published in 1948 and the second, much enlarged, edition in 1956. Whereas the first edition had only a few passing references to Freud, the second has a thirty-seven page chapter devoted to "Freud's Psychodynamics." Recognizing that an orderly exposition of a psychoanalytic learning theory is not possible, Hilgard decided to "rest content with examining in somewhat piecemeal fashion suggestions from psychoanalysis that bear upon learning" (p. 290). In this context he examined parallels between psychoanalytic and conventional interpretations of learning: pleasure principle and law of effect, the reality principle and trial-and-error learning, and the repetition compulsion in relation to theories of habit strength. He also reviewed psychoanalytic conceptions that have influenced learning experiments and theories (anxiety as a drive; unconscious influences on word associations; repression, forgetting, and recall; fixation; regression; aggression and its displacement) and gave suggestions from psychoanalysis which have been little represented in psychological studies of learning (stages of development in relation to learning, obstacles to learning, psychodynamics of thinking, and therapy as learning). Various experiments in repression and recall, and repression and recognition thresholds, were examined as illustrative of the laboratory use of psychodynamic concepts. In his closing estimate of Freud's contribution to learning, Hilgard remarked that "The goads from psychoanalysis to broaden the content studied within learning, to recognize the range of motivational determiners, including unconscious ones, and to build toward an ego psychology are acceptable ones, and the acceptance of these challenges has already proved rewarding" (p. 324).

From our point of view the striking change between these two editions only eight years apart reflects the same kind of change in attitude which we saw represented in the two editions of Boring's history.

READINGS

Let us turn now to "readings." Rand (1912), Robinson and Richardson-Robinson (1923, 1929), Dennis (1948), Marx (1951), and Helson (1951) in the broad range of psychology, and Taylor (1926), Tomkins (1943), Reed, Alexander, and Tomkins (1958), and Brand (1954) in abnormal psychology and personality, comprise the outstanding "readings" of the period. J. McV. Hunt's (1944) two-volume work may also be considered as belonging in the same group.

The 1912 volume compiled by Rand contains passages from forty-three psychologists from Anaxagoras to Wundt, but does not include anything related to Freud or psychoanalysis. The Robinson and Richardson-Robinson (1923) *Readings* has only indirect material on Freud in a three-page excerpt from Holt's *Freudian Wish*. The later (1929) edition of their volume contains the same Holt excerpt and a few others from J. B. Watson and F. L. Wells on topics close to psychoanalysis. Neither Freud nor psychoanalysis is mentioned in the index. Dennis' *Readings,* although published in 1948, contains nothing of relevance to psychoanalysis.

Marx's and Helson's collections, however, both written in 1951, do offer considerable material on Freud and psychoanalysis. Marx's volume is essentially "a collection of recent papers on problems of scientific theory construction in psychology (Part One), and an anthology of representative writings from the most prominent contemporary psychological theorists (Part Two)" (p. v). The first part of the book, dealing with the construction of theory, includes the Kris paper on "Psychoanalytic Propositions," and Gustav Bergmann's "Psychoanalysis and Experimental Psychology." The second part, on theoretical foundations, has a series on psychodynamics which begins with an excerpt from Freud's *The Problem of Anxiety* and continues with selections by Franz Alexander, Horney, Saul

Rosenzweig, A. H. Maslow, Neal Miller (frustration-aggression hypothesis), Mowrer, and Maier—all writings that derive at least in part from Freudian theory.

Helson's volume is not quite a "readings," but a symposium composed of chapters written by a selected group of authors who were asked to participate. This collection has only fifteen chapters as compared with the forty-five in Marx's volume. The writers of the several chapters are more strictly academic psychologists and their presentations are much more systematic than those in the Marx volume. Freudian and psychoanalytic materials play a considerable role in the volume; in fact, Freud is among the four authors most mentioned, along with Hull, Lewin, and Thurstone. The material on Freudian themes appears particularly in the chapters on "Motivation" by F. W. Irwin, "Feeling and Emotion" by J. G. Beebe-Center, "Personality" by D. W. MacKinnon and A. H. Maslow, "Psychological Theory and Social Psychology" by D. Krech, and "Abnormal Psychology" by D. B. Klein.

Thus these two books of general readings made psychoanalytic material available in "ready" form.

The readings in abnormal psychology, psychopathology, and personality theory offer a mixed picture. Taylor's volume, published in 1926, is a kind of study in ambitendency. While Jastrow's introduction of some fourteen pages is heavily weighted with a discussion of Freud and psychoanalysis, and the various contributors refer frequently to Freud, Taylor's own selection process leaned very much in the opposite direction. Of the 225 short excerpts which constitute the body of the work, only one is Freud's: a selection from his discussion of "Errors" in *Introductory Lectures on Psycho-Analysis*, comprising only three pages out of some 749 pages of text.[19] There are a few articles on Freud and some of his concepts but, with the one exception just mentioned, they are all secondary sources. Prince, Janet, and Sidis are the authors most frequently quoted, with by far the greatest emphasis on Prince (twenty excerpts).

Tomkins' (1943) collection, *Contemporary Psychopathology*, is

[19] Taylor's (1962) recent article is a good example of this same tendency to minimize Freud. He does not appear to recognize the differences that exist among building blocks, or that originality almost always lies in *what one does* with the same (or similar) building blocks which are lying around. (See last part of footnote 31, Chapter 3.)

another matter entirely. The excerpts are much fuller—frequently complete—the emphasis is strictly dynamic, and it is permeated with Freudian influence. Reed, Alexander, and Tomkins' (1958) volume, which might be considered a highly revised edition of Tomkins' 1943 volume, is mainly a collection of papers published in the psychological and psychiatric field during the period 1952-1957. Freud has the greatest number of references in the index.

The volume by Brand (1954), which is primarily on personality theory, also has marked evidences of Freudian influence. Although Gordon Allport is actually referred to most frequently, Freud is second, with various aspects of psychoanalysis pervading the volume.

Even if Hunt's (1944) two-volume *Personality and the Behavior Disorders* is really a handbook (since it is composed of articles especially written for it), it has enough affinity to the "readings" to be considered in this group. Whether because of its subject, the special sensitivity of the editor to historical developments, the recognition of the need for making psychoanalysis part of psychology, or all of these, the two volumes contain much material on Freud. In fact, from a purely quantitative standpoint, there are twice as many references to Freud in the index as there are to the next closest author. Although the volumes range from theoretical approaches to personality through experimental and sociological determinants of personality to biological and organic determinants of personality, it has some chapters which have a particular psychoanalytic flavor. Important among these are: Mowrer and Kluckhohn on "Dynamic Theory of Personality," Robert White on "Interpretation of Imaginative Productions," Thomas French on "Clinical Approach to the Dynamics of Behavior," Leon Saul on "Physiological Effects of Emotional Tension," Sears on "Experimental Analysis of Psychoanalytic Phenomena," Rosenzweig on "An Outline of Frustration Theory," Ribble on "Infantile Experience in Relation to Personality Development," Lois Murphy on "Childhood Experience in Relation to Personality Development," Blanchard on "Adolescent Experience in Relation to Personality and Behavior," and Appel on "Psychiatric Therapy."

Dictionaries

Another source of influence are the dictionaries. Baldwin's encyclopedic *Dictionary of Philosophy and Psychology* (J. M. Baldwin, 1900-1902, 1905) is of course a classic of great importance. Since it appeared before Freud was well-known in the English-speaking countries, it contains nothing of Freud in the first two volumes of articles, and only a few of Freud's works are listed in the Rand bibliography which comprises the third volume.

In 1934 a *Dictionary of Psychology* was published under the editorship of Howard C. Warren, with the help of a distinguished Advisory Board and a large group of collaborators. This reference work was indeed an important contribution to psychology. It contained more than 8,500 carefully defined items, and gave excellent coverage of psychoanalysis.

Decidedly less ambitious undertakings were P. L. Harriman's (1947) *The New Dictionary of Psychology* and the Penguin volume of James Drever (Sr.), *A Dictionary of Psychology* (1952). While Harriman gave longer definitions, he covered only some 3,000 words; whereas Drever defined about 5,000 terms somewhat more briefly. Both books contain a substantial number of words from psychoanalysis.

Horace English published *A Student's Dictionary of Psychological Terms* in 1928. There was apparently considerable call for the small volume because it went through a series of editions before the appearance of Warren's dictionary in 1934. The coverage of the most common psychoanalytic terms was reasonably complete. However, it was Horace and Ava Champney English's (1958) *A Comprehensive Dictionary of Psychological and Psychoanalytical Terms: A Guide to Usage* which provided psychologists with an unusually comprehensive and complete coverage of psychoanalytic terms, in the context of an excellent presentation of general psychological terms. In spite of occasional lapses, it is a dictionary of which psychologists can indeed be proud—a combination of dictionary and psychological "Fowler."

In the histories, readings, and dictionaries we have discussed, we have seen evidences of real recognition and acceptance. Although many barriers and reluctances still remain, psychoanalysis has on the whole come to be regarded as a legitimate part of psychology.

Summary

In this chapter we have ranged widely in the search for evidences of Freud's influence. We have considered on the one hand material immediately concerned with psychoanalysis, and on the other hand material only indirectly concerned with psychoanalysis, its focus being psychology in general. Of the more direct material, we examined such sources as general appraisals of psychoanalysis, surveys of experiments testing psychoanalytic theories, and the evaluation of special psychoanalytic themes. Our survey of general source material included particularly histories, readings, and dictionaries of psychology.

Increased understanding and exploration of psychoanalytic theory itself, some absorption of Freudian influences, and a beginning awareness of the crucial methodological problem are becoming evident in the direct material. In a particular instance (Rapaport) we can see that even deep immersion in psychoanalytic theory has its limitations, although it provides some insight about the possible contributions of psychoanalysis to general psychology.

The more general psychological sources—material primarily of a reference character and therefore more or less constantly before the student—provide a much clearer picture of the influence of Freud. We find historians, collectors of readings, and lexicographers to be among the most sensitive to the role of potentially important ideas. It is in this group that we find what is apparently the least ego involvement and the greatest readiness to examine the total scene. They are the ones who have shown the greatest recognition of Freud's contribution, and even of his greatness as a psychologist.

7

CONCLUSIONS

Freud, after a period of intensive work in various fields of medicine and physiology, turned his attention to problems more directly related to the understanding of human nature. He saw psychological phenomena differently from both his predecessors and contemporaries. When he reported what he saw, he was generally greeted with skepticism. Thereafter, through his long, active, and markedly productive[1] life he developed his ideas in isolation, assisted only by a group who identified strongly with him. In such circumstances, how did his vast influence on the psychology of which he had never been a part come about?

Using a broad definition of influence as a guide in our attempt to answer this question, we found that ideas which demonstrably originated in the Freudian body of theory and observation have indeed permeated virtually the whole range of psychology. In fact, we have seen that with the cumulative growth of this influence, Freud has become the most prominent name in the history of psychology. Nevertheless, this growth in influence has not, at least so far as psychology is concerned, been continuous: it has had its ebbs and flows, its enhancements and abatements, its leaps and halts.

A separation existed between psychoanalysis and psychology in spite of their common heritage from the Helmholtz tradition—a tradition which permeated the biological and physiological sciences when Freud started his work. It would seem that this gulf actually arose out of the different way in which each viewed its commitment to the Helmholtz program. Psychology did not recognize Freud's serious commitment to the "forces equal in dignity" part of the

[1] See Flugel (1951, pp. 291-292).

Helmholtz school oath as parallel to their own concern with the first part of this oath, the part which called for a "reduction to physical-chemical forces." Its own early focus on the "rigor" demanded by the latter led psychology to skip almost entirely the naturalistic stage usual in the development of a science and to identify itself with the "exact" of a hypothetical Science, rather than with the "meaningful" that psychoanalysis had chosen. Since psychology had not come to terms with defining the proper place and time for exact measurement and quantification, there arose confusion in the use and meaning of the terms "good" and "bad" science—"bad" science being taken to be that which characterized psychoanalysis. The "naturalistic" method which fitted psychoanalysis so well was derogated as "unscientific."

Despite superficial indications to the contrary, Freud, in his broad philosophic orientation, appears to have gone back to the spirit of the Enlightenment with its integration of intellect and affect, rather than adhering to either the Romantic Period's marked overemphasis on affect or to the later nineteenth century's heavy emphasis on intellect alone. It was inevitable that some vestigial aspects of the Romantic Period in which he grew up remained. However, these aspects were not intrinsic. It is only those persons identified with that movement, and those who are the strongest and most rigid exponents of the narrower Helmholtz view, who emphasize the Romantic trend in Freud. In contrast to the Romantic approach, Freud's was introspective rather than intuitive, deterministic rather than indeterministic, based on observation rather than on speculation, empirical rather than deductive. Although his approach substituted the consulting room for the laboratory, his data came from the *analyst's* chair rather than from the *arm*chair.

Pressures from the twentieth century *Zeitgeist*, both the "direct" pressures of the views expressed by psychoanalysts in their writings, and the "indirect" pressures of students, colleagues in other fields, and the popular and semipopular literature on psychoanalysis, forced psychologists to establish contact with psychoanalysis. Their initial responses ranged from complete rejection to complete acceptance, and at practically all levels were accompanied by conflict and hesitancy. Psychologists' reactions to Freud certainly in part were based on weaknesses in psychoanalysis: the lack of theoretical systematization, the poor translations of Freud's works, the inadequacy of the secondary sources, and the tone of presentation of psychoanalysis by Freudian students. But psychology had its own weaknesses, many of which grew out of its self-consciousness as a young discipline attempting to take its place among the established sciences. Academic psychology, having patterned itself after these sciences, had turned prematurely to rigorous experiment, and in the process had artificially restricted its content.

Nonetheless, our general discussion and our closer examination of the special areas of the unconscious and motivation revealed considerable evidence of accumulating Freudian influence. In this we professed to see a pattern. That Freud introduced important new areas and a new view of man to psychology has been almost universally accepted. In indirect, and at times even devious, ways, psychology has become pervaded by Freud's ideas of the role of the unconscious and its manifestations, of motivation (particularly its goal-directedness), his idea of the genetic approach, and his principle of psychological determinism. It has, however, most frequently been his conceptions, rather than his concepts and theories, that have received attention. His concepts have usually been modified, often into "common-sense" versions, and too often without awareness that a modification had been made.

Freud's methods—those developed in the process of working out his theories—have been rejected by psychologists. For a long time psychology had few alternative methods available for testing his concepts. Consequently, acceptance of Freud's conceptions has been essentially based on a sort of "psychologist-as-clinician" knowledge, rather than on the rigorous criteria prevalent in experimental psychology.

While Freud's influence on psychology has become increasingly great, it has not been accompanied by proportionate conversance; acceptance of his conception of man has been accompanied by relatively less acceptance of the means by which it was derived, its concepts, or its complexities. In sum, Freud has had great impact, but not an influence that has been accompanied by true understanding.

It was for these reasons, as well as those we presented in the comparison of Darwin and Freud with which we opened our essay, that we were compelled to conclude that Freud had a more difficult time in being accepted. Nevertheless, in the view of some,

Freud has still left us with "the most important body of thought committed to paper in the twentieth century" (Rieff, 1959, p. x). This view appears to be valid if we have reference to the life sciences. It has even been suggested that the twentieth century may go down in history as the "Freudian Century" (Nelson, 1957, p. 9). It would perhaps be more nearly correct if only the first half of the century were so characterized. We must not forget the cataclysmic importance achieved by nuclear physics in the latter half of the century.

In which areas of psychology has Freud's influence been greatest? If we were to use the most convenient categorical system at hand, the one recently adopted by *Psychological Abstracts*, we might list the following fields of psychology as most markedly affected: abnormal, personality, developmental, industrial and social, and psychotherapy. Some areas of experimental psychology (motivation, emotion, memory, and imagination) have also been substantially affected, and others (learning, thinking, and perception) have obviously been at least "touched." For a more graphic representation of these evaluations, we might apply the rating system Murphy used in his presentation to the Division of Clinical Psychology, on the occasion of the Freud Centennial in 1956 (Murphy, 1956). According to this system, our ratings are: Experimental—learning 2, thinking 2, perception 2, imagination 4, motivation and emotion 4, memory 4; Physiological 0;[2] Animal 2; Developmental 4; Social 3; Personality 5; Therapy 4-5; Abnormal 5; and Industrial 4. It will be noted that our list and ratings do not differ substantially from Murphy's.

Having looked at the historical background of the present position of psychoanalysis, it remains for us to examine briefly some of the problems and prospects for the future, as psychoanalysis takes its place as part of psychology. One of us, in attempting a systematization of psychoanalytic theory, has presented the main lines of the problems that lie ahead (Rapaport, 1959, pp. 155-167). We shall outline some of these arguments, adding relevant points where

[2] Pribram's (1962) recent article examining Freud's "Project" is, however, an especially promising study relating present-day neuropsychological thinking to Freudian ideas.

appropriate. We urge the reader to refer to the original for a detailed discussion.

The obstacles to the integration of psychoanalysis with psychology are of two types: practical obstacles that lie in both psychology and psychoanalysis, and certain theoretical obstacles that arise from the nature of their common field of study.

The practical obstacles lying within psychology are various. We have already noted some of the problems arising from psychology's self-consciousness,[3] a self-consciousness which was reflected in a preoccupation with *"the* scientific method" and experimental design at the cost of substantive concern. There has been, too, a tendency in psychology toward addiction to a "single theory" or to a "single method," a trend closely associated to the prevalence of "schools." Another obstacle is the extension to problems in psychology of what Adelson (1956) has called the notion of "perfectibility"—the natural American propensity to be optimistic (see Shakow, 1960b). Although this attitude of optimism has become most obviously involved in problems in therapy, it can also be seen in theories about the basic nature of man (for instance, Maslow, 1962).[4] These theories have developed largely in reaction to an exaggerated concern with the pathological, but tend to neglect the negative forces with which individuals must contend. Psychoanalytic ego psychology appears to have dealt with this area in a much more realistic fashion.

Psychoanalysis, too, has its practical obstacles. The first of these is a problem which we considered earlier: the lack of a systematic theoretical literature, especially on the general psychoanalytic theory. Although this situation is to some extent being alleviated by the work of persons like Rapaport (1955, 1959) and Gill (1963), it still remains an obstacle to theoretical progress. Another handicap is the training offered by psychoanalytic institutes. Its almost exclusive limitation to physicians, its essentially "night school"[5] character, its emphasis on private practice which does not foster

---

[3] For earlier discussions of these points, see Shakow (1953, 1956).

[4] It is surprising that in this work Maslow makes no reference to psychoanalytic ego psychology or ego psychologists.

[5] With some exceptions, such as the Chicago Psychoanalytic Institute and the Boston Psychoanalytic Institute, which have week end classes. But all institutes have the disadvantage of being part-time and do not afford the opportunity for serious full-time concentration.

theoretical interest[6] and development, and results in a limited number and kind of patient, are all handicaps to theoretical progress. It is not surprising, therefore, that some demand has grown up in recent years for relatively independent institutes to be associated with both medical schools and with graduate departments of psychology (Shakow, 1962).

In addition to the two kinds of practical problems we have considered, there are a number of theoretical obstacles arising from the very nature of the subject matter and the field which psychoanalysis and psychology have in common. Regard for the individual's legal and moral rights is a major empirical barrier to the observation and manipulation of behavior inside and outside the laboratory. This problem also has important theoretical aspects: the effects of such trespass upon the subject, the observer, and the observation.[7] There is, too, the "hierarchy" problem. Much experimentation lies ahead before laws of hierarchic transformation are developed which will permit adequate handling of field problems taken into the laboratory. Still another problem grows out of the fact that a large proportion of psychological phenomena occur only in the contact of one person with one or more others. The method of participant observation has been developed to deal with this problem, but the implications of this method have not yet been theoretically formulated,[8] and the lack of such systematization has in turn retarded the theory's development.[9] A final obstacle is that of mathematization, including quantification.

Some progress has been made in the attempt to deal with these various problems. First efforts are being made toward handling the difficulties created by participant observation through the development of alternative techniques. Knowledge of dyadic and other social situations is being advanced by the use of techniques for

[6] As Boring said about his analyst: "He was, moreover, dealing solely and particularly with ME and not with the human mind in general. It was I, not he, who wanted to make the generalizations" (Boring, 1940, p. 6).

[7] See Sternberg, Chapman, and Shakow (1958), Shakow (1960a), and Cohen and Cohen (1961) for a detailed discussion of some aspects of this problem.

[8] See, however, S. Bernfeld (1941), and Gross (1951).

[9] This problem is considered in Sternberg, Chapman, and Shakow (1958) and in Shakow (1960a) in the context of a discussion of sound-film recording, which does not involve participant observation. Another variant, involving the use of closed-circuit television as a possible way to circumvent some of the problems of participation, is considered in Shakow (1959b).

studying "organized complexity," interdisciplinary teams, and modern computational devices (Weaver, 1948). The "hierarchy" problem has offered more difficulties because the theoretical aspects of hierarchic transformation have not been developed. This difficulty is, of course, somewhat alleviated by the fact that not all problems need to be taken to the laboratory. Although as many problems as possible should be brought under laboratory control, efforts to deal rigorously with field situations should be continued and increased.[10] A start toward dealing with quantification would be a survey of "objective studies" of psychoanalysis. Instead of centering on the *results* of the studies, however, such a survey would give special attention to the *methods,* the *target variables,* and the *techniques* by which these variables were quantified.

Over a decade ago one of us had the opportunity to take stock of mid-century trends in what was broadly defined as the area of experimental psychology (Shakow, 1953). At that time a number of trends appeared conspicuous. One of these was the growing awareness by psychology of its own overconcern with its formal disciplinary aspects, and the resultant ego-[11] rather than task-orientation.[12] Together with this awareness were noted early signs of revolt against this preoccupation with our neighbors' presumed interest in our affairs. Another important trend noted was the growing interest in Jamesian "more nutritious objects of study," reflected in increasing attention to molar studies, accompanied by a diligent search for methods to handle the "organized complexity" involved.

Rapaport (1959) has made some important complementary points. More recently, Koch, in his Epilogue to the third volume of *Psychology: A Study of a Science* (Koch, 1959, pp. 729-788), has

[10] See Barker (1963). Also see the discussion of Soskin's paper in "Proceedings of the Twenty-Fifth Anniversary Meeting of the Society for Research in Child Development" (1960, pp. 216-217). See also Hilgard, Gill, and Shakow (1953).
[11] One view of some of the results of this ego-orientation is revealed in Broad's (1933, p. 476) extreme statement: "Poor dear Psychology, of course, has never got far beyond the stage of mediaeval physics, except in its statistical developments, where the labours of the mathematicians have enabled it to spin out the correlation of trivialities into endless refinements. For the rest it is only too obvious that, up to the present, a great deal of Psychology consists mainly of muddle, twaddle, and quacksalving, trying to impose itself as science by the elaborateness of its technical terminology and the confidence of its assertions."
[12] This theme is also considered in Shakow (1949, pp. 203-204) in terms of "purity."

presented a more systematic statement of a similar point of view. In his "concluding perspective," based on his review of the formulations made by the thirty-four contributors to the first three volumes of the *Study,* Koch says:

> *It can in summary be said that the results of Study I set up a vast attrition against virtually all elements of the Age of Theory* [approximately the 1930-1955 period] *code.* . . . [None of the contributors] is prepared to retreat one jot from the objectives and disciplines of scientific inquiry, but most are inclined to re-examine reigning stereotypes about the *character* of such objectives and disciplines. There is a longing, bred on perception of the limits of recent history and nourished by boredom, for psychology to embrace . . . problems over which it is possible to feel intellectual passion. . . .
>
> *For the first time in its history, psychology seems ready—or almost ready—to assess its goals and instrumentalities with primary reference to its own indigenous problems.* . . .
>
> This preparedness to face the indigenous must be seen as no trivial deflection in the line of history. . . .
>
> . . . at the time of *its* inception, *psychology was unique in the extent to which its institutionalization preceded its content and its methods preceded its problems.* If there are keys to history, this statement is surely a key to the brief history of our science. . . . Never had inquiring men been so harried by social need, cultural optimism, extrinsic prescription, the advance scheduling of ways and means, the shining success story of the older sciences.
>
> The "scientism" that many see and some decry in recent psychology was thus with it from the start. It was conferred by the timing of its institutionalization. If psychology had been born a century, three centuries earlier, it would have been less "scientistic." There would have been that much less science, and science-of-science to emulate. Those who use the term "scientism" dismissively are sensing a problem but decrying the inevitable. Yet, few who fairly look at the brief history of our science could agree that the *balance* between extrinsically defined tradition and creative innovation—prescription and production—has for any sizeable interval been optimal. From the earliest days of the experimental pioneers, man's stipulation that psychology be adequate to *science* outweighed his commitment that it be adequate to man. . . . It is, for instance, significant that a Freud, when he arrived, did not emerge from the laboratories of 19th century experimental psychology; nor was the ensuing tradition of work particularly hospitable to his ideas until rendered desperate by the human vacuum in its own content.
>
> . . . There is a new contextualism abroad, a new readiness to consider problem-centered curiosity a sufficient justification of

inquiry, but much effort is still invested in apologetically reconciling such impulses with Age of Theory code....

... What emerges from the critique of Age of Theory ideology made by our authors is a far more open and liberated conception of the task of psychology, the role of its investigators and systematists, than we have enjoyed in recent history [Koch, 1959, pp. 783-786].

Why do we make so much of these developments? Because they have direct reference to a central aspect of Freud's influence: the long delay in integration of his ideas and the many vicissitudes hindering the achievement of their appropriate place in psychology. But in making these points about the past, are we not, as Koch says, "decrying the inevitable"? Are we not trying to "hurry history," questioning the relentless march of historical forces, the forces of the dominant aspects of the *Zeitgeist*, which nothing could have changed? Those of us who have wished that the integration of Freud into psychology had been more rapid recognize that it would have required psychologists who were objective and task-oriented; who saw their central concern as the understanding of human nature; who reacted to Freud as a colleague (rather than as an outsider) equally interested in achieving this understanding; who accepted Freud as bringing to the field an insight into areas of crucial importance for psychology; who did their utmost to understand the theories and the methods which were being proposed; who marshaled the forces necessary for developing topics in these areas further, expanding the methods to make them more searching. In fact, earlier integration of psychoanalysis into psychology would have demanded that the psychologists of the period disregard both internal pressures and social pressures, would have demanded that they disregard both their own values and prejudices and those facets of the scientific *Zeitgeist* that impinged on them most closely. But, of course, it was the *Zeitgeist*, as could have been predicted, that disposed otherwise.[13]

It may be, of course, that just as the attainment of hybrid vigor requires different combinations of periods of inbreeding and outbreeding, so the optimal development of a science requires different

---

[13] We are placing the "responsibility" here primarily on the *Zeitgeist*. We have a sneaking notion that many more psychologists would have allied themselves with the aspect of the *Zeitgeist* which emphasized the "meaningful" if they had not been so overwhelmed by the "scientistic" *Zeitgeist*.

concentrations of attitudes at different periods in its development. If this is so, then psychology has certainly gone through its period of "inbreeding." We have been through a period which has been weighted heavily with the strongly held narrownesses and limited commitments we have described, as well as with the "negatives" which Boring discusses with such tolerance (Boring, 1942, p. 613). Perhaps these were inevitable for the period.

Can it be, however, that an atmosphere favorable for the "outbreeding" which some wished for this earlier period, but which the mainstream of the *Zeitgeist* was not ready to support, is now in the process of developing? Can it be that we, with Koch, are correct in our judgment[14] that now the main force of the scientific *Zeitgeist* is changing and asserting itself in an emphasis on meaningfulness, even though the new atmosphere is still permeated with the smog of tradition, the heritage of an irreversible history?

As the effects of its early negative characteristics—which we, however, cannot help believing any science needs in at least some degree during all phases of its growth—subside, psychology seems to be developing more positive qualities. These include a readiness to face substantive aspects of problems, with insistence upon only the degree of rigor necessary to protect the substance; an appreciation of the psychologist's personal motivations for entering the field (see Roe, 1953), and an appreciation of the stage of psychology's scientific development (see, for example, Adrian, 1946, and R. C. Tolman, 1947); a readiness to participate in a group commitment to a field where tolerance for tentativeness needs to be great; above all, an ability to recognize the value of a variety of approaches to psychology,[15] even if one's personal commitment is to one particular approach. These are the qualities of mature psychologists who have to work with an inevitably adolescent psychology.

[14] We must, however, keep in mind Boring's admonition (1948, p. 84) mentioned earlier on pp. 178-179.
[15] See R. B. Perry (1938, p. 79). Speaking of James, he said: "Had he known the psychology of today, he would have said, 'The tent of psychology should be large enough to provide a place for the bohemian and clinical speculations of a Freud, or the rigorous physiological methods of a Lashley, or the bold theoretical generalizations of a Köhler, or the useful statistical technique of a Spearman. Only time will tell which of these, or whether any of these, will yield the master hypothesis which will give to psychology that explanatory and predictive power, that control of the forces of nature, which has been achieved by the older sciences.'"

Freud has at times been compared with various great "idea" men—Anaximander, Confucius, Jesus, Leonardo, Newton, Kierkegaard, Kant, Darwin, Marx, Pasteur, Einstein; with great *"conquistadores"*—Moses, Hannibal, Columbus, Magellan, Captain Cook; and with great "methods" men such as Socrates. It is actually not surprising that the number and range, indeed, even the exaltedness, of the comparisons are so great. Besides the difficulty of categorizing great men simply by finding their counterparts, there is the difficulty of keeping individual emotions out of the situation. From one point of view, Freud *was,* despite his own denials, a great "idea" man, whose ideas revolutionized[16] not only psychology but a large part of twentieth century thought. From another point of view, Freud *was* a *conquistador,* a great discoverer who opened up and explored hitherto unprobed areas in man. And again, Freud *was* a great "methods" man (see S. Bernfeld, 1949, pp. 183-184), as the "free association" method attests.[17]

---

[16] In line with Kuhn's (1962) discussion of paradigms, Freud may be said to have been truly a "revolutionist," for he replaced an older paradigm with a newer one. Those who do so are the persons who are called "great men." Also see Boring's (1963) Presidential Address, "Eponym as Placebo," at the XVII International Congress of Psychology.

[17] And we would be negligent in not adding that Freud was a great "faults" man as well. That Freud had a number of traits that might be considered negative needs pointing out for the implications they may—or may not—have for the evaluation of his theories. Jones (1955, Chapter XVI) discusses most of them, including his preoccupation with personal secrecy, his indiscreetness, his tendency to make black-and-white judgments of people, his dependence upon and overestimation of others. The last was, not surprisingly, accompanied by "defensive" imperviousness to their views.

In quite another class of "faults" lie Freud's presumed or actual personal problems (about many of which Puner [1947] speaks), and the "subjective prejudices" which led to his overemphasis on sex (about which Jung [1962] reminisced toward the end of his life). Taken at one level, whatever the retrospective falsification involved in Jung's memories after some half a century, we must admit that no matter how necessary the emphasis on sex may have been to compensate for its previous neglect, and how much of this can be explained by the broad definition given sex in Freud's system, the early overemphasis cannot be denied. It led to many perhaps unnecessary misunderstandings which only later developments, particularly the more recent emphases in ego psychology and the efforts of the neo-Freudians, are helping to correct. This particular problem is a most complicated one which we cannot enter into here.

But taken at another level, most of these arguments are essentially puerile, and relevant at only a minor level of discourse. They are obviously irrelevant at the crucial level with which we are concerned, the one dealing with the fundamental importance and soundness of theories. Theories in psychology, especially motivational theories, *must* come out of man's struggle with himself. They are too near the center of man's being to be developed "objectively," without regard for content, and divorced from living. Theories in the biological and natural

But one thing characterized Freud above all: the constantly changing, developing nature of his theoretical system. He continually checked his hypotheses and theories against his observations, always ready to adjust them in reply to the demands of new facts. (There was, of course, an element of natural reluctance about revising his views, particularly in cases where new data originated outside of his own experience.) In all his correcting and revising he was constantly building, basing new ideas on new or old theories and hypotheses, even going back to long abandoned ideas if new data warranted.

Should we not try to emulate him by avoiding the extremes of either accepting his theories as dogma merely because they are his, or rejecting these same theories merely to indicate our independence from him? Can we not follow his own essential concern for congruence between fact and theory, building in part on what he has already given us, examining his views and testing them to the fullest, and developing new theories as needed?

What use are *psychologists*—all those professionally involved with human nature—to make of Freudian thinking? The answer lies essentially in the recognition that Freudian thinking is part of man's conquest of nature—the understanding of human nature. Psychoanalysis, like psychology of which it is a part, is not the possession of any group, not the property of the members of any organized association; it belongs to man. Being an "early Freudian" or a "trained Freudian" may carry certain rewards and certain claims in other settings, but has no relevance here. For psychoanalysis is part of the heritage which great men provide. As the discipline most directly involved, it is up to psychology to understand, develop, and build on this heritage, making the changes that imagination coupled with careful observation and experiment indicate.

---

sciences, though equally subject to determination by generalized needs, are much less likely to be contentually affected by the personalities of their originators. But psychology's subject matter is by its very nature associated with the "muck"—the repository of needs, memories, perceptions, feelings—that constitutes the history of our being. By their objective examination, however, psychologists compare and transform this muck, and from such processes general theories develop.

Bibliography

Ach, N. (1905), *Über die Willenstätigkeit und das Denken.* Göttingen: Vandenhoeck & Ruprecht. Translated in part as Determining Tendencies; Awareness. In Rapaport, ed. (1951), pp. 15-38.
Adelson, J. (1956), Freud in America: Some Observations. *Amer. Psychologist,* 11:467-470.
Adrian, E. D. (1946), The Mental and the Physical Origins of Behaviour. *Int. J. Psycho-Anal.,* 27:1-6.
────── (1954), Science and Human Nature. Supplement to *Nature,* 174:433-437.
Alexander, F. (1940), A Jury Trial of Psychoanalysis. *J. Abn. Soc. Psychol.,* 35:305-323.
────── & French, T. M. (1946), *Psychoanalytic Therapy: Principles and Application.* New York: Ronald Press.
────── & Healy, W. (1935), *Roots of Crime: Psychoanalytic Studies.* New York: Knopf.
Allen, F. L. (1931), *Only Yesterday.* New York: Harper.
Allport, F. (1924), *Social Psychology.* Boston: Houghton Mifflin.
Allport, G. W. (1937a), *Personality: A Psychological Interpretation.* New York: Holt.
────── (1937b), The Functional Autonomy of Motives. *Amer. J. Psychol.,* 50:141-156.
────── (1940), The Psychologist's Frame of Reference. *Psychol. Bull.,* 37:1-28.
────── ed. (1941), *Psychoanalysis as Seen by Analyzed Psychologists, a Symposium.* Washington, D.C.: American Psychological Association, 1953.
────── (1943), The Ego in Contemporary Psychology. *Psychol. Rev.,* 50:451-478.
────── (1946), Personality, a Symposium. III. Geneticism *versus* Ego-structure in Theories of Personality. *Brit. J. Educ. Psychol.,* 16:57-68.
────── (1947), Scientific Models and Human Morals. *Psychol. Rev.,* 54:182-192.
────── (1951), Dewey's Individual and Social Psychology. In *The Philosophy of John Dewey,* ed. P. A. Schlipp. New York: Tudor, pp. 263-290.
Alper, T. G. (1946a), Memory for Completed and Incompleted Tasks as a Function of Personality. *J. Abn. Soc. Psychol.,* 41:403-420.
────── (1946b), Task-Orientation vs. Ego-Orientation in Learning and Retention. *Amer. J. Psychol.,* 59:236-248.
────── (1948), Task-Orientation and Ego-Orientation as Factors in Reminiscence. *J. Exp. Psychol.,* 38:224-238.
Amacher, M. P. (1962), The Influence of the Neuroanatomy, Neurophysiology and Psychiatry of Freud's Teachers on His Psychoanalytic Theories. Unpublished doctoral dissertation. University of Washington.
Angell, J. R. (1907), The Province of Functional Psychology. *Psychol. Rev.,* 14:61-91.
────── (1936), James Rowland Angell. In *A History of Psychology in Autobiography,* Vol. 3, ed. C. Murchison. Worcester, Mass.: Clark University Press, pp. 1-38.

Aron, W. (1956), Fartzachenungen vegen upshtam fun Sigmund Freud un vegen zein yidishkeit. (Notes on Sigmund Freud's Ancestry and Jewish Contacts). *Yivo Bleter,* 40:166-174.
Bakan, D. (1958), *Sigmund Freud and the Jewish Mystical Tradition.* Princeton, N.J.: Van Nostrand.
Baldwin, B. T. (1914), The Normal Child: Its Physical Growth and Mental Development. *Pop. Sci. Monthly,* 85:559-567.
——— (1921), The Physical Growth of Children from Birth to Maturity. *University of Iowa Studies in Child Welfare,* 1(1). Iowa City: University of Iowa Press.
——— & Stecher, L. I. (1924, 1925), *The Psychology of the Preschool Child.* New York: Appleton.
Baldwin, J. M. (1901-1902, 1905), *Dictionary of Philosophy and Psychology,* 3 Vols. London: Macmillan.
——— (1904), *The Story of the Mind.* New York: Appleton.
——— (1913), *History of Psychology,* 2 Vols. New York: Putnam.
——— (1915), *Mental Development in the Child and the Race.* New York: Macmillan.
Barber, B. (1961), Resistance by Scientists to Scientific Discovery. *Science,* 134:596-602.
Barclay, J. R. (1959), Franz Brentano and Sigmund Freud: A Comparative Study in the Evolution of Psychological Thought. Unpublished doctoral dissertation. University of Michigan.
Barker, R. G., ed. (1963), *The Stream of Behavior: Explorations of Its Structure and Content.* New York: Appleton-Century-Crofts.
——— Dembo, T., & Lewin, K. (1941), Frustration and Regression: An Experiment with Young Children. *University of Iowa Studies in Child Welfare,* 18(1). Studies in Topological and Vector Psychology II. Iowa City: University of Iowa Press.
Barzun, J. (1958), *Darwin, Marx, Wagner: Critique of a Heritage,* 2nd ed. Garden City, N.Y.: Doubleday.
Beach, F. A., & Jaynes, J. (1954), Effects of Early Experience upon the Behavior of Animals. *Psychol. Bull.,* 51:239-263.
Beebe-Center, J. G. (1932), *The Psychology of Pleasantness and Unpleasantness.* New York: Van Nostrand.
Benjamin, J. D. (1950), Approaches to a Dynamic Theory of Development, Round Table, 1949. 2. Methodological Considerations in the Validation and Elaboration of Psychoanalytical Personality Theory. *Amer. J. Orthopsychiat.,* 20:139-156.
Bernard, L. L. (1921), The Misuse of Instinct in the Social Sciences. *Psychol. Rev.,* 28:96-119.
——— (1923), Instincts and the Psychoanalysts. *J. Abn. Psychol. and Soc. Psychol.,* 17:350-366.
——— (1924), *Instinct: A Study in Social Psychology.* New York: Holt.
Bernfeld, S. (1941), The Facts of Observation in Psychoanalysis. *J. Psychol.,* 12:289-305.
——— (1944), Freud's Earliest Theories and the School of Helmholtz. *Psychoanal. Quart.,* 13:341-362.
——— (1949), Freud's Scientific Beginnings. *Amer. Imago,* 6:163-196.
——— (1951), Sigmund Freud, M.D., 1882-1885. *Int. J. Psycho-Anal.,* 32:204-217.
Bernfeld, S. C. (1952), Correspondence: Discussion of Buxbaum (1951). *Bull. Menninger Clin.,* 16:67-72.
Bibring, E. (1936), The Development and Problems of the Theory of the Instincts. *Int. J. Psycho-Anal.,* 22:102-131, 1941.

Birenbaum, G. (1930), Das Vergessen einer Vornahme. *Psychol. Forsch.*, 13:218-284.
Bleuler, E. (1911), *Die Psychoanalyse Freuds*. Leipzig: Deuticke.
───── (1912), Das autistische Denken. *Jahrb. Psychoanal. Psychopathol. Forsch.*, 4:1-39.
Blum, G. S. (1953), *Psychoanalytic Theories of Personality*. New York: McGraw-Hill.
───── (1961), *A Model of the Mind*. New York: Wiley.
Boring, E. G. (1929), *A History of Experimental Psychology*. New York: Century.
───── (1940), Was This Analysis a Success? *J. Abn. Soc. Psychol.*, 35:4-10.
───── (1942), *Sensation and Perception in the History of Experimental Psychology*. New York: Appleton-Century.
───── (1948), Book Review: W. Dennis, ed., "Current Trends in Psychology." *Psychol. Bull.*, 45:75-84.
───── (1950a), Great Men and Scientific Progress. *Proc. Amer. Phil. Soc.*, 94:339-351.
───── (1950b), *History of Experimental Psychology*, 2nd ed. New York: Appleton-Century-Crofts.
───── (1953), A History of Introspection. *Psychol. Bull.*, 50:169-189.
───── (1954a), Psychological Factors in the Scientific Process. *Amer. Scientist*, 42:639-645.
───── (1954b), Book Review: E. Jones, "The Life and Work of Sigmund Freud." Vol. 1: The Formative Years and the Great Discoveries. *Psychol. Bull.*, 51:433-437.
───── (1955), Dual Role of the Zeitgeist in Scientific Creativity. *Sci. Monthly*, 80:101-106.
───── (1961), Book Review: L. L. Whyte, "The Unconscious before Freud." *Contemp. Psychol.*, 6:238.
───── (1963), Eponym as Placebo. In *History, Psychology, and Science: Selected Papers*, ed. R. I. Watson & D. T. Campbell. New York: Wiley, pp. 5-25.
Brand, H., ed. (1954), *The Study of Personality*. New York: Wiley.
Braun, O. (1909), *Eduard von Hartmann*. Stuttgart: Frommanns Verlag.
Brenman, M., & Gill, M. (1948), Research in Psychotherapy, Round Table, 1947. *Amer. J. Orthopsychiat.*, 18:92-118.
Brenner, C. (1955), *An Elementary Textbook of Psychoanalysis*. New York: International Universities Press.
Brentano, F. (1874), *Psychologie vom empirischen Standpunkt*. Leipzig: Felix Meiner, 1924.
Brett, G. S. (1921), *A History of Psychology*. Vol. 3: Modern Psychology. London: Allen & Unwin.
Breuer, J. (1895), Studies on Hysteria. III: Theoretical. *Standard Edition*, 2:183-251. London: Hogarth Press, 1955.
───── & Freud, S. (1893), Studies on Hysteria. I: On the Psychical Mechanism of Hysterical Phenomena: Preliminary Communication. *Standard Edition*, 2:1-17. London: Hogarth Press, 1955.
───── ───── (1893-1895), Studies on Hysteria. *Standard Edition*, Vol. 2. London: Hogarth Press, 1955.
Brierley, M. (1934-1947), *Trends in Psychoanalysis*. London: Hogarth Press, 1951.
Brill, A. A. (1912), *Psychanalysis: Its Theories and Practical Application*. Philadelphia: Saunders.
───── (1939), The Introduction and Development of Freud's Work in the United States. *Amer. J. Sociol.*, 45:318-325.
Brinton, C. (1959), *A History of Western Morals*. New York: Harcourt, Brace.

Broad, C. D. (1933), The "Nature" of a Continuant. In *Readings in Philosophical Analysis*, ed. H. Feigl & W. Sellars. New York: Appleton-Century-Crofts, 1949, pp. 472-481.
Brooks, V. W. (1952), *The Confident Years: 1885-1915*. New York: Dutton.
Brophy, B. (1962), *Black Ship to Hell*. New York: Harcourt, Brace & World.
Brosin, H. W. (1960), Evolution and Understanding Diseases of the Mind. In *Evolution After Darwin*. Vol. 2: The Evolution of Man, ed. S. Tax. Chicago: University of Chicago Press, pp. 373-422.
Brown, J. F. (1940), *The Psychodynamics of Abnormal Behavior*, with the collaboration of K. A. Menninger. New York: McGraw-Hill.
Brun, R. (1936), Sigmund Freuds Leistungen auf dem Gebiete der organischen Neurologie. *Schw. Arch. Neur. Psychiat.*, 37:200-207.
Bruner, J. S. (1956), Freud and the Image of Man. *Amer. Psychologist*, 11:463-466.
Bry, I., & Rifkin, A. H. (1962), Freud and the History of Ideas: Primary Sources, 1886-1910. In *Science and Psychoanalysis*. Vol. 5: Psychoanalytic Education, ed. J. H. Masserman. New York: Grune & Stratton, pp. 6-36.
Burnham, J. C. (1958), Psychoanalysis in American Civilization before 1918. Unpublished doctoral dissertation. Stanford University.
―――― (1960), Sigmund Freud and G. Stanley Hall: Exchange of Letters. *Psychoanal. Quart.*, 29:307-316.
―――― (unpublished ms.), On the Early History of American Psychiatry's Relationship with Psychoanalysis. To be published in *Psychological Issues*. New York: International Universities Press.
Burrow, T. (1958), *A Search for Man's Sanity: The Selected Letters of Trigant Burrow*. New York: Oxford University Press.
Butterfield, H. (1949), *The Origins of Modern Science*. London: G. Bell, 1950.
Buxbaum, E. (1951), Freud's Dream Interpretation in the Light of His Letters to Fliess. *Bull. Menninger Clin.*, 15:197-212.
―――― (1952), Correspondence: Reply to S. C. Bernfeld (1952). *Bull. Menninger Clin.*, 16:73.
Cargill, O. (1941), *Intellectual America*. New York: Macmillan.
Caron, A. J., & Wallach, M. A. (1957), Recall of Interrupted Tasks under Stress: A Phenomenon of Memory or of Learning? *J. Abn. Soc. Psychol.*, 55:372-381.
Carter, G. S. (1957), *A Hundred Years of Evolution*. London: Sidgwick & Jackson.
Cartwright, D. (1959), Lewinian Theory as a Contemporary Systematic Framework. In *Psychology: A Study of a Science*. Vol. 2: General Systematic Formulations, Learning and Special Processes, ed. S. Koch. New York: McGraw-Hill, pp. 7-91.
Cassirer, E. (1955), *The Philosophy of the Enlightenment*. Boston: Beacon Press.
Claparède, E. (1903), *L'Association des Idées*. Paris: Octave Doin.
―――― (1920), Freud et la Psychanalyse. *Rev. Genève*, 1:846-864.
―――― (1930), Edouard Claparède. In *A History of Psychology in Autobiography*, Vol. 1, ed. C. Murchison. Worcester, Mass.: Clark University Press, pp. 63-97.
Coan, R. W., & Zagona, S. V. (1962), Contemporary Ratings of Psychological Theorists. *Psychol. Rec.*, 12:315-322.
Cohen, R. A., & Cohen, M. B. (1961), Research in Psychotherapy: A Preliminary Report. *Psychiatry*, 24:46-61.
Colby, K. M. (1955), *Energy and Structure in Psychoanalysis*. New York: Ronald Press.
Comfort, A. (1960), Darwin and Freud. *Lancet*, Vol. 2 for 1960:107-111.
Cranefield, P. F. (1957), The Organic Physics of 1847 and the Biophysics of Today. *J. Hist. Med.*, 12:407-423.

——— (1958), Josef Breuer's Evaluation of His Contribution to Psycho-Analysis. *Int. J. Psycho-Anal.,* 39:319-322.
——— (1959), The Nineteenth-Century Prelude to Modern Biophysics. *Proceedings of the First National Biophysics Conference.* New Haven: Yale University Press, pp. 19-26.
Curti, M. (1943), *The Growth of American Thought.* New York: Harper.
Dallenbach, K. M. (1955), Phrenology Versus Psychoanalysis. *Amer. J. Psychol.,* 68:511-525.
Darlington, C. D. (1959a), The Origin of Darwinism. *Sci. Amer.,* 200:60-66.
——— (1959b), *Darwin's Place in History.* Oxford: Blackwell.
Darwin, C. (1859), *On the Origin of the Species by Means of Natural Selection, or the Preservation of Favoured Races in the Struggle for Life.* London: J. Murray.
Darwin, F., ed. (1887), *The Life and Letters of Charles Darwin,* Vol. 1. New York: Appleton.
——— ed. (1950), *Charles Darwin's Autobiography.* New York: Schuman.
Dembo, T. (1931), Der Ärger als dynamisches Problem. *Psychol. Forsch.,* 15:1-144.
Dennis, W. (1942), Piaget's Questions Applied to a Child of Known Environment. *J. Genet. Psychol.,* 60:307-320.
——— (1943), Animism and Related Tendencies in Hopi Children. *J. Abn. Soc. Psychol.,* 38:21-36.
——— ed. (1948), *Readings in the History of Psychology.* New York: Appleton-Century-Crofts.
Dessoir, M. (1912), *Outlines of the History of Psychology.* New York: Macmillan.
Dewey, J. (1920), *Reconstruction in Philosophy.* New York: Holt.
——— (1922), *Human Nature and Conduct.* New York: Holt.
Dillenberger, J. (1960), *Protestant Thought and Natural Science.* Garden City, N.Y.: Doubleday.
Dingle, H. (1952), *The Scientific Adventure.* London: Pitman. New York: Philosophical Library, 1953.
Dollard J. (1935), *Criteria for the Life History.* New Haven: Yale University Press.
——— (1937), *Caste and Class in a Southern Town.* New Haven: Yale University Press.
——— (1964), Yale's Institute of Human Relations: What Was It? *Ventures,* 3 (Winter):32-40.
——— & Miller, N. E. (1950), *Personality and Psychotherapy.* New York: McGraw-Hill.
——— ——— Doob, L. W., Mowrer, O. H., & Sears, R. R. (1939), *Frustration and Aggression.* New Haven: Yale University Press.
Dorer, M. (1932), *Historische Grundlagen der Psychoanalyse.* Leipzig: Felix Meiner.
Drever, J. (1917), *Instinct in Man.* Cambridge: University Press.
——— (1952), *A Dictionary of Psychology.* London: Penguin Books, 1953.
du Bois-Reymond, E. H. (1918), *Jugendbriefe von Emil du Bois-Reymond an Eduard Hallmann.* Berlin: Reimer.
——— (1927), *Zwei grosse Naturforscher des 19. Jahrhunderts. Ein Briefwechsel zwischen Emil du Bois-Reymond und Karl Ludwig.* Leipzig: Barth.
Dummer, E. S., ed. (1927), *The Unconscious, A Symposium.* New York: Knopf.
Dunlap, K. (1914), The Pragmatic Advantage of Freudo-Analysis (A Criticism). *Psychoanal. Rev.,* 1:149-152.
——— (1920), *Mysticism, Freudianism and Scientific Psychology.* St. Louis: Mosby.
——— (1930), Response Psychology. In *Psychologies of 1930,* ed. C. Murchison. Worcester, Mass.: Clark University Press, pp. 309-323.

——— (1932), Knight Dunlap. In *A History of Psychology in Autobiography,* Vol. 2, ed. C. Murchison. Worcester, Mass.: Clark University Press, pp. 35-61.
——— (1934), *Civilized Life.* Baltimore: Williams & Wilkins.
Earnest, E. (1950), *S. Weir Mitchell.* Philadelphia: University of Pennsylvania Press.
Eastman, M. (1942), Visit in Vienna: The Crotchety Greatness of Sigmund Freud. In *Heroes I Have Known: Twelve Who Lived Great Lives.* New York: Simon & Schuster, pp. 261-273.
Eiseley, L. (1959), *Darwin's Century.* London: Victor Gollancz.
Ellegård, A. (1958), *Darwin and the General Reader.* Göteborg: Göteborgs Universitets Årsskrift.
Ellenberger, H. F. (1956), Fechner and Freud. *Bull. Menninger Clin.,* 20:201-214.
Ellis, A. (1950), An Introduction to the Principles of Scientific Psychoanalysis. *Genet. Psychol. Monog.,* 41:147-212.
English, H. B. (1928), *A Student's Dictionary of Psychological Terms.* Yellow Springs, Ohio: Antioch Press.
——— & English, A. C. (1958), *A Comprehensive Dictionary of Psychological and Psychoanalytical Terms: A Guide to Usage.* New York: Longmans, Green.
Erikson, E. H. (1950), Growth and Crises of the Healthy Personality. In "Identity and the Life Cycle." *Psychological Issues,* 1(1):50-100. New York: International Universities Press, 1959.
——— (1955), Freud's 'The Origins of Psycho-Analysis.' *Int. J. Psycho-Anal.,* 36:1-15.
——— (1956a), The First Psychoanalyst: Crisis and Discovery. *The Yale Review,* 46:40-62.
——— (1956b), The Problem of Ego Identity. In "Identity and the Life Cycle." *Psychological Issues,* 1(1):101-164. New York: International Universities Press, 1959.
——— (1961), The Roots of Virtue. In *The Humanist Frame,* ed. J. Huxley. New York: Harper, pp. 145-165.
Escalona, S. (1952), Problems in Psycho-Analytic Research. *Int. J. Psycho-Anal.,* 33:11-21.
Eulau, H. (1951), Mover and Shaker: Walter Lippmann as a Young Man. *Antioch Rev.,* 11:291-312.
Eysenck, H. J., ed. (1961a), *Handbook of Abnormal Psychology.* New York: Basic Books.
——— (1961b), Communicating with Caliban. In *Guildhall Lectures 1960.* London: University of London Press, pp. 41-83.
Fenichel, O. (1934), *Outline of Clinical Psychoanalysis.* New York: Norton.
——— (1945), *The Psychoanalytic Theory of Neurosis.* New York: Norton.
——— (1946), Some Remarks on Freud's Place in the History of Science. *Collected Papers,* 2:362-366. New York: Norton, 1954.
Feuer, L. S. (1960), The Standpoints of Dewey and Freud: A Contrast and Analysis. *J. Indiv. Psychol.,* 16:119-136.
Fielding, W. J. (1923), *Health and Self-Mastery Through Psycho-Analysis and Autosuggestion.* Boston: Lothrop, Lee & Shepard.
Fine, R. (1962), *Freud: A Critical Re-Evaluation of His Theories.* New York: McKay.
Flugel, J. C. (1930), Psychoanalysis; Its Status and Promise. In *Psychologies of 1930,* ed. C. Murchison. Worcester, Mass.: Clark Univeristy Press, pp. 374-394.
——— (1945), *Man, Morals and Society.* London: Penguin Books, 1955.
——— (1951), *A Hundred Years of Psychology,* 2nd ed. London: Duckworth.

Forcey, C. B. (1954), Intellectuals in Crisis: Croly, Weyl, Lippmann and the *New Republic,* 1900-1919. Unpublished doctoral dissertation. University of Wisconsin.
Fortier, R. H. (1953), The Response to Color and Ego Functions. *Psychol. Bull.,* 50:41-63.
French, T. M. (1933), Interrelations between Psychoanalysis and the Experimental Work of Pavlov. *Amer. J. Psychiat.,* 89:1165-1203.
—— (1941), Goal, Mechanism and Integrative Field. *Psychosom. Med.,* 3:226-252.
—— (1942), Some Psychoanalytic Applications of the Psychological Field Concept. *Psychoanal. Quart.,* 11:17-32.
Frenkel-Brunswik, E. (1954), Psychoanalysis and the Unity of Science. *Proc. Amer. Acad. Arts and Sciences,* 80:271-347.
Freud, A. (1931), Psychoanalysis of the Child. In *A Handbook of Child Psychology,* ed. C. Murchison. Worcester, Mass.: Clark University Press, pp. 555-567.
—— (1936), *The Ego and the Mechanisms of Defence.* New York: International Universities Press, 1946.
Freud, E. L., ed. (1960), *Letters of Sigmund Freud.* New York: Basic Books.
Freud, S. (1886), Report on My Studies in Paris and Berlin. *Int. J. Psycho-Anal.,* 37:2-7, 1956.
—— (1887-1902), *The Origins of Psycho-Analysis: Letters to Wilhelm Fliess, Drafts and Notes: 1887-1902.* London: Imago, 1954.
—— (1891), *On Aphasia.* London: Imago, 1953.
—— (1893), Charcot. *Standard Edition,* 3:7-23. London: Hogarth Press, 1962.
—— (1895a [1894]), On the Grounds for Detaching a Particular Syndrome from Neurasthenia under the Description "Anxiety Neurosis." *Standard Edition,* 3:85-117. London: Hogarth Press, 1962.
—— (1895b), A Reply to Criticisms of My Paper on Anxiety Neurosis. *Standard Edition,* 3:119-139. London: Hogarth Press, 1962.
—— (1895c), Project for a Scientific Psychology. In Freud (1887-1902), pp. 347-445.
—— (1896), The Aetiology of Hysteria. *Standard Edition,* 3:187-221. London: Hogarth Press, 1962.
—— (1898), Sexuality in the Aetiology of the Neuroses. *Standard Edition,* 3:259-285. London: Hogarth Press, 1962.
—— (1900a), The Interpretation of Dreams. *Standard Edition,* 4 & 5. London: Hogarth Press, 1953.
—— (1900b), *The Interpretation of Dreams.* New York: Macmillan, 1913.
—— (1900c), The Interpretation of Dreams. *The Basic Writings of Sigmund Freud.* New York: Modern Library, 1938, pp. 179-549.
—— (1901), The Psychopathology of Everyday Life. *Standard Edition,* 6. London: Hogarth Press, 1960.
—— (1905a), Jokes and Their Relation to the Unconscious. *Standard Edition,* 8. London: Hogarth Press, 1960.
—— (1905b), Three Essays on the Theory of Sexuality. *Standard Edition,* 7:125-245. London: Hogarth Press, 1953.
—— (1906), Psycho-Analysis and the Establishment of the Facts in Legal Proceedings. *Standard Edition,* 9:97-114. London: Hogarth Press, 1959.
—— (1910 [1909]), Five Lectures on Psycho-Analysis. *Standard Edition,* 11:3-56. London: Hogarth Press, 1957.
—— (1911), Formulations on the Two Principles of Mental Functioning. *Standard Edition,* 12:213-226. London: Hogarth Press, 1958.
—— (1912a), The Dynamics of Transference. *Standard Edition,* 12:97-108. London: Hogarth Press, 1958.

——— (1912b), A Note on the Unconscious in Psycho-Analysis. *Standard Edition*, 12:255-266. London: Hogarth Press, 1958.
——— (1913), The Claims of Psycho-Analysis to Scientific Interest. *Standard Edition*, 13:163-190. London: Hogarth Press, 1955.
——— (1914a), On the History of the Psycho-Analytic Movement. *Standard Edition*, 14:1-66. London: Hogarth Press, 1957.
——— (1914b), On Narcissism: An Introduction. *Standard Edition*, 14:67-102. London: Hogarth Press, 1957.
——— (1915a), Instincts and Their Vicissitudes. *Standard Edition*, 14:109-140. London: Hogarth Press, 1957.
——— (1915b), The Unconscious. *Standard Edition*, 14:159-215. London: Hogarth Press, 1957.
——— (1915c), A Metapsychological Supplement to the Theory of Dreams. *Standard Edition*, 14:217-235. London: Hogarth Press, 1957.
——— (1916-1917 [1915-1917]), Introductory Lectures on Psycho-Analysis. *Standard Edition*, 15 & 16. London: Hogarth Press, 1963.
——— (1917), A Difficulty in the Path of Psycho-Analysis. *Standard Edition*, 17:135-144. London: Hogarth Press, 1955.
——— (1920), Beyond the Pleasure Principle. *Standard Edition*, 18:1-64. London: Hogarth Press, 1955.
——— (1921), Group Psychology and the Analysis of the Ego. *Standard Edition*, 18:65-143. London: Hogarth Press, 1955.
——— (1922), Dreams and Telepathy. *Standard Edition*, 18:195-220. London: Hogarth Press, 1955.
——— (1923), The Ego and the Id. *Standard Edition*, 19:1-66. London: Hogarth Press, 1961.
——— (1925a [1924]), The Resistances to Psycho-Analysis. *Standard Edition*, 19:211-224. London: Hogarth Press, 1961.
——— (1925b [1924]), An Autobiographical Study. *Standard Edition*, 20:1-74. London: Hogarth Press, 1959.
——— (1926a), Inhibitions, Symptoms and Anxiety. *Standard Edition*, 20:75-175. London: Hogarth Press, 1959.
——— (1926b), The Question of Lay Analysis. *Standard Edition*, 20:177-258. London: Hogarth Press, 1959.
——— (1927), The Future of an Illusion. *Standard Edition*, 21:1-56. London: Hogarth Press, 1961.
——— (1930a [1929]), Civilization and Its Discontents. *Standard Edition*, 21:57-145. London: Hogarth Press, 1961.
——— (1930b), Introduction to the Special Psychopathology Number of *The Medical Review of Reviews*. *Standard Edition*, 21:254-255. London: Hogarth Press, 1961.
——— (1932), *New Introductory Lectures on Psycho-Analysis*. New York: Norton, 1933.
——— (1937), Analysis Terminable and Interminable. *Collected Papers*, 5:316-357. London: Hogarth Press, 1950.
——— (1939 [1937-1939]), *Moses and Monotheism*. New York: Knopf.
——— (1940 [1938]), *An Outline of Psychoanalysis*. New York: Norton, 1949.
Froude, J. A., ed. (1883), *Letters and Memorials of Jane Welsh Carlyle*, II. New York: Harper.
Galdston, I. (1956a), Freud and Romantic Medicine. *Bull. Hist. Med.*, 30:489-507.
——— (1956b), Freud's Influence in Contemporary Culture. *Bull. N.Y. Acad. Med.*, 32:908-919.
Gay, F. P. (1938), *The Open Mind: Elmer Ernest Southard, 1876-1920*. Chicago: Normandie House.

Gay, P. (1954), The Enlightenment in the History of Political Theory. *Pol. Sci. Quart.,* 69:374-389.
Gengerelli, J. A. (1957), The Limitations of Psychoanalysis—2. Dogma or Discipline? *Sat. Rev.,* March 23:9-11, 40.
Gibson, J. J. (1941), A Critical Review of the Concept of Set in Contemporary Experimental Psychology. *Psychol. Bull.,* 38:781-816.
Gill, M. M. (1963), Topography and Systems in Psychoanalytic Theory. *Psychological Issues,* 3(2). New York: International Universities Press.
———— & Brenman, M. (1947), Problems in Clinical Research, Round Table, 1946. *Amer. J. Orthopsychiat.,* 17:196-230.
———— ———— (1959), *Hypnosis and Related States: Psychoanalytic Studies in Regression.* New York: International Universities Press.
Gillispie, C. C. (1951), *Genesis and Geology.* Cambridge, Mass.: Harvard University Press.
Glixman, A. F. (1948), An Analysis of the Use of the Interruption-Technique in Experimental Studies of "Repression." *Psychol. Bull.,* 45:491-506.
Goethe, W. (1780), Die Natur (Aphoristisch.) (Um das Jahr 1780.) *Goethes Werke,* 36er Band. Stuttgart: J. G. Cotta'scher Verlag, 1867, pp. 218-221.
Goldman, E. (1934), *Living My Life.* New York: Knopf.
Gomperz, T., ed. (1880), *John Stuart Mills Gesammelte Werke.* Vol. 12: Über Frauenemancipation. Plato. Arbeiterfrage. Sozialismus. Tr. S. Freud. Leipzig: Fues's Verlag.
Gould, R. (1942), Repression Experimentally Analyzed. *Charact. & Pers.,* 10: 259-288.
Greene, J. C. (1959a), Darwin and Religion. *Proc. Amer. Philos. Soc.,* 103:716-725.
———— (1959b), *The Death of Adam.* New York: New American Library (Mentor Books), 1961.
Grinker, R. R. (1958), A Philosophical Appraisal of Psychoanalysis. In *Science and Psychoanalysis.* Vol. 1: Integrative Studies, ed. J. H. Masserman. New York: Grune & Stratton, pp. 126-142.
Gross, A. (1951), The Secret. *Bull. Menninger Clin.,* 15:37-44.
Groves, E. R. (1916a), *Moral Sanitation.* New York: Association Press.
———— (1916b), Freud and Sociology. *Psychoanal. Rev.,* 3:241-253.
Hacker, L. M., & Kendrick, B. B. (1949), *The United States Since 1865,* 4th ed. Appleton-Century-Crofts.
Hale, N. G., Jr. (1964), Popularizations of Freud in America through the 1920's. Forthcoming doctoral dissertation. University of California.
Hall, C. S. (1954), *A Primer of Freudian Psychology.* Cleveland: World.
———— & Lindzey, G. (1957), *Theories of Personality.* New York: Wiley.
Hall, G. S. (1891), Book Review: W. James, "Principles of Psychology." *Amer. J. Psychol.,* 3:578-591.
———— (1895a), Editorial. *Amer. J. Psychol.,* 7:3-8.
———— (1895b), Discussion and Correspondence: Experimental Psychology in America. *Science,* N. S. 2:734-735.
———— (1904), *Adolescence: Its Psychology.* New York: Appleton.
[————] (1909a), Twentieth Anniversary of Clark University. *Nation,* 89:284-285.
———— (1909b), Evolution and Psychology. In *Fifty Years of Darwinism. Modern Aspects of Evolution. Centennial Addresses in Honor of Charles Darwin before the AAAS.* New York: Holt, pp. 251-267.
———— (1923), *Life and Confessions of a Psychologist.* New York: Appleton.
Hamilton, G. V. (1914), A Study of Sexual Tendencies in Monkeys and Baboons. *J. Animal Behav.,* 4:295-318.
———— (1916), A Study of Perseverance Reactions in Primates and Rodents. *Behav. Monogr.,* 3(13).
———— (1925), *An Introduction to Objective Psychopathology.* St. Louis: Mosby.

——— (1929), *A Research in Marriage.* New York: Boni.
Hapgood, H. (1939), *A Victorian in the Modern World.* New York: Harcourt, Brace.
Harrell, W., & Harrison, R. (1938), The Rise and Fall of Behaviorism. *J. Gen. Psychol.,* 18:367-421.
Harriman, P. L. (1947), *The New Dictionary of Psychology.* New York: Philosophical Library.
Hart, B. (1910), The Conception of the Subconscious. *J. Abn. Psychol.,* 4:351-371.
——— (1912), *The Psychology of Insanity.* Cambridge: University Press.
——— (1926), The Conception of Dissociation. *Brit. J. Med. Psychol.,* 6:241-256.
Hartmann, H. (1939), *Ego Psychology and the Problem of Adaptation.* New York: International Universities Press, 1958.
——— (1948), Comments on the Psychoanalytic Theory of Instinctual Drives. *Psychoanal. Quart.,* 17:366-388.
——— (1950a), Comments on the Psychoanalytic Theory of the Ego. *The Psychoanalytic Study of the Child,* 5:74-96. New York: International Universities Press.
——— (1950b), Psychoanalysis and Developmental Psychology. *The Psychoanalytic Study of the Child,* 5:7-17. New York: International Universities Press.
——— (1952), The Mutual Influences in the Development of the Ego and Id. *The Psychoanalytic Study of the Child,* 7:9-30. New York: International Universities Press.
——— (1956a), Notes on the Reality Principle. *The Psychoanalytic Study of the Child,* 11:31-53. New York: International Universities Press.
——— (1956b), The Development of the Ego Concept in Freud's Work. *Int. J. Psycho-Anal.,* 37:425-438.
——— (1960), *Psychoanalysis and Moral Values.* New York: International Universities Press.
——— & Kris, E. (1945), The Genetic Approach in Psychoanalysis. *The Psychoanalytic Study of the Child,* 1:11-30. New York: International Universities Press.
——— ——— & Loewenstein, R. M. (1946), Comments on the Formation of Psychic Structure. *The Psychoanalytic Study of the Child,* 2:11-38. New York: International Universities Press.
——— ——— ——— (1949), Notes on the Theory of Aggression. *The Psychoanalytic Study of the Child,* 3/4:9-36. New York: International Universities Press.
——— ——— ——— (1953), The Function of Theory in Psychoanalysis. In *Drives, Affects, Behavior,* ed. R. M. Loewenstein. New York: International Universities Press, pp. 13-37.
H. D. (1956), *Tribute to Freud.* New York: Pantheon.
Healy, W. (1915), *The Individual Delinquent.* Boston: Little, Brown.
——— Bronner, A. F., & Bowers, A. M. (1930), *The Structure and Meaning of Psychoanalysis.* New York: Knopf.
Heidbreder, E. (1933), *Seven Psychologies.* New York: Appleton-Century.
——— (1940), Freud and Psychology. *Psychol. Rev.,* 47:185-195.
Heider, F. (1958), *The Psychology of Interpersonal Relations.* New York: Wiley.
Helson, H., ed. (1951), *Theoretical Foundations of Psychology.* New York: Van Nostrand.
Henderson, E. N. (1911), Do We Forget the Disagreeable? *J. Philos., Psychol., Sci. Meth.,* 8:432-437.
Hendrick, I. (1934), *Facts and Theories of Psychoanalysis.* New York: Knopf.
——— (1939), *Facts and Theories of Psychoanalysis,* 2nd ed. New York: Knopf.

——— (1958), *Facts and Theories of Psychoanalysis*, 3rd rev. ed. New York: Knopf.
Herma, H., Kris, E., & Shor, J. (1943), Freud's Theory of the Dream in American Textbooks. *J. Abn. Soc. Psychol.*, 38:319-334.
Hermann, I. (1934), *Die Psychoanalyse als Methode*. Vienna: Internationaler psychoanalytischer Verlag.
Hilgard, E. R. (1948), *Theories of Learning*. New York: Appleton-Century-Crofts.
——— (1949), Human Motives and the Concept of the Self. *Amer. Psychologist*, 4:374-382.
——— (1952), Experimental Approaches to Psychoanalysis. In *Psychoanalysis As Science*, ed. E. Pumpian-Mindlin. Stanford, Calif.: Stanford University Press, pp. 3-45.
——— (1956a), *Theories of Learning*, 2nd ed. New York: Appleton-Century-Crofts.
——— (1956b), Freud's Psychodynamics. In Hilgard (1956a), pp. 290-327.
——— (1957), Freud and Experimental Psychology. *Behav. Sci.*, 2:74-79.
——— Gill, M. M., & Shakow, D. (1953), A Planning Proposal for Research in Emotional Growth and Mental Health. (Behavioral Sciences Division of the Ford Foundation.) New York: Social Science Research Council (for private circulation).
Himmelfarb, G. (1959), *Darwin and the Darwinian Revolution*. Garden City, N.Y.: Doubleday.
Hitschmann, E. (1911), *Freud's Theories of the Neuroses*. New York: Nervous and Mental Disease Pub. Co., 1913.
Hoff, H., & Seitelberger, F. (1962), The History of the Neurological School of Vienna. *J. Nerv. Ment. Dis.*, 116:495-505.
Hoffman, F. J. (1957), *Freudianism and the Literary Mind*, 2nd ed. New York: Grove Press (Evergreen Books), 1959.
Hofstadter, R. (1955), *The Age of Reform: From Bryan to F.D.R.* New York: Knopf.
Holmes, O. W. (1871), *Mechanism in Thought and Morals*. Boston: Osgood.
Holt, E. B. (1915), *The Freudian Wish and Its Place in Ethics*. New York: Holt.
Hook, S., ed. (1960), *Psychoanalysis, Scientific Method, and Philosophy; a Symposium*. New York: Grove Press (Evergreen Books).
Hoppe, F. (1930), Erfolg und Misserfolg. *Psychol. Forsch.*, 14:1-62.
Hughes, H. S. (1958), *Consciousness and Society*. New York: Knopf.
Hulin, W. S. (1934), *A Short History of Psychology*. New York: Holt.
Hull, C. L. (1930), Knowledge and Purpose as Habit Mechanisms. *Psychol. Rev.*, 37:511-525.
——— (1931), Goal Attraction and Directing Ideas Conceived as Habit Phenomena. *Psychol. Rev.*, 38:487-506.
——— (1933), *Hypnosis and Suggestibility*. New York: Appleton-Century.
——— (1935), Book Review: E. L. Thorndike, "Fundamentals of Learning." *Psychol. Bull.*, 32:807-823.
——— (1936-1942), Hull Seminars: Notices, Memoranda, Abstracts of Proceedings, and Related Working Papers. Unpublished mimeographed material. On deposit, Yale University Library.
——— (1943), *Principles of Behavior*. New York: Appleton-Century.
——— (1952), Clark L. Hull. In *A History of Psychology in Autobiography*, Vol. 4, ed. E. G. Boring, H. S. Langfeld, H. Werner & R. M. Yerkes. Worcester, Mass.: Clark University Press, pp. 143-162.
——— (1962), Psychology of the Scientist: IV. Passages from the 'Idea Books' of Clark L. Hull. *Percept. Mot. Skills*, 15:807-882.
Humphrey, G. (1920), The Conditioned Reflex and the Freudian Wish. *J. Abn. Psychol.*, 14:388-392.
——— (1921), Education and Freudianism. *J. Abn. Psychol.*, 15:350-402.

——— (1922a), The Conditioned Reflex and the Elementary Social Reaction. *J. Abn. Soc. Psychol.,* 17:113-119.
——— (1922b), Book Reviews: S. Freud, "A General Introduction to Psychoanalysis." A. G. Tansley, "The New Psychology and Its Relation to Life." *J. Abn. Soc. Psychol.,* 17:224-227.
Hunt, J. McV. (1941), The Effects of Infant Feeding-Frustration upon Adult Hoarding in the Albino Rat. *J. Abn. Soc. Psychol.,* 36:338-360.
——— ed. (1944), *Personality and the Behavior Disorders,* 2 Vols. New York: Ronald Press.
——— Hunter, W. S., & Schlosberg, H. (1945), Raymond Royce Willoughby: 1896-1944. *Psychol. Rev.,* 52:113-115.
Hunter, J. D. (1925), The History and Development of Institutes for the Study of Children. In *The Child, the Clinic and the Court.* New York: New Republic, pp. 204-214.
Huxley, J. (1960), The Emergence of Darwinism. In *Evolution After Darwin.* Vol. 1: The Evolution of Life, ed. S. Tax. Chicago: University of Chicago Press, pp. 1-21.
Huxley, L. (1900), *Life and Letters of Thomas Henry Huxley,* Vol. 2. London: Macmillan.
Hyman, S. E. (1962), *The Tangled Bank.* New York: Atheneum.
Irvine, W. (1955), *Apes, Angels, and Victorians.* New York: McGraw-Hill.
Isaacs, S. (1930), *Intellectual Growth in Young Children.* New York: Harcourt, Brace.
——— (1933), *Social Development in Young Children.* New York: Harcourt, Brace.
Jacobson, E. (1953), Affects and Their Pleasure-Unpleasure Qualities, in Relation to the Psychic Discharge Processes. In *Drives, Affects, Behavior,* ed. R. M. Loewenstein. New York: International Universities Press, pp. 38-66.
James, W. (1884), On Some Omissions of Introspective Psychology. *Mind,* 9:1-26.
——— (1890), *The Principles of Psychology,* 2 Vols. New York: Holt.
——— (1902), *The Varieties of Religious Experience.* New York: Longmans, Green.
——— (1907), *Pragmatism.* London: Longmans, Green.
——— (1911), *Some Problems of Philosophy.* London: Longmans, Green.
——— (1920a), *Collected Essays and Reviews.* New York: Longmans, Green.
——— (1920b), *The Letters of William James,* Vol. 2. London: Longmans, Green.
——— Ladd, G. T., Baldwin, J. M., & Cattell, J. McK. (1895), Correspondence: Experimental Psychology in America. *Science,* N. S. 2:626-628.
Janet, P. (1889), *L'Automatisme Psychologique.* Paris: Alcan.
——— (1914), Psychoanalysis. *J. Abn. Psychol.,* 9:1-35; 153-187.
Jastrow, J. (1906), *The Subconscious.* New York: Houghton Mifflin.
——— (1930), Joseph Jastrow. In *A History of Psychology in Autobiography,* Vol. 1, ed. C. Murchison. Worcester, Mass.: Clark University Press, pp. 135-162.
——— (1932), *The House that Freud Built.* New York: Greenberg.
Jelliffe, S. E. (1931), Sigmund Freud as a Neurologist: Some Notes on His Earlier Neurobiological and Clinical Neurological Studies. *J. Nerv. Ment. Dis.,* 85:696-711.
Jones, E. (1913a), *Papers on Psycho-Analysis.* London: Baillière, Tindall & Cox.
——— (1913b), Book Review: W. Lippmann, "A Preface to Politics." *Imago,* 2:452-456.
——— (1948), *Papers on Psycho-Analysis,* 5th ed. Baltimore: Williams & Wilkins.
——— (1953), *The Life and Work of Sigmund Freud.* Vol. 1: The Formative Years and the Great Discoveries, 1856-1900. New York: Basic Books.

——— (1955), *The Life and Work of Sigmund Freud.* Vol. 2: Years of Maturity, 1901-1919. New York: Basic Books.
——— (1956), *Sigmund Freud: Four Centenary Addresses.* New York: Basic Books.
——— (1957), *The Life and Work of Sigmund Freud.* Vol. 3: The Last Phase, 1919-1939. New York: Basic Books.
Jung, C. G. (1907), The Psychology of Dementia Praecox. In *The Psychogenesis of Mental Disease.* London: Routledge & Kegan Paul, 1960, pp. 1-151.
——— (1962), Jung on Freud. *Atlant. Monthly,* 210:47-58.
Kaplan, A. (1957), Freud and Modern Philosophy. In Nelson, ed. (1957), pp. 209-229.
Kaufman, W. (1959), Book Review: D. Bakan, "Sigmund Freud and the Jewish Mystical Tradition." *Judaism,* 8:190-192.
——— (1960), *From Shakespeare to Existentialism.* Garden City, N.Y.: Doubleday (Anchor Books).
——— (1961), *The Faith of a Heretic.* Garden City, N.Y.: Doubleday.
Kazin, A. (1942), *On Native Grounds: An Interpretation of Modern American Prose Literature.* New York: Reynal & Hitchcock.
——— (1962), *Contemporaries.* Boston: Little, Brown.
Keith, A. (1935), Darwinism and Its Critics. *The Modern Thinker,* 6:51-61.
Kempf, E. J. (1917), A Study of the Anaesthesia, Convulsions, Vomiting, Visual Constriction, Erythema and Itching of Mrs. V. G. *J. Abn. Psychol.,* 12:1-24.
Koch, S. (1959), Epilogue. In *Psychology: A Study of a Science.* Vol. 3: Formulations of the Person and the Social Context, ed. S. Koch. New York: McGraw-Hill, pp. 729-788.
Kris, E. (1950), The Significance of Freud's Earliest Discoveries. *Int. J. Psycho-Anal.,* 31:1-9.
Kubie, L. (1953), Psychoanalysis as a Basic Science. In *Twenty Years of Psychoanalysis,* ed. F. Alexander & H. Ross. New York: Norton, pp. 120-145.
Kuhn, T. S. (1957), *The Copernican Revolution.* Cambridge, Mass.: Harvard University Press.
——— (1962), *The Structure of Scientific Revolutions.* Chicago: University of Chicago Press.
Langfeld, H. S. (1946), Edwin Bissell Holt, 1873-1946. *Psychol. Rev.,* 53:251-258.
Lasswell, H. D. (1960), Approaches to Human Personality: William James and Sigmund Freud. *Psychoanal. & Psychoanal. Rev.,* 47(3):52-68.
Lerner, E. (1937), *Constraint Areas and the Moral Judgment of Children.* Menasha, Wisconsin: Banta.
Levitt, M. (1960), *Freud and Dewey on the Nature of Man.* New York: Philosophical Library.
Lewin, B. D. (1962), Reminiscence and Retrospect. In *Fruition of an Idea: Fifty Years of Psychoanalysis in New York,* ed. M. Wangh. New York: International Universities Press, pp. 35-42.
——— & Ross, H. (1961), *Psychoanalytic Education in the United States.* New York: Norton.
Lewin, K. (1917), Die psychische Tätigkeit bei der Hemmung von Willensvorgängen und das Grundgesetz der Assoziation. *Z. Psychol.,* 77:212-247.
——— (1922a), Das Problem der Willensmessung und das Grundgesetz der Assoziation, I. *Psychol. Forsch.,* 1:191-302.
——— (1922b), Das Problem der Willensmessung und das Grundgesetz der Assoziation, II. *Psychol. Forsch.,* 2:65-140.
——— (1922c), *Der Begriff der Genese in Physik, Biologie und Entwicklungsgeschichte.* Berlin: Springer.

——— (1923), Über die Umkehrung der Raumlage auf dem Kopf stehender Worte und Figuren in der Wahrnehmung. *Psychol. Forsch.,* 4:210-261.

——— (1926), *Vorsatz, Wille und Bedürfnis mit Vorbemerkungen über die psychischen Kräfte und Energien und die Struktur der Seele.* Berlin: Springer. Translated in part as Intention, Will and Need. In Rapaport, ed. (1951), pp. 95-153.

——— (1927), Gesetz und Experiment in der Psychologie. *Symposion,* 1:375-421.

——— (1935), *A Dynamic Theory of Personality.* New York: McGraw-Hill.

——— (1937), Psychoanalysis and Topological Psychology. *Bull. Menninger Clin.,* 1:202-211.

——— & Sakuma, K. (1925), Die Sehrichtung monokularer und binokularer Objekte bei Bewegung und das Zustandekommen des Tiefeneffektes. *Psychol. Forsch.,* 6:298-357.

——— et al. (1926-1932), Untersuchungen zur Handlungs und Affekt Psychologie. *Psychol. Forsch.*

Lewis, N. D. C., & Landis, C. (1957), Freud's Library. *Psychoanal. Rev.,* 44: 327-328.

Lewy, E., & Rapaport, D. (1944), The Psychoanalytic Concept of Memory and Its Relation to Recent Memory Theories. *Psychoanal. Quart.,* 13:16-42.

Lippmann, W. (1913), *A Preface to Politics.* New York: Mitchell Kennerley.

——— (1915), Freud and the Layman. *New Republic,* April 17:9-10.

Loeb, J. (1899), *Comparative Physiology of the Brain and Comparative Psychology.* New York: Putnam, 1907.

Luhan, M. D. (1936), *Intimate Memories.* Vol. 3: Movers and Shakers. New York: Harcourt, Brace.

MacCurdy, J. T. (1922), *Problems in Dynamic Psychology: A Critique of Psychoanalysis and Suggested Formulations.* New York: Macmillan.

——— (1925), *The Psychology of Emotion.* New York: Harcourt, Brace.

MacKinnon, D. W., & Dukes, W. F. (1962), Repression. In *Psychology in the Making,* ed. L. Postman. New York: Knopf, pp. 662-744.

MacRae, D. (1954), A Test of Piaget's Theories of Moral Development. *J. Abn. Soc. Psychol.,* 49:14-18.

Madison, P. (1956), Freud's Repression Concept: A Survey and Attempted Clarification. *Int. J. Psycho-Anal.,* 37:75-81.

Martin, E. D. (1920), *The Behavior of Crowds.* New York: Harper.

Marx, M. H., ed. (1951), *Psychological Theory: Contemporary Readings.* New York: Macmillan.

Maslow, A. H. (1962), *Toward a Psychology of Being.* Princeton, N. J.: Van Nostrand.

——— & Mittelmann, B. (1941), *Principles of Abnormal Psychology.* New York: Harper.

——— ——— (1951), *Principles of Abnormal Psychology,* rev. ed. New York: Harper.

Matthews, F. H., Jr. (1955), Freud Comes to America: The Influence of Freudian Ideas on American Thought, 1909-1917. Unpublished master's thesis. University of California.

May, H. F. (1959), *The End of American Innocence.* New York: Knopf.

McClelland, D. C. (1957), Freud and Hull: Pioneers in Scientific Psychology. *Amer. Scientist,* 45:101-113.

McDougall, W. (1910), V. Instinct and Intelligence. *Brit. J. Psychol.,* 3:250-266.

——— (1914a), The Definition of the Sexual Instinct. *Proc. Roy. Soc. Med.,* 7:65-78.

——— (1914b), *An Introduction to Social Psychology,* 13th ed. Boston: Luce, 1918.

——— (1918), The Present Position in Clinical Psychology. *Proc. Roy. Soc. Med.,* 12:1-13.

——— (1920), Motives in the Light of Recent Discussion. *Mind,* 29:277-293.
——— (1923), *Outline of Psychology.* New York: Scribner's.
——— (1925), A Great Advance of the Freudian Psychology. *J. Abn. Soc. Psychol.,* 20:43-47.
——— (1926), *Outline of Abnormal Psychology.* New York: Scribner's.
——— (1930), William McDougall. In *A History of Psychology in Autobiography,* Vol. 1, ed. C. Murchison. Worcester, Mass.: Clark University Press, pp. 191-223.
——— (1936), *Psychoanalysis and Social Psychology.* London: Methuen.
——— (1938), The Relations between Dissociation and Repression. *Brit. J. Med. Psychol.,* 17:141-157.
Meltzer, H. (1930), Individual Differences in Forgetting Pleasant and Unpleasant Experiences. *J. Educ. Psychol.,* 21:399-409.
——— (1931a), The Forgetting of Pleasant and Unpleasant Experiences in Relation to Intelligence and Achievement. *J. Soc. Psychol.,* 2:216-229.
——— (1931b), Sex Differences in Forgetting Pleasant and Unpleasant Experiences. *J. Abn. Soc. Psychol.,* 25:450-464.
Merlan, P. (1945), Brentano and Freud. *J. Hist. Ideas,* 6:375-377.
——— (1949), Brentano and Freud—A Sequel. *J. Hist. Ideas,* 10:451.
Moore, R. (1957), *Charles Darwin.* London: Hutchinson.
Moore, T. V. (1919), Hypnotic Analogies. *Psychol. Monogr.,* 27:387-400.
——— (1921), The Parataxes: A Study of Certain Borderline Mental States. *Psychoanal. Rev.,* 8:252-283.
——— (1924), *Dynamic Psychology.* Philadelphia: Lippincott.
Mowrer, O. H. (1950), *Learning Theory and Personality Dynamics.* New York: Ronald Press.
Müller-Freienfels, R. (1935), *The Evolution of Modern Psychology.* New Haven: Yale University Press.
Munroe, R. L. (1955), *Schools of Psychoanalytic Thought.* New York: Dryden Press.
Murphy, G. (1929a), *An Historical Introduction to Modern Psychology.* New York: Harcourt, Brace.
——— ed. (1929b), *An Outline of Abnormal Psychology.* New York: Modern Library.
——— (1933), *General Psychology.* New York: Harper.
——— (1945), The Freeing of Intelligence. *Psychol. Bull.,* 42:1-19.
——— (1947), *Personality: A Biosocial Approach to Origins and Structure.* New York: Harper.
——— (1949), *Historical Introduction to Modern Psychology,* rev. ed. New York: Harcourt, Brace.
——— (1950), The Irrational in the International Picture. In *Feelings and Emotions: The Moosehart Symposium,* ed. M. L. Reymert. New York: McGraw-Hill, pp. 487-492.
——— (1956), The Current Impact of Freud upon Psychology. *Amer. Psychologist,* 11:663-672.
——— & Bachrach, A. J., eds. (1954), *An Outline of Abnormal Psychology,* rev. ed. New York: Modern Library.
——— & Jensen, F. (1932), *Approaches to Personality: Some Contemporary Conceptions Used in Psychology and Psychiatry.* New York: Coward-McCann.
——— & Murphy, L. B. (1931), *Experimental Social Psychology.* New York: Harper.
——— ——— & Newcomb, T. M. (1937), *Experimental Social Psychology,* rev. ed. New York: Harper.
Murray, H. A. (1938), *Explorations in Personality.* New York: Oxford University Press.

Myers, C. S., Morgan, C. L., Carr, H. W., Stout, G. F., & McDougall, W. (1910), Instinct and Intelligence. *Brit. J. Psychol.,* 3:209-270.
Nelson, B., ed. (1957), *Freud and the 20th Century.* New York: Meridian Books.
Nicoll, M., Rivers, W. H. R., & Jones, E. (1918), Why is the 'Unconscious' Unconscious? *Brit. J. Psychol.,* 9:230-256.
Northridge, W. L. (1924), *Modern Theories of the Unconscious.* New York: Dutton.
Nunberg, H. (1955), *Principles of Psychoanalysis.* New York: International Universities Press.
Oberndorf, C. P., ed. and trans. (1953), Autobiography of Josef Breuer (1842-1925). *Int. J. Psycho-Anal.,* 34:64-67.
Ofiesh, G. D. (1959), The History, Development, Present Status, and Purpose of the First (Introductory) Course in Psychology in American Undergraduate Education. Unpublished doctoral dissertation. University of Denver.
Ogburn, W. F. (1933), *Recent Social Trends in the United States: Report of the President's Research Committee on Social Trends,* 2 Vols. New York: McGraw-Hill.
Orlansky, H. (1949), Infant Care and Personality. *Psychol. Bull.* 46:1-48.
Park, D. G. (1931), Freudian Influence on Academic Psychology. *Psychol. Rev.,* 38:73-85.
Payne, S. M. (1956), Sir Arthur George Tansley, F. R. S., 1871-1955. *Int. J. Psycho-Anal.,* 37:197.
Payne, V. (1950), Psychology and Psychiatry at the Clark Conference of 1909. Doctor of Medicine dissertation. University of Wisconsin.
Pelikan, J. (1960), Creation and Causality in the History of Christian Thought. *J. Relig.,* 40:246-255.
Perry, R. B. (1935), *The Thought and Character of William James.* Vol. 2: Philosophy and Psychology. Boston: Little, Brown.
—————— (1938), *In the Spirit of William James.* New Haven: Yale University Press.
Peters, R. S., ed. (1953), *Brett's History of Psychology.* London: Allen & Unwin.
Pfister, O. (1913), *The Psychoanalytic Method.* New York: Moffat, Yard, 1917.
—————— (1923), *Some Applications of Psycho-Analysis.* London: Allen & Unwin.
Piaget, J. (1923), *The Language and Thought of the Child.* New York: Harcourt, Brace, 1926.
—————— (1924), *Judgment and Reasoning in the Child.* New York: Harcourt, Brace, 1928.
—————— (1927a), *The Child's Conception of the World.* New York: Harcourt, Brace, 1929.
—————— (1927b), *The Child's Conception of Physical Causality.* New York: Humanities Press, 1951.
—————— (1932), *The Moral Judgment of the Child.* Glencoe, Ill.: The Free Press, 1952.
—————— (1952), Jean Piaget. In *A History of Psychology in Autobiography,* Vol. 4, ed. E. G. Boring, H. S. Langfeld, H. Werner & R. M. Yerkes. Worcester, Mass.: Clark University Press, pp. 237-256.
Postman, L. (1947), The History and Present Status of the Law of Effect. *Psychol. Bull.,* 44:489-563.
Pribram, K. H. (1962), The Neuropsychology of Sigmund Freud. In *Experimental Foundations of Clinical Psychology,* ed. A. J. Bachrach. New York: Basic Books, pp. 442-468.
Prince, M. (1885), *The Nature of Mind and Human Automatism.* Philadelphia: Lippincott.
—————— (1891), Association Neuroses: A Study of the Pathology of Hysterical

Joint Affections, Neurasthenia and Allied Forms of Neuro-Mimesis. *J. Nerv. Ment. Dis.*, 16:257-282.

─── (1914), *The Unconscious.* New York: Macmillan.

─── (1939), *Clinical and Experimental Studies in Personality*, rev., enlarged (with Introduction and Notes) by A. A. Roback. Cambridge, Mass.: Sci-Art Publishers.

Proceedings of the Twenty-Fifth Anniversary Meeting of the Society for Research in Child Development (1960), *Child Developm.,* 31:187-239.

Puner, H. W. (1947), *Freud: His Life and His Mind.* New York: Dell, 1961.

Putnam, J. J. (1915), *Human Motives.* Boston: Little, Brown.

Ralph, J. (1921), *How to Psycho-Analyze Yourself.* Long Beach, Calif.: The Author.

Ramsey, G. V. (1953), Studies of Dreaming. *Psychol. Bull.,* 50:432-455.

Rand, B., ed. (1912), *The Classical Psychologists.* Boston: Houghton Mifflin.

Rapaport, D. (1942a), *Emotions and Memory.* Baltimore: Williams & Wilkins.

─── (1942b), Freudian Mechanisms and Frustration Experiments. *Psychoanal. Quart.,* 11:503-511.

─── (1944), The Scientific Methodology of Psychoanalysis. Six lectures given at the Topeka Institute of Psychoanalysis. Ms.

─── (1947), Dynamic Psychology and Kantian Epistemology. Paper presented at the staff seminar of the Menninger Foundation School of Clinical Psychology. Ms.

─── (1949), Interpersonal Relations, Communication, and Psychodynamics. Paper presented at the Menninger Foundation General Seminar. Ms.

─── (1950a), On the Psycho-Analytic Theory of Thinking. *Int. J. Psycho-Anal.,* 31:161-170. Also in *Psychoanalytic Psychiatry and Psychology: Clinical and Theoretical Papers* [Austen Riggs Center, Vol. 1], ed. R. P. Knight & C. R. Friedman. New York: International Universities Press, 1954, pp. 259-273.

─── (1950b), *Emotions and Memory,* 2nd unaltered ed. New York: International Universities Press.

─── ed. (1951), *Organization and Pathology of Thought.* New York: Columbia University Press.

─── (1952), Book Review: O. H. Mowrer, "Learning Theory and Personality Dynamics." *J. Abn. Soc. Psychol.,* 47:137-142.

─── (1953a), Book Review: J. Dollard & N. E. Miller, "Personality and Psychotherapy: An Analysis in Terms of Learning, Thinking, and Culture." *Amer. J. Orthopsychiat.,* 23:204-208.

─── (1953b), On the Psycho-Analytic Theory of Affects. *Int. J. Psycho-Anal.,* 34:177-198. Also in *Psychoanalytic Psychiatry and Psychology: Clinical and Theoretical Papers* [Austen Riggs Center, Vol. 1], ed. R. P. Knight & C. R. Friedman. New York: International Universities Press, 1954, pp. 274-310.

─── (1953c), Discussion in *Mass Communications Seminar: Proceedings of an Interdisciplinary Seminar,* ed. H. Powdermaker. New York: Wenner-Gren Foundation, pp. 121-128.

─── (1955), *The Development and the Concepts of Psychoanalytic Ego Psychology.* Twelve seminars given at the Western New England Institute for Psychoanalysis. Multilithed.

─── (1957a), Cognitive Structures. In *Contemporary Approaches to Cognition: A Symposium Held at the University of Colorado,* J. Bruner et al. Cambridge, Mass.: Harvard University Press, pp. 157-200.

─── (1957b), *Seminars on Advanced Metapsychology,* 4 Vols. Western New England Institute for Psychoanalysis, ed. S. C. Miller et al. Multilithed.

─── (1957c), Priorities: Freud and Adler. *Contemp. Psychol.,* 2:303-304.

─── (1957-1959), *Seminars on Elementary Metapsychology,* 3 Vols. Western

New England Institute for Psychoanalysis and Austen Riggs Center, ed. S. C. Miller. Multilithed.
────── (1958a), A Historical Survey of Psychoanalytic Ego Psychology. In "Identity and the Life Cycle." *Psychological Issues,* 1(1):5-17. New York: International Universities Press, 1959.
────── (1958b), The Theory of Ego Autonomy: A Generalization. *Bull. Menninger Clin.,* 22:13-35.
────── (1959), The Structure of Psychoanalytic Theory: A Systematizing Attempt. In *Psychology: A Study of a Science.* Vol. 3: Formulations of the Person and the Social Context, ed. S. Koch. New York: McGraw-Hill, pp. 55-183. Also in *Psychological Issues,* 2(2). New York: International Universities Press, 1960.
────── (1960a), On the Psychoanalytic Theory of Motivation. In *Nebraska Symposium on Motivation,* ed. M. R. Jones. Lincoln: University of Nebraska Press, pp. 173-247.
────── (1960b), Psychoanalysis as a Developmental Psychology. In *Perspectives in Psychological Theory,* ed. B. Kaplan & S. Wapner. New York: International Universities Press, pp. 209-255.
────── & Gill, M. M. (1959), The Points of View and Assumptions of Metapsychology. *Int. J. Psycho-Anal.,* 40:153-162.
Reed, C. F., Alexander, I. E., & Tomkins, S. S., eds. (1958), *Psychopathology.* Cambridge, Mass.: Harvard University Press.
Rickers-Ovsiankina, M. (1928), Die Wiederaufnahme unterbrochener Handlungen. *Psychol. Forsch.,* 11:302-379.
Rieff, P. (1959), *Freud: The Mind of the Moralist.* New York: Viking Press.
Rivers, W. H. R. (1918), Dreams and Primitive Culture. *Bull. John Rylands Libr., Manchester,* 4:387-410.
────── (1920), *Instinct and the Unconscious,* 2nd ed. Cambridge: University Press, 1924.
────── (1923), *Conflict and Dream.* London: Kegan Paul, Trench, Trubner.
────── Myers, C. S., Jung, C. G., Wallas, G., Drever, J., & McDougall, W. (1919), Instinct and the Unconscious. *Brit. J. Psychol.,* 10:1-42.
Robinson, E. S., & Richardson-Robinson, F., eds. (1923), *Readings in General Psychology.* Chicago: University of Chicago Press.
────── ────── eds. (1929), *Readings in General Psychology,* 2nd ed. Chicago: University of Chicago Press.
Robinson, J. H. (1921), *The Mind in the Making.* New York: Harper.
Roe, A. (1953), A Psychological Study of Eminent Psychologists and Anthropologists, and a Comparison with Biological and Physical Scientists. *Psychol. Monogr.,* 67(2): Whole No. 352.
Rosenbaum, M. (1954), Freud-Eitingon-Magnes Correspondence: Psychoanalysis at the Hebrew University. *J. Amer. Psychoanal. Assn.,* 2:311-317.
Rosenzweig, S. (1933), Preferences in the Repetition of Successful and Unsuccessful Activities as a Function of Age and Personality. *Pedagog. Sem. & J. Genet. Psychol.,* 42:423-441.
────── (1935), Freud Versus the Libertine. *The Modern Thinker,* 6(3):13-19.
────── (1941), Need-Persistive and Ego-Defensive Reactions to Frustration as Demonstrated by an Experiment on Repression. *Psychol. Rev.,* 48:347-349.
────── (1943), An Experimental Study of "Repression" with Special Reference to Need-Persistive and Ego-Defensive Reactions to Frustration. *J. Exp. Psychol.,* 32:64-74.
────── (1945), Further Comparative Data on Repetition-Choice after Success and Failure as Related to Frustration Tolerance. *J. Genet. Psychol.,* 66:75-81.
────── (1956), The Cultural Matrix of the Unconscious. *Amer. Psychologist,* 11:561-562.

―――― (1960), The Rosenzweig Picture-Frustration Study, Children's Form. In *Projective Techniques with Children,* ed. A. I. Rabin & M. R. Haworth. New York: Grune & Stratton, pp. 149-176.
―――― (1964), *Psychology in Historical Perspective,* in collaboration with E. G. Boring, J. Huxley, & W. Overholser. New York: Harper, in press.
―――― & Mason, G. (1934), An Experimental Study of Memory in Relation to the Theory of Repression. *Brit. J. Psychol.,* 24:247-265.
Ross, D. (1965), A Biography of G. Stanley Hall. Forthcoming doctoral dissertation. Columbia University.
Rosvold, H. E. (1955), Calvin Perry Stone: 1892-1954. *Amer. J. Psychol.,* 68:326-329.
Schoenwald, R. L. (1952), Sigmund Freud: The Origins and Early Development of a Social Theory. Unpublished doctoral dissertation. Harvard University.
Schur, M. (1953), The Ego in Anxiety. In *Drives, Affects, Behavior,* ed. R. M. Loewenstein. New York: International Universities Press, pp. 67-103.
―――― (1958), The Ego and the Id in Anxiety. *The Psychoanalytic Study of the Child,* 13:190-220. New York: International Universities Press.
Schwalbe, G. (1909), "The Descent of Man." In *Darwin and Modern Science,* ed. A. C. Seward. Cambridge: University Press, pp. 112-136.
Schwartz, G., & Bishop, P. W. (1958), *Moments of Discovery.* Vol. 1: The Origins of Science. New York: Basic Books.
Schwarz, G. (1927), Über Rückfälligkeit bei Umgewöhnung, I. *Psychol. Forsch.,* 9:86-158.
―――― (1933), Über Rückfälligkeit bei Umgewöhnung, II. *Psychol. Forsch.,* 18:143-190.
Sears, R. R. (1936a), Experimental Studies of Projection: I. Attribution of Traits. *J. Soc. Psychol.,* 7:151-163.
―――― (1936b), Functional Abnormalities of Memory with Special Reference to Amnesia. *Psychol. Bull.,* 33:229-274.
―――― (1937a), Experimental Studies of Projection: II. Ideas of Reference. *J. Soc. Psychol.,* 8:389-400.
―――― (1937b), Initiation of the Repression Sequence by Experienced Failure. *J. Exp. Psychol.,* 20:570-580.
―――― (1943), *Survey of Objective Studies of Psychoanalytic Concepts.* New York: Social Science Research Council.
―――― (1944), Experimental Analysis of Psychoanalytic Phenomena. In Hunt, ed. (1944), pp. 306-332.
―――― (1959), Personality Theory: The Next Forty Years. *Child Developm. Monogr.,* 24(5): Serial No. 74.
Severn, E. (1917), *The Psychology of Behaviour: A Practical Study of Human Personality and Conduct with Special Reference to Methods of Development.* New York: Dodd, Mead.
Shaffer, L. F., & Shoben, E. J., Jr. (1956), *The Psychology of Adjustment,* 2nd ed. Boston: Houghton Mifflin.
Shakow, D. (1948), Clinical Psychology: An Evaluation. In *Orthopsychiatry, 1923-1948: Retrospect and Prospect,* ed. L. G. Lowrey & V. Sloane. New York: American Orthopsychiatric Association, pp. 231-247.
―――― (1949), Psychology and Psychiatry: A Dialogue. *Amer. J. Orthopsychiat.,* 19:191-208; 381-396.
―――― (1953), Some Aspects of Mid-Century Psychiatry: Experimental Psychology. In *Mid-Century Psychiatry,* ed. R. R. Grinker. Springfield, Ill.: Thomas, pp. 76-103.
―――― (1956), The Improvement of Practicum Training and Facilities. In *Psychology and Mental Health,* ed. C. R. Strother. Washington, D.C.: American Psychological Association, pp. 53-75.
―――― (1959a), Discussion of L. S. Kubie, A New Model for Human Psycho-

logical Processes. Paper presented at a Joint Meeting of the Washington Psychiatric Society and Washington Psychoanalytic Society. Ms.

—— (1959b), Research in Child Development: A Case Illustration of the Psychologist's Dilemma. *Amer. J. Orthopsychiat.*, 29:45-59.

—— (1960a), The Recorded Psychoanalytic Interview as an Objective Approach to Research in Psychoanalysis. *Psychoanal. Quart.*, 29:82-97.

—— (1960b), Psicopatologia y Psicologia: Nota Sobre Tendencias. *Rev. Psicol. Gen. Apl., Madrid,* 15:835-837.

—— (1962), Psychoanalytic Education of Behavioral and Social Scientists for Research. In *Science and Psychoanalysis.* Vol. 5: Psychoanalytic Education, ed. J. H. Masserman. New York: Grune & Stratton, pp. 146-161.

—— (1964), Ethics for a Scientific Age—Some Moral Aspects of Psychoanalysis. To be published in *Psychoanal. & Psychoanal. Rev.*

Shapley, H. (1958), *Of Stars and Men.* Boston: Beacon Press.

Sidis, B. (1898), *The Psychology of Suggestion.* New York: Appleton.

—— (1914), *The Foundations of Normal and Abnormal Psychology.* Boston: Badger.

—— & Goodhart, S. P. (1904), *Multiple Personality.* New York: Appleton.

Silberer, H. (1912), Über die Symbolbildung. *Jahrb. Psychoanal. Psychopathol. Forsch.,* 3:661-723. Translated in part as On Symbol-Formation. In Rapaport, ed. (1951), pp. 208-233.

Simon, E. (1957), Sigmund Freud, the Jew. In *Year Book II:* Publication of the Leo Baeck Institute of Jews from Germany. London: East and West Library, pp. 270-305.

Simpson, G. G. (1960), The World into Which Darwin Led Us. *Science,* 131:966-974.

Skinner, B. F. (1954), Critique of Psychoanalytic Concepts and Theories. *Sci. Monthly,* 79:300-305.

Sliosberg, S. (1934), Zur Dynamik des Ersatzes in Spiel- und Ernstsituationen. *Psychol. Forsch.,* 19:122-181.

Solley, C. M., & Murphy, G. (1960), *Development of the Perceptual World.* New York: Basic Books.

Spearman, C. (1937), *Psychology Down the Ages,* 2 Vols. London: Macmillan.

Spence, K. W. (1952), Clark Leonard Hull: 1884-1952. *Amer. J. Psychol.,* 65:639-646.

Sternberg, R. S., Chapman, J., & Shakow, D. (1958), Psychotherapy Research and the Problem of Intrusions on Privacy. *Psychiatry,* 21:195-203.

Stoodley, B. H. (1959), *The Concepts of Sigmund Freud.* Glencoe, Ill.: The Free Press.

Sullivan, M. (1932), *Our Times: The United States 1900-1925.* Vol. 4: The War Begins, 1909-1914. New York: Scribner's.

Symonds, P. M. (1931), *Diagnosing Personality and Conduct.* New York: Century.

—— (1946), *The Dynamics of Human Adjustment.* New York: Appleton-Century.

Tansley, A. G. (1920), *The New Psychology and Its Relation to Life.* London: Allen & Unwin.

Taylor, W. S., ed. (1926), *Readings in Abnormal Psychology and Mental Hygiene.* New York: Appleton.

—— (1928), *Morton Prince and Abnormal Psychology.* New York: Appleton.

—— (1962), Psychoanalysis Revised or Psychodynamics Developed? *Amer. Psychologist,* 17:784-788.

Terman, L. M. (1932), Lewis M. Terman. In *A History of Psychology in Autobiography,* Vol. 2, ed. C. Murchison. Worcester, Mass.: Clark University Press, pp. 297-331.

BIBLIOGRAPHY

―― (1948), Kinsey's "Sexual Behavior in the Human Male": Some Comments and Criticisms. *Psychol. Bull.,* 45:443-459.
Thorndike, E. L. (1898), Animal Intelligence: An Experimental Study of the Associative Processes in Animals. *Psychol. Rev. Monogr. Suppl.,* 2: Whole No. 8.
―― (1911), *Animal Intelligence.* New York: Macmillan.
―― (1913), *Educational Psychology.* Vol. 2: The Psychology of Learning. New York: Teachers College, Columbia University.
―― (1927), The Law of Effect. *Amer. J. Psychol.,* 39:212-222.
―― (1933), A Proof of the Law of Effect. *Science,* 77:173-175.
Thurstone, L. L. (1924), Contributions of Freudism to Psychology. I. Influence of Freudism on Theoretical Psychology. *Psychol. Rev.,* 31:175-183.
―― (1952), L. L. Thurstone. In *A History of Psychology in Autobiography,* Vol. 4, ed. E. G. Boring, H. S. Langfeld, H. Werner & R. M. Yerkes. Worcester, Mass.: Clark University Press, pp. 295-321.
Tinker, M. A., Thuma, B. D., & Farnsworth, P. R. (1927), Minor Studies from the Psychological Laboratory of Stanford University. II. The Rating of Psychologists. *Amer. J. Psychol.,* 38:453-455.
Tolman, E. C. (1920), Instinct and Purpose. *Psychol. Rev.,* 27:217-233.
―― (1922), Can Instincts Be Given Up in Psychology? *J. Abn. Soc. Psychol.,* 17:139-152.
―― (1923), The Nature of Instinct. *Psychol. Bull.,* 20:200-218.
―― (1942), *Drives Toward War.* New York: Appleton-Century.
―― (1943), A Drive-Conversion Diagram. *Psychol. Rev.,* 50:503-513.
―― (1945), A Stimulus-Expectancy Need-Cathexis Psychology. *Science,* 101:160-166.
―― (1949a), There Is More Than One Kind of Learning. *Psychol. Rev.,* 56:144-155.
―― (1949b), The Nature and Functioning of Wants. *Psychol. Rev.,* 56:357-369.
―― (1952), Edward Chace Tolman. In *A History of Psychology in Autobiography,* Vol. 4, ed. E. G. Boring, H. S. Langfeld, H. Werner & R. M. Yerkes. Worcester, Mass.: Clark University Press, pp. 323-339.
Tolman, R. C. (1947), A Survey of the Sciences. *Science,* 106:135-140.
Tomkins, S. S., ed. (1943), *Contemporary Psychopathology.* Cambridge, Mass.: Harvard University Press.
Tridon, A. (1921), *Psychoanalysis, Sleep, and Dreams.* New York: Knopf.
Trilling, L. (1955), *Freud and the Crisis of Our Culture.* Boston: Beacon Press.
―― (1957), *The Liberal Imagination.* Garden City, N.Y.: Doubleday (Anchor Books).
Troland, L. T. (1920), A System for Explaining Affective Phenomena. *J. Abn. Psychol.,* 14:376-387.
―― (1928), *The Fundamentals of Human Motivation.* New York: Van Nostrand.
―― (1932), *The Principles of Psychophysiology.* Vol. 3: Cerebration and Action. New York: Van Nostrand.
Ugurel-Semin, R. (1952), Moral Behavior and Moral Judgment of Children. *J. Abn. Soc. Psychol.,* 47:463-474.
Van der Heide, C. (1952), Correspondence: Discussion of Buxbaum (1951). *Bull. Menninger Clin.,* 16:66-69.
Van Teslaar, J. S., ed. (1924), *An Outline of Psychoanalysis.* New York: Boni & Liveright.
Waelder, R. (1960), *Basic Theory of Psychoanalysis.* New York: International Universities Press.
Walker, N. (1957), A New Copernicus? In Nelson, ed. (1957), pp. 22-30.

Wallin, J. E. W. (1914), *The Mental Health of the School Child.* New Haven: Yale University Press.
——— (1927), *Clinical and Abnormal Psychology.* London: Harrap.
——— (1955), *The Odyssey of a Psychologist: Pioneering Experiences in Special Education, Clinical Psychology, and Mental Hygiene with a Comprehensive Bibliography of the Author's Publications.* Wilmington 4, Delaware: The Author.
Warren, H. C. (1934), *Dictionary of Psychology.* New York: Houghton Mifflin.
Watson, J. B. (1913), Psychology as the Behaviorist Views It. *Psychol. Rev.,* 20:158-177.
——— (1916), The Psychology of Wish Fulfillment. *Sci. Monthly,* 3:479-487.
——— (1919), *Psychology From the Standpoint of a Behaviorist.* Philadelphia: Lippincott.
——— (1936), John Broadus Watson. In *A History of Psychology in Autobiography,* Vol. 3, ed. C. Murchison. Worcester, Mass.: Clark University Press, pp. 271-281.
——— & Watson, R. R. (1928), *Psychological Care of Infant and Child.* New York: Norton.
Watson, R. I. (1953), A Brief History of Clinical Psychology. *Psychol. Bull.,* 50:321-346.
Weaver, W. (1948), Science and Complexity. *Amer. Scientist,* 36:536-544.
Weber, A. O., & Rapaport, D. (1941), Teleology and the Emotions. *Philos. Sci.,* 8:69-82.
Wells, F. L. (1912), Critique of Impure Reason. *J. Abn. Psychol.,* 7:89-93.
——— (1913a), On Formulation in Psychoanalysis. *J. Abn. Psychol.,* 8:217-227.
——— (1913b), Book Review: A. A. Brill, "Psychoanalysis. Its Theories and Practical Application." *J. Abn. Soc. Psychol.,* 7:447-449.
——— (1913c), Book Review: S. Freud, "The Interpretation of Dreams." *J. Philos., Psychol., Sci. Meth.,* 10:551-555.
——— (1916), Mental Regression: Its Conception and Types. *Psychiat. Bull. N.Y. State Hosp.,* 1:445-492.
——— (1917a), *Mental Adjustments.* New York: Appleton.
——— (1917b), A Summary of Material on the Topical Community of Primitive and Pathological Symbols. ("Archeopathic" Symbols). *Psychoanal. Rev.,* 4:47-63.
——— (1924), *Pleasure and Behavior.* New York: Appleton.
——— (1935a), Social Maladjustments: Adaptive Regression. In *A Handbook of Social Psychology,* ed. C. Murchison. Worcester, Mass.: Clark University Press, pp. 845-915.
——— (1935b), Attitude Measurement and "The Dunlap Dilemma." *Science,* 81:227.
Wheeler, W. M. (1921), On Instincts. *J. Abn. Psychol.,* 15:295-318.
——— (1923), The Dry-Rot of Our Academic Biology. *Science,* 57:61-71.
White, A. D. (1896), *A History of the Warfare of Science with Theology in Christendom,* 2 Vols. New York: Appleton.
White, R. W. (1948), *The Abnormal Personality.* New York: Ronald Press.
——— (1956), *The Abnormal Personality,* 2nd ed. New York: Ronald Press.
——— (1959), Motivation Reconsidered: The Concept of Competence. *Psychol. Rev.,* 66:297-333.
——— (1963), Ego and Reality in Psychoanalytic Theory. *Psychological Issues,* 3(3). New York: International Universities Press.
Whyte, L. L. (1960), *The Unconscious before Freud.* New York: Basic Books.
Wightman, W. P. D. (1953), *The Growth of Scientific Ideas.* New Haven: Yale University Press.
Willey, B. (1960), *Darwin and Butler: Two Versions of Evolution.* New York: Harcourt, Brace.

Willoughby, R. R. (1929), An Adaptive Aspect of Dreams. *J. Abn. Soc. Psychol.*, 24:104-107.
——— (1931), The Efficiency of Short Psychoanalyses. *J. Abn. Soc. Psychol.*, 26:125-130.
——— (1932), A Scale of Emotional Maturity. *J. Soc. Psychol.*, 3:3-36.
——— (1933a), Book Review: M. Klein, "The Psycho-Analysis of Children." *J. Soc. Psychol.*, 4:257-261.
——— (1933b), A Note on a Child's Dream. *J. Genet. Psychol.*, 42:224-228.
——— (1935), Magic and Cognate Phenomena: An Hypothesis. In *A Handbook of Social Psychology*, ed. C. Murchison. Worcester, Mass.: Clark University Press, pp. 461-519.
——— (1940), Some Articulations between Psychoanalysis and the Rest of Psychology. *J. Abn. Soc. Psychol.*, 35:45-55.
Wilm, E. C. (1925), *The Theories of Instinct*. New Haven: Yale University Press.
Wilson, L. N. (1914), *G. Stanley Hall: A Sketch*. New York: G. E. Stechert.
Wisdom, J. O. (1943), Determinism and Psycho-Analysis. *Int. J. Psycho-Anal.*, 24:140-147.
Witmer, H. L. (1940), *Psychiatric Clinics for Children*. New York: Commonwealth Fund.
Witmer, L. (1909), Mental Healing and the Emmanuel Movement (Conclusion). 4. As a System of Psychology and Philosophy. *Psychol. Clinic*, 2:282-300.
Wittels, F. (1931), *Freud and His Time*. New York: Liveright.
Wolff, P. H. (1960), The Developmental Psychologies of Jean Piaget and Psychoanalysis. *Psychological Issues*, 2(1). New York: International Universities Press.
Wood, A. B. (1941), Another Psychologist Analyzed. *J. Abn. Soc. Psychol.*, 36:87-90.
Woodworth, R. S. (1917), Some Criticisms of the Freudian Psychology. *J. Abn. Psychol.*, 12:174-194. Also in *Psychological Issues*. New York: Columbia University Press, 1939, pp. 192-211.
——— (1918), *Dynamic Psychology*. New York: Columbia University Press.
——— (1927), A Justification of the Concept of Instinct. *J. Abn. Soc. Psychol.*, 22:3-7. Also in *Psychological Issues*. New York: Columbia University Press, 1939, pp. 136-140.
——— (1931), *Contemporary Schools of Psychology*. New York: Ronald Press.
——— (1932), Robert S. Woodworth. In *A History of Psychology in Autobiography*, Vol. 2, ed. C. Murchison. Worcester, Mass.: Clark University Press, pp. 359-380.
——— (1948), *Contemporary Schools of Psychology*, rev. ed. New York: Ronald Press.
——— (1958), *Dynamics of Behavior*. New York: Holt.
Zeigarnik, B. (1927), Das Behalten erledigter und unerledigter Handlungen. *Psychol. Forsch.*, 9:1-85.
Zilboorg, G., & Henry, G. W. (1941), *A History of Medical Psychology*. New York: Norton.

INDEX

INDEX

Abnormal psychology, 70, 72
Abraham, K., 14
Ach, N., 121, 125, 126, 159
Acher, R., 162
Act psychology, 119, 120, 159
Action readiness, 125
Adaptation, 37, 40
Adelson, J., 195
Adler, A., 62, 67, 72, 106, 146, 184
Adrian, E. D., 15, 201
Affect and action psychology, 9, 121
Affective
  -conative, 33, 47, 72, 85
  in psychoanalysis, 45, 72, 86, 192
  in the Enlightenment, 31, 47
  vs. rational, 72; *see also* Rationalism
Agassiz, L., 18
Alexander, F., 76, 77, 78, 91, 186
Alexander, F. M., 73
Alexander, I. E., 186, 188
Allen, F. L., 58
Allers, R., 168
Allport, F., 148-149
Allport, G. W., 73, 77, 78, 116, 120, 131, 153, 188
Alper, T. G., 131
Amacher, M. P., 45
American culture
  early twentieth century, 55-58, 95
  optimism in, 195
  relation of professionals to intellectuals in, 82-83
American Journal of Psychology, 68
American Orthopsychiatric Association, 180
American psychology; *passim*
  instinct in, 147 ff.
  main trend in, 40-41, 52-53, 53-54
Amnesias, 110

Angell, J. R., 8, 36, 37, 79-80
Animal psychology, 152, 170, 179
Animal studies, 132, 135, 139, 177
Anthropocentrism, 15, 16
Anxiety, 86, 106-107
  signal, 107
Aphasia, 45-46
Appel, K., 188
Applied psychology, 37, 40, 51
Aron, W., 30
Aschaffenburg, G., 20
Association, 69, 105, 114, 121, 162
  and will, 125
Association experiments, 89
Association neurosis and psychosis, 105
Association psychology, 119, 124, 159
Attraction and repulsion, forces of, 34, 40, 49
Autism, 122, 174-175
Automatic writing, 104
Autonomy, 153

Bachrach, A. J., 76
Bain, A., 115
Bakan, D., 79
Baldwin, B. T., 37
Baldwin, J. M., 134, 185, 189
Barber, B., 28
Barclay, J. R., 43, 120
Barker, R. G., 129, 197
Barzun, J., 14, 19, 26, 27
Beach, F. A., 177-178
Bechterev, V. M., 50, 134
Beebe-Center, J. G., 132, 187
Behavior
  adaptation and purpose in, 114-115 *passim*, 136, 175

229

Behavior (*continued*)
  in psychoanalytic theory, 166
  observable, 40
Behaviorism, 39-41, 49, 51, 69, 72, 116, 118, 134, 147-149, 149-150; *see also* Watson, J. B.
Behaviorist frame of reference, 134, 169
Benjamin, J. D., 10, 88
Bentham, J., 115
Bergmann, G., 186
Bernard, L. L., 147-148, 159
Bernays, M., 43
Bernfeld, S., 34, 41, 42, 43, 45, 49, 50, 196, 201
Bernfeld, S. C., 44
Bernheim, H., 8
Bibring, E., 86
Birenbaum, G., 126, 127, 128, 153
Bisexuality, 46, 101
Bishop, P. W., 17
Blanchard, P., 74, 188
Bleuler, E., 22, 122, 174
Blum, G. S., 92, 131
Body and mind, 34, 113, 179
Bonaparte, M., 28, 46
Boring, E. G., 3-4, 6, 11, 16, 34, 36, 37, 41, 42, 50, 51, 119, 127, 162, 180, 183, 185, 200, 201
  analysis, 77, 196
  and the *Zeitgeist*, 5, 52, 101
  historical opinion of Freud, 52, 73, 181-182, 186
  on Freud's method, 48
  on history of behaviorism and functionalism, 39
  on introspection, 40, 179
  on Lewin, 127, 128
  on "religiousness" in science, 13, 40
  review, 178-179
Bowers, A. M., 90-91, 92, 115
Brand, H., 186, 188
Braun, O., 101
Brenman, M., 88, 104
Brenner, C., 86
Brentano, F., 8, 42-43, 79, 101, 119, 120, 159
Brett, G. S., 183
Breuer, J., 8, 27, 28, 42, 43, 44, 102, 103, 105, 120

Brief psychoanalysis, 76
Brierley, M., 21
Brill, A. A., 56, 66, 87, 88, 89, 155
Brinton, C., 31, 57, 59, 66, 78, 84, 87
British philosophy; *see* Hedonism
British psychology, 6
Broad, C. D., 197
Bronner, A. F., 90-91, 92, 115
Brooks, V. W., 56, 58
Brophy, B., 88
Brosin, H. W., 31
Brown, J. F., 74, 77, 92, 183
Brücke, E., 8, 34, 35, 42, 47
Brun, R., 43
Bruner, J. S., 32
Bruno, G., 17
Brunswik, E., 149
Bry, E., 21
Bumke, O., 20
Burnham, J. C., 4, 9-10, 33, 38, 57, 62, 65, 67, 89, 106, 154
Burrow, T., 135
Butler, S., 29
Butterfield, H., 17
Buxbaum, E., 44

Cadman, S. P., 63
Calkins, M., 67
Calvin, J., 17
Cannon, W. B., 136
Cargill, O., 58
Caron, A. J., 131
Carpenter, W. B., 7, 18, 100, 101
Carter, G. S., 30
Cartwright, D., 126-127
Cassirer, E., 32, 46-47
Cathexis, 150
  attention, 161
Cattell, J. McK., 40, 51
Causality; *see* Determinism
Censor, 90
Censorship, 99, 100
Chambers, R., 18
Chapman, J., 196
Charcot, J. M., 8, 27, 43, 102, 104
Chemical; *see* Physical-chemical
Chicago School, 36
Child guidance clinics, 91
Child psychology, 178, 182
Circular reactions, 134

INDEX

Claparède, E., 120, 121-123, 159
Clark University, 65-66
Clergy
   and Darwinism, 18-19, 21-22
   and psychoanalysis, 21-22
   status of, 19, 22
Clinical evidence; see Experimental evidence
Clinical psychology, 51, 52, 73-74, 84-85, 178, 179-180, 182
Coan, R. W., 73
Coconscious, 102
Cognition, 33, 48, 85, 161, 174-175
Cohen, M. B., 196
Cohen, R. A., 196
Colby, K. M., 87
Collins, J., 20
Comfort, A., 15
Complex, origin of term, 89
Concept, definition of, 8
Conception, definition of, 8
Conditioning, 114
   and law of effect, 134, 136
   and psychoanalysis, 69, 134, 135, 138, 159; see also Hull Seminars
Condorcet, 47
Conflict, 104
Consciousness, 73, 74, 110, 144
   and behaviorists, 40
   and introspection, 179
   as a sense organ, 179
Constitution; see Nature and nurture, in Freud's theory
Controls, 47
Copernicus, 14 ff., 50, 73
Crane, S., 56
Cranefield, P. F., 34-35, 53, 103
Croce, B., 31
Crook, D., 76
Crook, M., 76
Curti, M., 56, 58

Dallenbach, K. M., 17
Darlington, C. D., 17, 29
Darwin, C., 14-32 passim, 50, 67, 183, 201
   Butler attacks, 29
   correspondence, 28
   response to controversy, 29
   works: *Descent of Man*, 29; *On the Origin of the Species*, 18-20, 27, 28-29, 37, 67; other, 27
   see also Darwinism; Freud and Darwin
Darwin, F., 29
Darwinism
   influence in psychology, 37, 38, 41, 147, 181, 182
   in United States, 38
   late opposition to, 17
   reception of, 18-20
   see also Clergy; Religion
Day residues, 127
Debs, E., 56
Defense, 99, 154
   mechanisms of, 62, 115, 150
Delage, I., 150
Dell, F., 56
Dembo, T., 9, 125, 126, 129, 131
Dennis, W., 124, 186
Dercum, F., 21
Dessoir, M., 185
Determining tendencies, 121, 125
Determinism, 119
   and Freud, 32, 46, 47, 48, 104, 114, 193
   and Helmholtz school, 34
   vs. teleology, 114
   see also Mechanism
Development, human, 37, 152
Dewey, J., 8, 36, 73-74
Diderot, D., 47
Dillenberger, J., 19
Dingle, H., 173
Dissociation, 68, 103, 104, 109, 110
Distortion, 99, 100, 142-143
Dodge (Luhan), M., 56, 58
Dollard, J., 9, 116, 131, 137, 138, 139, 140, 141, 142, 150, 159, 176, 178
Dorer, M., 101
Dream, 123, 124, 127, 142-143, 150-151, 156, 170, 175
   literature, 78
   studies, 150-151, 161, 175-176
Dreiser, T., 56
Drever, J., 109-110, 121, 147, 189
Drive, 136, 159
   acquisition of, 152-153
   concepts of, 9, 141, 153, 159
   in conditioning, 136
Du Bois, C., 176

INDEX

Dubois, P., 21
du Bois-Reymond, E. H., 34, 35, 45, 47
Dukes, W. F., 131, 163
Dummer, E. S., 110-111
Dunlap, K., 111-112, 118, 148, 161, 162-163, 165
Du Prel, C., 43
Durkheim, E., 31
Dynamic psychology, 38, 52, 85, 107, 124, 135, 146, 180
and Freud, 10, 51-52, 69, 73, 98, 154-158
pressures toward, 64
term, 151

Early experience, 116
studies of, 176, 177-178
Earnest, E., 21
Eastman, M., 56
Ebbinghaus, H., 43, 47, 52
Ego, 16, 23-24, 25, 82, 86, 99, 110-111, 124, 158, 176, involvement, 180: vs. task-involvement, studies of, 131
Egocentrism, 15
Ego psychology, 111, 152, 161, 185
Allport, 131
psychoanalytic, 81, 86, 103, 104, 156, 157, 167-168, 195, 201
Eighteenth century; see Enlightenment
Einstein, A., 26, 201
Eiseley, L., 16, 18, 25
Elisabeth, Fräulein, case of, 103
Ellegård, A., 18, 19
Ellenberger, H. F., 42
Ellis, A., 161, 164-165
Emmy, Frau, case of, 103
Emotions, 51, 112, 132, 159
Empiricism, 50
in psychoanalysis, 108, 112, 166
Energy, 115, 131
English, A. C., 189
English, H. B., 189
Enlightenment, 33, 42, 46-47, 83
and Freud, 31-32, 46-47, 192
Entropy, 113
Environment, 37, 134, 147-148; see also Nature-nurture; Empiricism
Epigenesis vs. preformation, 9

Epistemology, 33, 50
Freud, 32, 50, 125
Lewin, 125
Piaget, 121, 124, 125
Erikson, E. H., 11, 15, 21, 44, 45, 87, 129, 138, 141, 176, 182
Eros and Thanatos, 49
Ethics, 33; see also Psychoanalysis, ethical implications of
Escalona, S., 10
Ethnocentrism, 16
Ethology, 161
Eulau, H., 59
European psychoanalysts, 6
European psychology, 5-6
Exner, S., 42
Existentialism, 6
Experimental evidence and clinical evidence, 75, 129-130
Experimental method, 35
and functionalism, 37
in physiology, 34, 35, 36
in psychoanalysis, 48, 156
in psychology, 36, 48
related to understanding, 173
see also Method
Experimental psychology, 122
mid-century trends in, 197
see also Psychology
Eysenck, H. J., 50, 131

Farber, L. H., 176
Farnsworth, P. R., 73
Fear; see Anxiety
Fechner, G., 8, 34, 37, 42, 52, 183
Feigenbaum, D., 83, 84
Fenichel, O., 16, 61, 86, 90, 92
Ferenczi, S., 66, 123
Feuer, L. S., 74
Fick, A., 41
Fielding, W. J., 61, 63
Fine, R., 92
Fisher, C., 176
Fixation, 128, 170
Fleischl, E., 42
Fleming, A., 17
Fliess letters, 29, 102, 120; see also Freud, correspondence
Fliess, W., 14, 29, 42, 44, 46, 99, 101, 102, 120
Flournoy, T., 67, 68

Flugel, J. C., 21, 36, 90, 101, 182-183, 191
Forcey, C. B., 58
Forgetting of intentions, 127-128, 129; *see also* Repression
Förster, O., 20
Fortier, R. H., 176
Frazer, J., 154
French, T. M., 76, 134, 135, 188
Frenkel-Brunswik, E., 31-32, 74, 77
Freud, A., 90, 167
Freud, E. L., 30
Freud, S., *passim*
and clinical work, 43
and Darwin, 15, 67, 73, 147, 181-182, 193, 201: and professional colleagues, 22; as writers, 26-27; chronological relationship of, 16, 17, 31; correspondence compared, 29, 30; cultural contexts of, 21-22, 30-31; early presentations of theory, 26-27, 73; methods and evidence, 28; response to controversy, 30; social and scientific status, 30
and earlier and contemporary theories, 7-8, 9, 52, 100-108, 119-121
and James compared, 51-52
and Jewish mystical tradition, 79
and Lamarckism, 32
and later motivation theories, 9, 52, 121-142
and philosophers, 79
and physiology, 43
and professional colleagues, 20-21, 22, 44
and psychical research, 83
and romanticism, 32, 46-47
and the occult, 32, 83
and the physiological, 43-44, 44-45, 46
and the psychological, 27, 43-44, 44-45, 49
areas of influence rated, 194
as anti-intellectual, 31-32
as a writer, 26-27, 155
attitude toward experiment, 129-130
attitude toward psychology, 79-81, 96
attitude toward strangers, 130
changes in theoretical views, 86, 202
comparisons with other historical figures, 14-16, 70, 73, 118, 201
contacts with academic psychology, 42-43
correspondence, 29-30; *see also* Fliess letters
early career, 42-43
early influences: Brentano, 42-43, 101, 120; Breuer, 27, 42, 43, 102, 103; Brücke, 42; Charcot, 27, 43; Fliess, 42, 44, 46; other, 15, 42, 45, 101, 120
family intellectual background, 30
followers, 22, 79-80, 80-81, 107
in the history of psychology, 69, 73, 181-182
Janet attack, 102-103
library, 41, 43
personal qualities, 50, 68, 69, 74, 101, 201
self-analysis, 44
use of anthropomorphic language, 115, 145
works: "A Difficulty in the Path of Psycho-Analysis," 14; *An Autobiographical Study*, 86; *The Ego and the Id*, 86; *Five Lectures on Psycho-Analysis*, 88, 89; *Group Psychology and the Analysis of the Ego*, 78; *Inhibitions, Symptoms and Anxiety*, 86, 107; "Instincts and Their Vicissitudes," 113, 146; *The Interpretation of Dreams*, 20, 21, 27-28, 59, 78, 86, 87, 89, 90, 101, 102, 112, 120, 154-155; *Introductory Lectures on Psycho-Analysis*, 86, 89; *Jokes and Their Relation to the Unconscious*, 20, 90; *Moses and Monotheism*, 26; "On the Grounds for Detaching a Particular Syndrome from Neurasthenia under the Description 'Anxiety Neurosis,'" 106; *On the History of the Psycho-Analytic Movement*, 86; *The Origins of Psycho-Analysis: Letters to*

Freud, S. (*continued*)
  works (*continued*)
    Wilhelm Fliess, Drafts and Notes: 1887-1902, 29, 102, 120; "Project for a Scientific Psychology," 45, 194; *The Psychopathology of Everyday Life,* 20, 90; "A Reply to Criticisms of My Paper on Anxiety Neurosis," 106; "Sexuality in the Aetiology of the Neuroses," 20; *Three Essays on the Theory of Sexuality,* 20, 113, 146
  see also Psychoanalysis
Frost, E., 72
Froude, J. A., 25
Frustration
  -aggression hypothesis, 176
  experiments, 131
Fugues, 104
Functionalism, 36-39, 68, 114, 148
  and dynamic psychology, 51-52
  and Freud, 8, 38-39, 40, 41, 51
  and Hull, 136
  and instinct, 148
Functional point of view, 85

Galdston, I., 41-42, 46-47
Galton, F., 18, 183
Gates, A. I., 61, 62
Gay, F. P., 21
Gay, P., 32, 47
Genetic approach, 67, 124, 193
Gengerelli, J. A., 17
Geocentrism, 15
German professors, 30
Gestalt psychology, 36, 116, 128; *see also* Lewin, K.
Gibson, J. J., 125
Gill, M. M., 4, 79, 87, 88, 93, 98-100, 104, 105, 195, 197
Gillispie, C. C., 19
Givler, R. C., 62
Glixman, A. F., 131
Goethe, W., 32, 42
Goldman, E., 56
Gomperz, T., 79
Goodhart, S. P., 106
Gorer, G., 176
Gould, R., 131
Graham, C. H., 76

Gray, A., 18
Greene, J. C., 19, 30
Griesinger, W., 101, 120
Grinker, R. R., 130
Gross, A., 196
Groves, E. R., 33

Habit, 74, 138, 153, 174
  and instinct, 38-39, 151-152
Hacker, L. M., 56, 58
Haeckel, E., 19
Hale, Nathan G., Jr., 26, 58
Hall, C. S., 61, 86, 92
Hall, G. S., 37, 40, 43, 65-67, 68, 71, 72, 96, 150, 180
Hall, R. G., 66
Hallowell, A. I., 178
Hamilton, G. V., 134-135
Hapgood, H., 41
Harrell, W., 148
Harriman, P. L., 189
Harrison, R., 148
Hart, B., 61, 88, 89, 101, 104
Hartmann, E. v., 7, 101, 109
Hartmann, H., 11, 21, 51, 86, 87, 94, 100, 101, 130, 137, 153, 167, 168
Harvard Psychological Clinic, 130, 131, 146, 157, 180
H. D., 56
Healy, W., 52, 65, 90-91, 92, 115
Hebb, D. O., 177
Hedonism, 115-116, 120
  and law of effect, 132, 133
  and psychoanalysis, 132-133, 134, 144-145
  pro and anti, 115-116
Heidbreder, E., 15, 63-64, 72-73, 94, 171, 181
Heider, F., 9, 126, 157
Heilbronner, K., 20
Heine, H., 32
Helmholtz, H. v., 34, 35, 36, 47, 52, 73, 100, 101, 181, 182
Helmholtz program, 33-35, 35-54 *passim*
  and physiology, 34-35, 53
  Freud's commitment, 41-46
  implications of commitments, 82, 191-192; *see also* Psychology, exact science in

INDEX

Helmholtz program (*continued*)
  philosophy of, 34
  psychology's commitment, 36-41
  ways of fulfillment, 47
Helmholtz School of Medicine, 34
Helson, H., 186, 187
Henderson, E. N., 133
Hendrick, I., 61, 90, 92
Henry, G. W., 184
Herbart, J. F., 7, 15, 79, 100, 101, 119, 159
Hering, E., 8, 100
Herma, H., 9, 118, 178
Hermann, I., 88
Herschel, J., 18
Hilgard, E. R., 62, 167, 171, 172-173, 174, 185-186, 197
Himmelfarb, G., 14, 17
Hitschmann, E., 61, 88, 89
Hoarding, 177
Hoch, A., 154, 158
Hoff, H., 45
Hoffman, F. J., 11, 12, 58, 59
Hofstadter, R., 56, 58, 66
Holbach, P., 47
Holmes, O. W., 100
Holt, E. B., 8, 33, 52, 61, 68-69, 90, 134, 186
Hook, S., 79
Hooker, J., 18
Hoppe, F., 131
Hormic psychology; see McDougall, W.
Horney, K., 107, 186
Hughes, H. S., 30, 31, 47
Hulin, W. S., 185
Hull, C. L., 9, 52, 92, 95, 134, 135-142, 150, 159, 175, 187
Hull seminars, 137-142, 159
Humanism, 184
Human nature, interest in, 10, 73, 98
Hume, D., 50
Humphrey, G., 62-63, 70, 89-90, 134
Hunt, J. McV., 75, 168, 176, 177, 186, 188
Hunter, J. D., 91
Hunter, W. S., 75
Huschka, M., 176
Huxley, J., 17
Huxley, L., 26

Huxley, T. H., 18, 19, 26, 27
Hyman, S. E., 26-27
Hypnagogic experiments, 158
Hypnosis, 104, 106, 137
Hysteria, 20, 102

Id, 25, 108
Ideas
  active, 119, 120, 121, 159
  and association, 119, 120, 132
  new, 16-17, 78-79, 142
Idiographic approach, 131
Impulse
  and cognition, 174-175
  and ideas, 120, 132
Individual differences, 37, 40
Infancy and childhood, 10, 72; see also Early experience
Inference *vs.* direct experience, 179
Influence
  and new religious systems, 12-13
  and new scientific theories, 12-13
  and the artist, 11
  and the scientist, 11-12, 143
  and understanding, 10, 12
  criteria and definition, 12
  Freud's characterized, 9-10, 97, 191, 193
  nature of, 125, 149, 171
  problem of assessment of, 7-13
Inhibition, 38-39
  of energy, 99, 100
Instinct, 86, 144
  and Darwin's influence, 147
  and Dewey, 74
  and habit, 38-39, 73, 74, 151-152
  and intellect, 109
  and the unconscious, 109-110, 121
  anti-, 147, 148, 159
  controversy over, 142-152
  Freud on, 49, 113; see also Instinctual drive
Instinctual drive, 51
  Freud's concept, 86, 117, 134: and association, 105; and Hull's theory, 136; and Lewin's theory, 131; compared with instinct conception, 159; description, 112-113
  use of term, 51

236 INDEX

Intelligence, Piaget's sensorimotor theory, 121, 124
Intentionalism, 119
Interrupted tasks, studies of, 127-128, 129, 153
Introspection, 36, 39-40, 149
  and related dichotomies, 179
Irrational
  and Freud, 31-32
  in man, 10, 23-24, 25, 31, 144
  see also Rationalism
Irvine, W., 19, 29
Irwin, F. W., 187
Isaacs, S., 122
Isserlin, M., 20

Jacobson, E., 86
James, W., 36, 43, 50, 145, 200
  and clinical psychology, 180
  and dynamic psychology, 51-52
  and Freud, 67-68, 79, 83
  and Woodworth, 150
  anticipation of Freud, 8, 38-39
  in history of psychology, 73, 182
  neglect of, 38
  on psychophysics, 37, 38
  personal qualities, 137
  Principles of Psychology, 38
  Witmer attacks, 85
Janet, P., 8, 66, 68, 72, 102-104, 105, 106, 107, 109, 110, 123, 130, 187
Jaspers, K., 20
Jastrow, J., 61, 63, 91-92, 161, 163-164, 187
Jaynes, J., 177-178
Jelliffe, S. E., 43
Jennings, H. S., 135
Jensen, F., 76
Jones, E., 14-15, 21, 22, 27, 28, 29-30, 32, 40, 41, 42, 46, 48, 49, 50, 52, 58, 66, 67, 74, 83, 86, 87, 88, 89, 92, 101, 103, 104, 107-108, 109, 121, 122, 123, 130, 201
Jung, C. G., 22, 49, 50, 62, 66, 67, 72, 89, 90, 103, 105, 108, 109, 130, 144, 146, 154, 163, 165, 184, 201

Kant, I., 50, 79, 201
Kaplan, A., 79
Kardiner, A., 176
Kaufman, W., 32, 74, 79
Kazin, A., 46, 58
Keith, A., 17
Kelly, E. L., 178
Kelvin, 18
Kempf, E. J., 134
Kendrick, B. B., 56, 58
Kenworthy, M., 110
Kingsley, C., 19
Klein, D. B., 187
Klopstock, F. G., 12
Kluckhohn, C., 178, 188
Koch, S., 165, 197-199, 200
Koffka, K., 111
Köhler, W., 200
Kraepelin, E., 20
Krech, D., 187
Kris, E., 9, 15, 44, 45, 46, 86, 87, 94, 100, 118, 178, 186
Kubie, L., 10
Kuhn, T. S., 17, 184-185, 201
Külpe, O., 52
Kuo, Z. Y., 148, 159
Kuttner, A. B., 59

La Barre, W., 176
Ladd, G. T., 114
Lamettrie, J., 47
Landis, C., 43, 77
Lange, L., 52
Langfeld, H. S., 68-69
Lashley, K. S., 200
Lasswell, H. D., 51
Law of effect, 121
  and conditioning, 134, 136
  and hedonism, 115, 132-133, 133-134
  and psychoanalysis, 132, 133-134
  description, 132
Law of momentary interest, 121
Lay, W., 69
Learning theorists, 116
Learning theory and psychoanalysis, 150, 169, 185; see also Hull seminars; Conditioning
LeBon, G., 78
Leeper, R., 76
Leibnitz, G., 100, 101

Le Lay, Y., 122
Lerner, E., 124
Level of aspiration studies, 131
Levitt, M., 73, 74
Levy, D. M., 176
Lewin, B. D., 83, 87
Lewin, K., 9, 52, 80, 121, 125-132, 133, 134, 142, 146, 153, 159, 166, 187
Lewis, N. D. C., 43
Lewy, E., 86
Libido, 115, 150
Lindzey, G., 92
Lippmann, W., 33, 56, 58, 59
Lipps, T., 8, 79, 179
Loeb, J., 41, 135
Loewenstein, R. M., 87
London, J., 56
Lorenz, K., 177
Lowell, J. R., 94
Lubbock, J., 18
Ludwig, C., 34, 35, 41, 47
Luther, M., 17
Lyell, C., 18

MacCurdy, J. T., 158
MacRae, D., 124
MacKinnon, D. W., 131, 168, 187
Madison, P., 168
Magnes, J. L., 80
Maier, N., 187
Martin, E. D., 58
Marx, M. H., 186-187
Maslow, A. H., 92, 187, 195
Mason, G., 129
Materialism
  and Freud, 32
  in biology, 31
Matthews, F. H., Jr., 26
Maudsley, H., 43
May, H. F., 56, 58
May, M., 135, 137, 138, 141-142
McClelland, D. C., 136
McDougall, W., 78, 90, 106, 107, 110, 130, 142, 143, 144, 157, 183
  and hedonism, 116, 145
  and Woodworth, 153
  at Harvard, 146
  Cattell attack, 40-41
  on dissociation, 104
  relationship to psychoanalysis, 52, 70, 116, 118, 121, 135, 143-146, 159
McGranahan, D., 77
Mead, M., 178
Mechanism, 31, 33, 119
  and Freud, 114, 144-145
  vs. vitalism, 35
  see also Defense, mechanisms of
Mechanistic-deterministic point of view, 35
Medical psychology, 146, 184
Melanchthon, 17
Meltzer, H., 133
Memory, 86
Menninger Clinic, 180
Mental elements, 36
Mental operations, 37
Merlan, P., 42-43
Method
  and behaviorism, 39-40
  and scientists' personalities, 31, 49-50
  and subject matter of fields, 36, 37-38, 40, 47-48, 49, 53-54, 193, 195, 196, 197, 198-199
  and theoretical understanding, 133
  hierarchy problem, 196, 197
  in psychoanalysis and psychology, 53, 82
  in psychology, 72
  laboratory, and field situations, 196, 197
  of Freud and Darwin, 28
  problems of, 72, 151, 176, 178: with psychoanalysis, 10, 64, 84, 95, 133, 153-154, 168, 170-173 *passim*, 180, 190
  see also Subject matter of fields, and method; various specific methods
Meyer, A., 130, 135, 143, 154, 158
Meynert, T., 8, 101, 120
Mill, J., 115
Mill, J. S., 48, 79, 115, 120
Miller, N. E., 9, 71, 116, 135, 137, 138, 140, 141-142, 150, 159, 187
Mitchell, S. W., 21
Mittelmann, B., 92
Mivart, St. G., 18

INDEX

Models, psychological, in psychoanalysis, 93, 166
Moll, A., 20
Moore, R., 19
Moore, T. V., 158
Moral philosophy, 33, 34, 45
Morality
 changes in, 57
 see also Psychoanalysis, moral implications of
Mosbacher, E., 87
Motivation, 10, 51, 112-160, 151, 153, 193
 and parapraxes, 81-82
 hierarchic conceptions, 125, 159, 168
 in Hull's theory, 135-136
 in Lewin's theory, 125
 in Piaget's theory, 124-125, 159
 in psychoanalysis, 73, 124-125, 159; *see also* Instinctual drive
 secondary, 170
 see also Instinct; Instinctual drive
Motor psychology, 68-69, 90
Mowrer, O. H., 9, 116, 139, 141, 142, 150, 159, 187, 188
Müller, G. E., 47, 50, 52
Müller-Freienfels, R., 184
Multiple personalities, 104
Munn, N., 76
Munroe, R. L., 92
Münsterberg, H., 43, 85
Murchison, C., 90
Murdock, G. P., 138
Murphy, G., 36, 72, 74, 76-77, 92, 96, 122, 174-175, 181, 182, 183, 185, 194
Murphy, L. B., 76, 122, 188
Murray, H. A., 4, 52, 74, 77, 130, 131, 145, 146, 157-158
Myers, C. S., 109, 147

Nachmansohn, M., 176
Narcissism
 and psychoanalysis and Darwinism, 23-26
 historic blows to, 15-16
Nativism, 159
 in psychoanalysis, 108, 112, 169
 see also Nature and nurture
Natural philosophy, 33, 42

Naturalism, 31, 33
Naturalistic observation, 47, 50, 53
 and psychoanalysis, 47, 48, 192
 and psychology, 38, 53, 192
 and the Helmholtz school, 34, 35
Nature and nurture
 controversy over, 116
 in Freud's theory, 116-117, 124, 159
 in Piaget's theory, 124, 159
 in Thorndike's theory, 132
 see also Instinct; Environment
Nature of evidence, 28
Naturphilosophie, 42, 47
Needs, 157, 174-175
 genuine, 125, 126
 quasi-, 126
Nelson, B., 15, 194
Neo-Freudians, 107, 115, 116, 201
Neuropsychology, 194
Neurosis, 100, 103, 104, 106-107, 139, 143
 war, 143
Newcomb, T. M., 76
Newton, I., 140, 201
Nicoll, M., 108, 109
Nietzsche, F., 32
Nineteenth century
 attitudes, 19, 31, 147, 192
 philosophy, 33; *see also* Helmholtz program
 see also Romantic Period
Norris, F., 56
Northridge, W. L., 101
Nunberg, H., 86, 92
Nurture; *see* Nature and nurture

Oberndorf, C. P., 43
Observational method; *see* Naturalistic observation
Oedipus complex, 148, 154
Ofiesh, G. D., 72
Ogburn, W. F., 58
Oppenheim, H., 20
Orlansky, H., 176-177
Owen, R., 18

Paradigms, 201
Parapraxes, 156
Parataxes, 158
Park, D. G., 71-72

Participant observation, 28, 196
Pavlov, I., 50, 134, 137
Payne, S. M., 60
Payne, V., 66
Pelikan, J., 19
Perception, 112, 124, 161
Periodicity, 46
Perry, R. B., 50, 67-68, 200
Personality, 70, 72, 132, 157, 182
Pestalozzi, R., 42
Peters, R. S., 183-184
Pfister, O., 26, 61, 89, 154
Phobia, 107
Physical-chemical
  forces, 34, 35
  method, 34, 35, 36, 44, 48
Physical-mathematical method, 34
Physics, 36
  field force concept of, 126
Physiology and Helmholtz School of Medicine, 34-35, 53
Piaget, J., 121-125, 134, 142, 159, 174
Pinel, P., 184
Pleasure principle, 113, 129, 174
  and hedonism, 115, 116, 132-133
Poe, E. A., 94
Pohorilles, N. E., 101
Positivism, 31, 33
Postman, L., 132
Pötzl, O., 130, 168, 176
Preconscious, 99
Prescott, F. C., 59
Presses, 157
Pribram, K. H., 45, 194
Primary process, 99
Prince, M., 8, 65, 80-81, 102, 104-105, 107-108, 145, 154, 157, 187
Projective testing, 157
Psychiatry, 31, 53, 91, 180
Psychoanalysis, *passim*
  American interpretation of, 26
  and "bad science," 170, 172
  and romantic love, 56
  attempts to systematize, 165-167; *see also* Hull Seminars
  early references to, 106, 148-149
  ethical implications of, 21, 25-26, 33, 90
  experimental studies of, 132-133:
  Freud on, 129, 130; surveys of, 168-173, 174; *see also* Method, problems of, with psychoanalysis
  fourfold nature, 93, 94
  future problems and prospects, 194-197
  general theory of, 86; *see also* written sources of, general theory in and clinical theory of, 93
  in America, 83-84
  initial reception, 20-22
  medical tradition of, 82-83, 96
  metapsychology of; *see* general theory of
  origins of theory, 86
  oversimplifications and distortions of, 22, 58; *see also* Psychoanalysis, written sources of
  related experimental studies, 124, 131
  related psychological points of view, 166
  sources of anxiety in, 23-26
  symbolic theory, 162
  therapy, 88, 93
  training in America, 83-84, 96, 195-196
  weaknesses in, 192-193
  written sources of: clinical theory in, 86, 89, 92, 93; general theory in, 86-87, 89, 92, 93, 195; periodicals, 58; popular and semi-popular sources, 61, 62-63, 90, 95, 96; primary sources, 61, 65, 82, 86-87, 88, 96; psychoanalytic journals, 10; secondary sources, 61, 65, 81, 82, 84, 87-93, 96; translations, 59, 78, 87, 89, 96, 155; unsystematic nature, 63, 64, 73, 86, 140, 173, 195; *see also* Textbooks; Psychological literature related to psychoanalysis
  see also Psychoanalytic method; Reactions to psychoanalysis; Sexuality in psychoanalysis; Subject matter of fields
Psychoanalytic method, 10, 48, 69, 88, 133, 139, 144, 155, 182, 192, 201

Psychoanalytic method (*continued*)
  and biology, 182
  and clinical theory, 93
  and psychologists, 88, 96, 193
Psychological Abstracts, 75
Psychological Bulletin, 174
Psychological literature related to psychoanalysis
  articles and reviews, 154-156, 174-180
  dictionaries, 189, 190
  general appraisals, 72, 161-167, 190
  histories, 73, 180-186
  Journal of Abnormal and Social Psychology, 9
  readings, 186-187, 189, 190
Psychologists, *passim*
  academic, 149
  analyzed, 77-78
  importance of psychopathological material for, 70, 82
  professional guilts, 64, 95
Psychology, *passim*
  concern about itself, 64, 193, 197
  courses in 59-60, 62, 72
  exact science in, 40, 64, 69, 114, 115, 184, 192, 197-199
  "new psychology," pressures for, 59, 60-61, 95
  schools of, 195
  trends in, 197-200
  see also Subject matter of fields
Psychophysics, 34, 36, 37, 38, 49
Psychoses, 103, 107
Psychotaxes, 158
Psychotherapy, 178, 195; *see also* Psychoanalysis, therapy
  cathartic therapy, 102
Puner, H. W., 201
Puritanism, 55, 57, 95
Putnam, J. J., 26, 108

Quantification, 192, 196, 197

Ralph, J., 61, 63
Ramsay, A., 18
Ramsey, G. V., 175-176
Rand, B., 186, 189
Rank, O., 79, 115, 146
Rapaport, D., 1-2, 49, 50, 51, 79, 86, 87, 88, 93, 94, 100, 103, 104, 105, 111, 112, 113, 115, 116, 124, 125, 126, 127, 128, 129, 131, 132, 134, 141, 161, 165-167, 167-168, 190, 194, 195, 197
Rationalism
  and Freud, 23, 31-32, 72, 83
  in European and American intellectuals, 83
  in the Enlightenment, 31
Reactions to psychoanalysis
  ambivalence, 62, 64, 67
  in psychiatry, 65
  in psychology, *passim,* 64-65, 65-78, 96-97
  opposition, 9, 10, 17, 20-21, 22, 56; late, 17
  receptivity, 8, 9-10, 22, 41, 56, 74-77, 118, 142, 178
Reality, 49, 50, 53
Reality factors, 157
Reality principle, 129
Reed, C. F., 186, 188
Reedy, W. M., 57
Reflex, 134, 152
Regression, 129, 170
Reinforcement, 136
Religion
  and Copernican theory, 17
  and Darwinism, 17, 19, 21, 25, 31
  and psychoanalysis, 56
  and science, 18-19, 21-22; *see also* Clergy
Religious therapy, 83
Repression, 57, 99, 104, 110, 117, 143, 164, 168, 169
  and experimental studies, 129, 132-133, 167-168
  and forgetting, 128, 162-163
Resistance, 81-82
  to psychoanalysis, 81-82, 93, 96, 156
Retroflex, 134
Ribble, M. A., 188
Richardson-Robinson, F., 186
Rickers-Ovsiankina, M., 9, 125, 126, 127, 128, 129, 153
Rieff, P., 22, 45, 194
Rifkin, A. H., 21

INDEX

Rivers, W. H. R., 108, 109, 142-143, 144, 147
Riviere, J., 87
Robinson, E. S., 186
Robinson, J. H., 58
Roe, A., 200
Roffenstein, G., 176
Rogers, C. R., 172, 178
Róheim, G., 176
Romanes, G., 43
Romantic Period, 192; *see also* Freud, and romanticism
Rorschach, H., 176
Rosenbaum, M., 80
Rosenzweig, S., 26, 101, 129-131, 187, 188
Ross, D., 66, 68
Ross, H., 83
Rosvold, H. E., 72
Russian objectivists, 50

Sachs, B., 21
Sachs, H., 77, 137
Sakuma, K., 126
Sapir, E., 137, 138
Saul, L., 188
Schachtel, E. G., 176
Schelling, F. v., 42
Schlosberg, H., 75
Schoenwald, R. L., 43, 45
Schopenhauer, A., 14, 79
Schreiner, O., 56
Schroetter, K., 176
Schur, M., 4, 51, 86, 129-130
Schwalbe, G., 29
Schwartz, G., 17
Schwarz, G., 128-129
Science, 33
 development of a, 173, 199-200
 discoveries in, 173
 European and American attitudes toward, 83
 "good" and "bad," 173
 in Britain, 21-22
 in nineteenth century school, 19
 philosophy of, 173
 revolutions in, 184-185
 Western faith in, 32
 see also Religion, and science; influence, and new scientific theories

Scopes trial, 17
Sears, R. R., 135, 137-138, 141, 142, 167, 168-171, 172, 173, 178, 188
Sechenov, I. M., 50
Secondary process, 99
Sedgwick, A., 19
Seitelberger, F., 45
Sensory psychology, 36
Sentiments, 157
Severn, E., 61, 63
Sexuality in psychoanalysis, 21, 23, 117, 143, 162
 infantile, 20, 72
 interest in, 111, 135, 148, 164
 overemphasis of, 80, 81, 116, 144, 145, 156, 201
Shaffer, L. F., 61, 92
Shakow, D., 10, 24, 39, 40-41, 52, 53, 57, 70, 77, 84, 85, 91, 146, 149, 157, 173, 195, 196, 197
Shand, A. F., 157
Shapley, H., 16
Shoben, E. J., Jr., 92
Sholem, G., 79
Shor, J., 9, 118, 178
Sidis, B., 8, 21, 65, 101, 102, 104, 105-107, 187
Silberer, H., 26, 103, 158
Simon, E., 14
Simpson, G. G., 24-25, 27
Sinclair, U., 56
Skinner, B. F., 48
Sliosberg, S., 129
Social frame of reference, 42, 135
Social psychology, 72, 182
Sociology, 65
Solley, C. M., 77
Somatic compliance, 105
Sommer, R., 20
Soskin, W., 197
Southard, E. E., 21
Southey, R., 37
Spearman, C., 183, 184-185, 200
Spence, K. W., 9, 136
Spencer, H., 37, 115, 183
Spielmeyer, W., 20
Spielrein, S., 49, 123
Starr, M. A., 21
Stecher, L. I., 37
Steffens, L., 56

Stengel, E., 45-46
Stern, W., 21
Sternberg, R. S., 196
Stimulus, 113
Stone, C., 72
Stoodley, B. H., 42, 45
Strachey, J., 27, 42, 49, 87, 98, 102-103
Structuralist point of view, 52
Structuralists, 36, 39, 180
Stumpf, C., 43
Subception, 112
Subconscious, 8, 71
   theories contemporary with Freud, 8, 102-107
Subject matter of fields
   Darwin's, 28
   ethics, 33
   moral philosophy, 45
   psychoanalysis, 28, 33, 39, 45, 47-48, 49, 53, 54, 69, 70, 82, 166, 196
   psychology, 33, 36, 45, 48, 53, 54, 82, 114, 195, 197, 198, 202: behaviorism, 40; functionalism, 37-38
   see also Method, and subject matter of fields
Sublimation, 117
Substitution, 110, 129
Sullivan, H. S., 107, 115, 138, 158
Sullivan, M., 56-57, 58
Sumner, W. G., 154
Suppression; see Repression
Symbolism, 103; see also Dream
Symonds, P. M., 61, 74, 77, 92

Tansley, A. G., 60, 89, 90
Tarbell, I., 56
Taylor, W. S., 80, 108, 186, 187
Teleology, 119
   and Freud, 114, 116
   vs. determinism, 113-114
Teler, I., 168
Tension systems, 9, 126, 131, 159
Terman, L. M., 70-71, 72, 88, 137, 178
Textbooks
   elementary, of psychoanalysis, 86
   psychoanalysis in psychological, 62, 71-72, 92, 148, 158

Thomas, W. I., 110
Thorndike, E. L., 8, 9, 115, 120-121, 132, 133, 135 ff., 142, 151, 159, 175
Thought, 86
   stream of, 39
   syncretistic, 123
Thuma, B. D., 73
Thurstone, L. L., 70, 153, 187
Tinker, M. A., 73
Titchener, E. B., 13, 36, 162
Tobler, G. C., 42
Tolman, E. C., 52, 59, 118, 149-150, 159
Tolman, R. C., 200
Tomkins, S. S., 186, 187-188
Topographic theory, 79
Topological psychologists, 131-132
Tridon, A., 61, 63
Trilling, L., 32
Troland, L. T., 134, 135
Tropistic psychology, 41
Trotter, W., 90

Ugurel-Semin, R., 124
Unconscious, 10, 31, 67, 73-74, 98-112, 181
   and instinct, 109-110
   and introspectable, 179
   earlier theories of, 7-8, 100-102
   Freud's theory, 23, 72, 143, 164, 184, 193: as threatening, 25, 26; description, 98-100; development of, 27, 98-99, 102; non-repressed, 99, 100, 108; relation to other theories, 79; see also Subconscious; repressed, 99, 100, 108
   symposia on, 108-111
   vs. conscious, 179

Van der Heide, C., 44
Van Teslaar, J. S., 61, 63
Victoria Institute, 17, 19
Victorian Era, 19
Victorianism, 31, 56, 95
Vitalism, 119
   and Freud, 114, 115
   anti, 34, 35, 47, 48
Vogt, O., 20
Voltaire, 47

Waelder, R., 51, 61, 86, 92
Walker, N., 15
Wallace, A. R., 16, 18
Wallach, M. A., 131
Wallas, G., 109
Wallin, J. E. W., 84-85
Warren, H. C., 189
Watson, J. B., 39, 40, 69, 111, 118, 134, 135, 148, 159, 186
Watson, R. I., 179-180
Watson, R. R., 40, 148
Weaver, W., 197
Weber, A. O., 116
Weber, M., 31
Wells, F. L., 4, 57, 62, 93, 163, 186
   and psychoanalysis, 61, 69, 80, 154-157: on *The Interpretation of Dreams*, 87, 154-155
   dynamic psychology, origin of term, 151
   notation of James' anticipation of Freud, 38
Werner, H., 124
Weyer, J., 184
Weygant, W., 20
Wheeler, W. M., 31, 60-61
Whewell, W., 18
White, A. D., 19
White, R. W., 92, 153, 188
White, W. A., 110-111
Whiting, J., 138, 178
Whyte, L. L., 52, 79, 100, 101
Wightman, W. P. D., 17
Wilberforce, S., 19
Willey, B., 29
Willoughby, R. R., 74, 75-77, 92
Wilm, E. C., 147
Wilson, L. N., 66
Wisdom, J. O., 79
Wish, 68, 90, 134, 135, 155
Witmer, H. L., 91

Witmer, L., 52, 84, 85
Wittels, F., 42
Wolf, A., 176
Wolfe, W. B., 184
Wolff, P., 125
Wood, A. B., 77
Woodworth, R. S., 51, 52, 69
   and James, 8, 38, 150-151
   and motivation, 150-153, 159
   and psychoanalysis, 69, 80, 125, 181: understanding of, 53, 104, 117, 134
   anticipations, 150-151, 153
Worcester State Hospital, 180
Wundt, W., 43, 47, 50, 52, 181, 183, 186
Wundtian-Kraepelinian approach, 85
Würzburg School, 52, 126

Yale University, 95, 137-138; *see also* Hull seminars
Yerkes, R. M., 135

Zagona, S. V., 73
Zeigarnik, B., 125, 126, 127-128, 129, 153
Zeitgeist, 5, 45, 101, 125, 181
   and Freud, 8, 45, 52, 58-59, 95, 101, 125, 181, 192
   and Lewin, 125
   and McDougall, 146
   and Piaget, 125
   and psychologists, 59, 61, 95, 192, 199, 200
   and Sears, 169
   vs. personal qualities, 45, 52
Ziehen, T., 20, 43
Zilboorg, G., 184
Zinn, E., 138
Zürich group, 22, 89

ABOUT THE AUTHORS

DAVID SHAKOW received his Ph.D. from Harvard University in 1942. From 1928 to 1946 he was Director of Psychological Research at the Worcester State Hospital. In 1946 he became Professor of Psychology in the Department of Psychiatry of the University of Illinois School of Medicine where he remained until 1954. During the years 1948-1954 he was also Professor of Psychology at the University of Chicago. Since 1954 he has been Chief of the Laboratory of Psychology of the National Institute of Mental Health. His research has been mainly in the experimental psychology of schizophrenia and in psychotherapy. He is the author of "The Nature of Deterioration in Schizophrenic Conditions" and numerous papers on the psychology of schizophrenia.

DAVID RAPAPORT received his Ph.D. in psychology at the University of Budapest in 1938. He was Head of the Department of Psychology and Director of the Research Department at the Menninger Foundation, and, from 1948 to 1960, Research Associate and Senior Staff Member at the Austen Riggs Center, Stockbridge, Massachusetts. His writings include *Emotions and Memory, Diagnostic Psychological Testing, Organization and Pathology of Thought*, and "The Structure of Psychoanalytic Theory: A Systematizing Attempt" [*Psychological Issues,* 2(2)]. Dr. Rapaport died December 14, 1960.